IMAGES
of America

Along the Union River

I0792676

IMAGES
of America

ALONG THE UNION RIVER

Connee Jellison

ARCADIA
PUBLISHING

ISBN 978-0-7385-6476-0

Published by Arcadia Publishing
Charleston, South Carolina

Printed in the United States of America

For all general information contact Arcadia Publishing at:
Telephone 843-853-2070
Fax 843-853-0044
E-mail sales@arcadiapublishing.com
For customer service and orders:
Toll-Free 1-888-313-2665

Visit us on the Internet at www.arcadiapublishing.com

Contents

Acknowledgments

I am particularly indebted to my close friends and family who have "cleared the decks" for me so that I might put this book together. Thanks to all who shared their personal photo books and preserved the material over the years.

Special thanks to the following: the Ellsworth Public Library, and Patricia Foster and Charlene Clemons in particular; the Bangor Public Library; the Dedham Historical Society and great historian Eunice Ladd; the Otis Historical Society and the Mariaville Historical Society, especially Joanne and Arthur Dority, Mathel Bell, Geneva Frost, and Beverly Bragg; the Amherst Historical Society, with special thanks to Elizabeth Bragg Martin; the Surry Historical Society and Wayne Smith in particular; the Clifton Historical Society, with gratefulness to Alma Comins Williams and Mary Foster Bragg. I wish to thank Patsy Wilbur Jordan for providing invaluable resources, and extend my appreciation to the following: Honorable Herbert Silsby II, Carolyn Wood, Millard Giles, Joanne Anderson LaBlanc, Carole Luchetti, Thelma Bennoch Cyr, Mark Honey, Carl Humphrey, Arnold Hanscom, JoAnn Fletcher, Ed Honey, Milton Jellison, Sally Mathews, David N. Jellison, Asa "Bud" Mace, Roland A. Wilbur Sr., Muriel Wilbur, Evelyn Bragdon, Merle Jordan, Martha Peabody Jordan, Mary Mace Simeon, Richard Sumner, and the late Evelyn Gray Huckins, Clifton historian.

Introduction

While this author has spent most of her life in and around the towns along the Union River, there is still a great deal left to discover, as I learned while gathering material for this book.

We are all cousins along the river, it seems, or at least a land of third cousins stemming from the fact that the few who did venture to the mouth of the Union River sent out their sons and daughters upcountry to clear their own lands. Common bonds of family and hardships on the frontier made for the close-knit wholeness that exists even today.

All of the towns covered in this book lie within a 25-mile radius of Ellsworth. The most common bond is the Union River. Three out of every ten acres in the county are drained by brooks or streams which join to form the river. Sixty-nine thousand acres of lakes, ponds, and streams lie within these seven or eight towns and one half of them lie within the river's drainage system. Three major branches, called East, West, and Middle, have their beginnings in Penobscot County. The West Branch is the largest, draining 175 square miles.

There are few dams on the river, the largest being the 65-foot dam that created Leonard Lake in Ellsworth City proper. The old Brimmer Dam which created Graham Lake further north has recently been modernized.

On January 28, 1793, a man by the name of William Bingham changed the area forever when he purchased 1,107,398 acres of what was to become Hancock and Washington Counties. His land agent, General David Cobb, offered the lands for sale, and soon Bingham and his partner, Alexander Baring, were broadcasting an idea of theirs to install a greenhouse settlement to be erected at Mariaville Falls. John Fabrique of Connecticut was hired to manage the mill. While this dream did not flourish, it brought settlers to the area and soon towns were cropping up all along the river.

Settlement began at the mouth of the river, where towns shared yet another tie: their borders. Soon lands were annexed from one settlement to another; some inhabitants petitioned to separate their land and other lands were "taken out of" the original grants. In 1832, Tisdale, Hewins and Flowers of Boston purchased two lots of land at Amherst for $500 and put up a tannery. Another tannery was installed at Mariaville. These two operations provided work for hundreds of new settlers. When the two operations burned around 1900, the land owners turned to farming, harvesting blueberries, and raising cattle. Others moved to summer colonies west and south of the river.

These towns survive to this day, and the people still farm and depend on the larger towns for year-round employment.

One

Beginning at the Falls:
Ellsworth Falls and Fletcher's Landing

The earliest records, deeds, and wills indicate that part of the city of Ellsworth known today as "The Falls," which registered but little upon the flow of people to the south and east, was at one time the center upon which the area revolved. Here the Union River narrowed at places to make erecting a dam easy. Other bends became mill sites with a cribwork of legs and stones harnessing the water. The Union River derived further strength from Branch Pond Stream and the flow from Reed's Pond to the north. Lumber planing mills, stave mills, sawmills, and shingle mills soon brought more men to the area. What Samuel, Robert, and Benjamin Milliken started in 1769, when they purchased lands on the Union River from William Maxfield while yet living in Scarborough, never crossed their minds. The huge drawing card of plenty of water power brought hundreds of families here. When Benjamin Jellison built the first mill dam, called Middle Dam, before 1775, his interests insured the future of what was to become Ellsworth, Maine, the largest city in land area in the United States. The early deeds of such men as Fletcher, Jordan, Maddocks, Moore, Lord, Smith, Garland, and Flood, to name a few, are still preserved and provide a genealogical bonanza. So, the title of this section could be paraphrased "The Beginning, at the Falls."

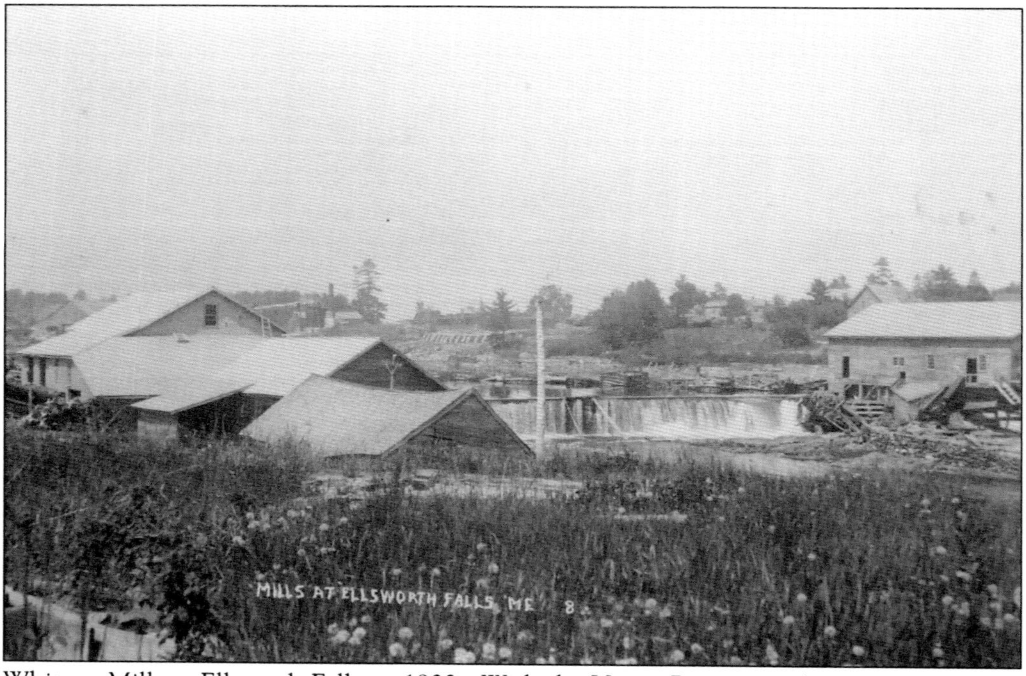

Whitney Mills at Ellsworth Falls, *c.* 1900s. With the Union River providing a strong flow of power, thousands of board feet of lumber were turned out. As many as seventeen such mills operated here at one time.

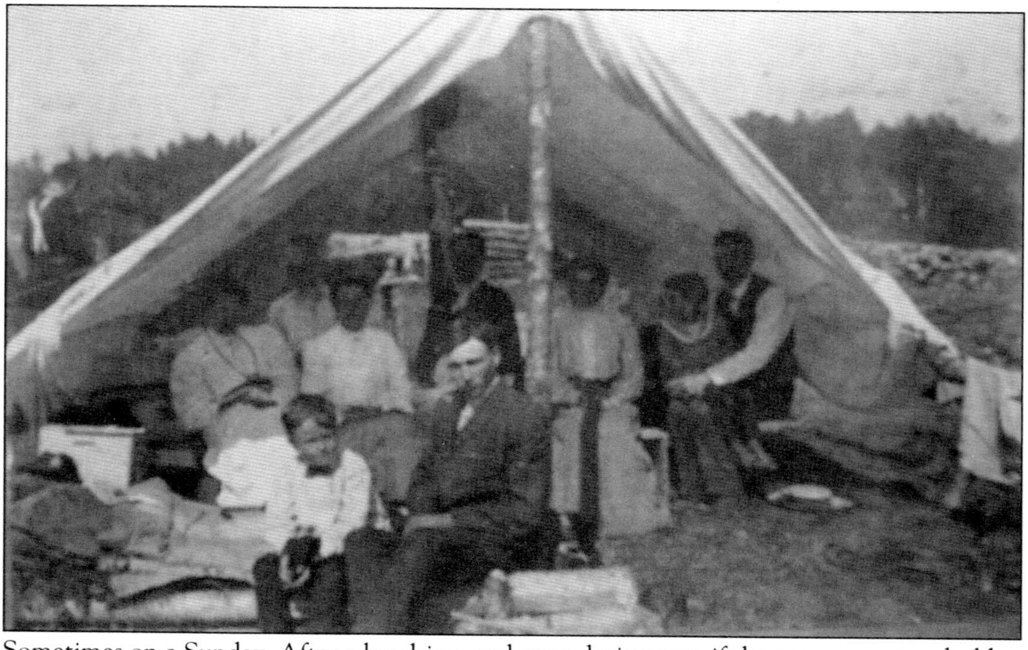
Sometimes on a Sunday. After a log drive, and even during one, if the crew came to a holdup in the river, families came to bring a bit of home-cooked food or just to see their loved ones. On the right a father holds his young son while another lad and his dad sit on a log bunk in the foreground.

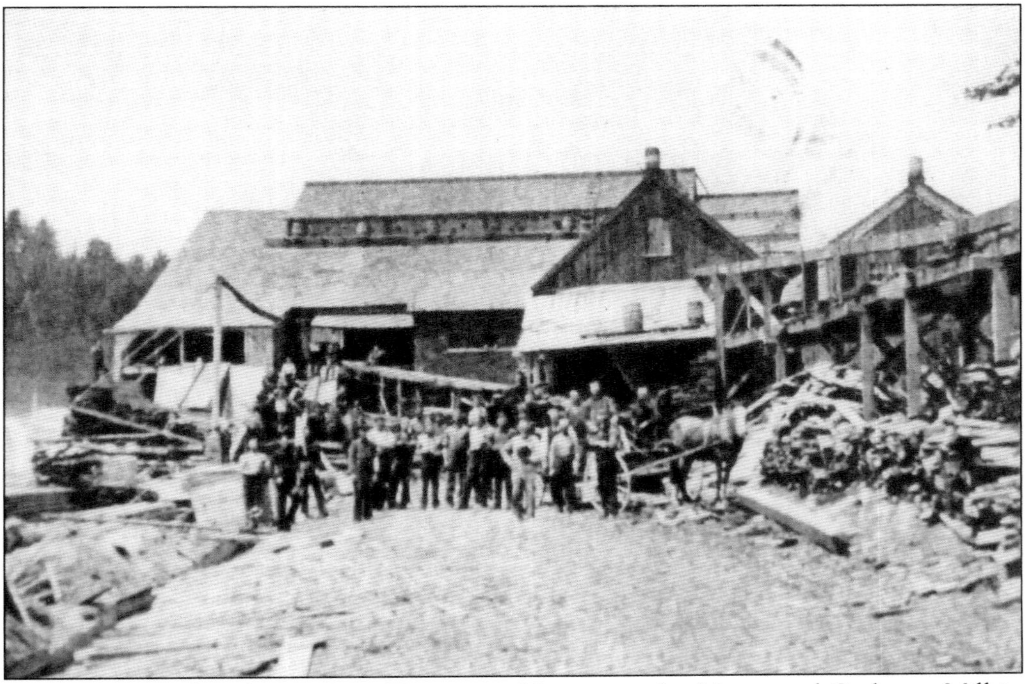

The Historic Mill and Dam Site. This is an old scene at the Mason and Cushman Mill in Ellsworth. It was first developed in 1768 when Benjamin Milliken and his brother Thomas built "Head Tide" Dam. The mill had a number of owners through the years, including Murch, Joy, Jones, and John Fabrique; Bingham, Peters and Pond; and Joseph Knapp and Colonel John Black. The building burned and was rebuilt several times, and was sold in 1859 by Milliken to Mason and Cushman. A clothing mill operated by Henry Bowen was at the same site.

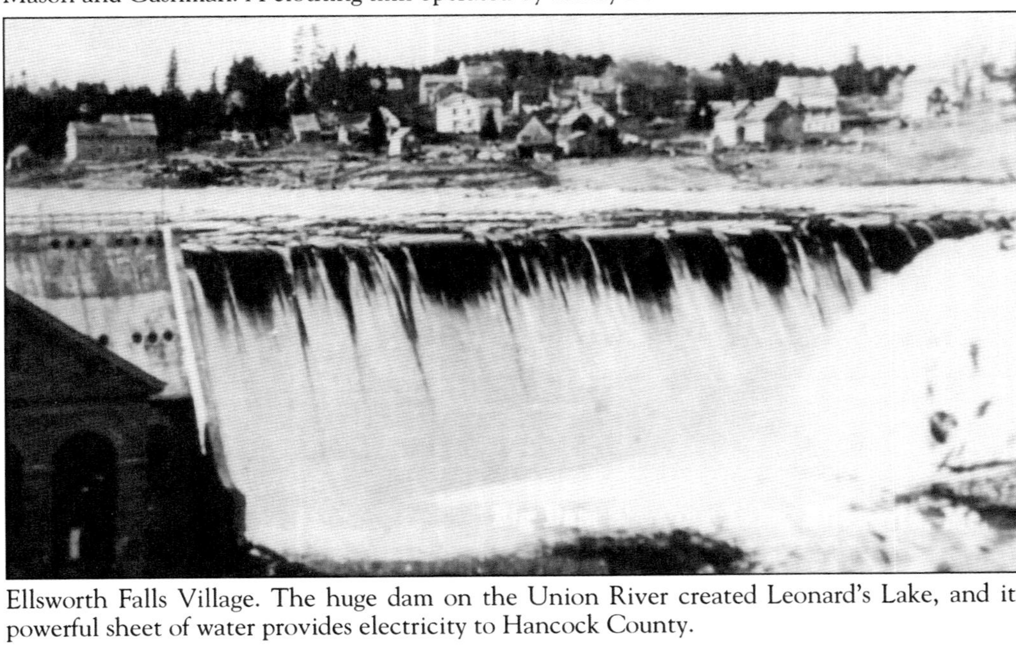

Ellsworth Falls Village. The huge dam on the Union River created Leonard's Lake, and its powerful sheet of water provides electricity to Hancock County.

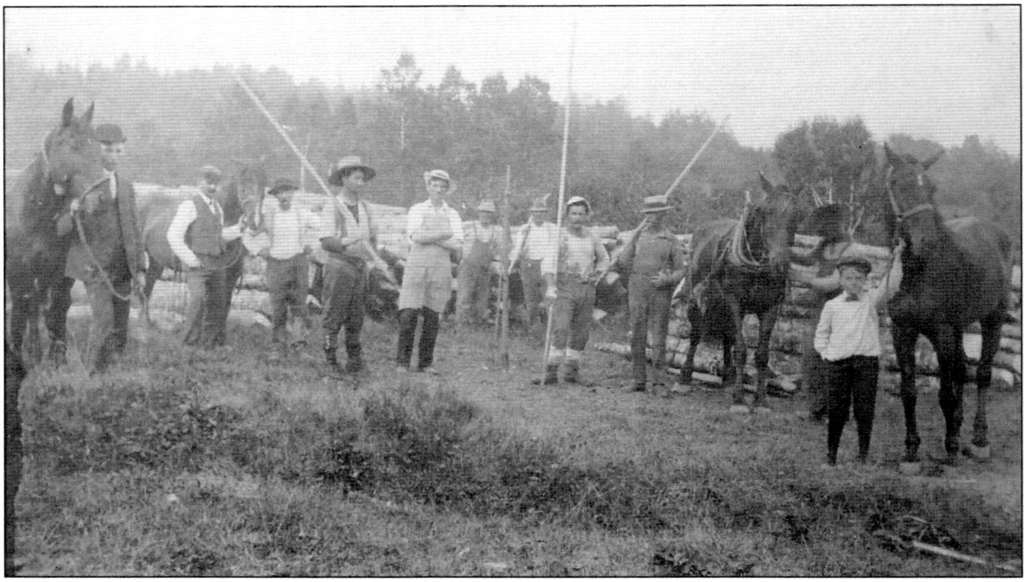

A Logging Operation on Union River, *c.* 1912. This scene is typical of a log landing on the river bank. Those men with long pics have pried the logs from the pile; the smaller piles were then twitched away by horses (see right center). The men in the background rest on iron-tipped peaveys which were much easier to handle then the pics. The man on the far left is Howard Caldwell Fletcher.

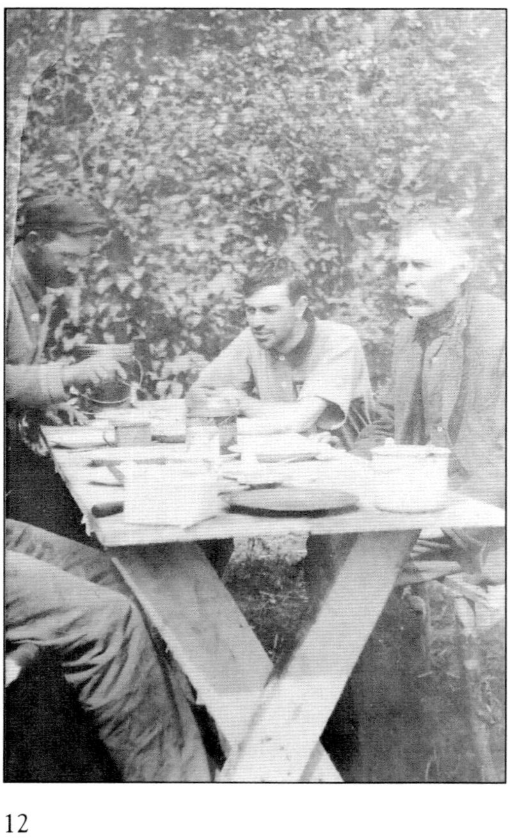

A Well-Deserved Lunch Break. Caldwell Fletcher, on the right, takes a two o'clock lunch break with the crew. Tin plates, cups, and lard-can serving dishes were the order of the day.

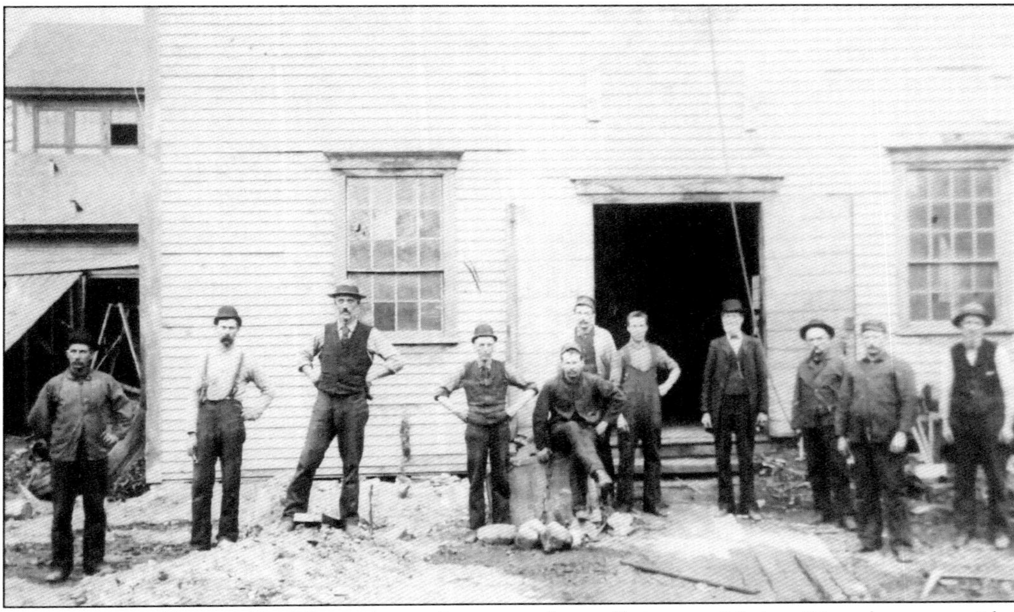

The Lower Mill, *c.* 1860s. Throughout the years, the mill sites on Union River have provided work for hundreds of men. A typical setup is shown here.

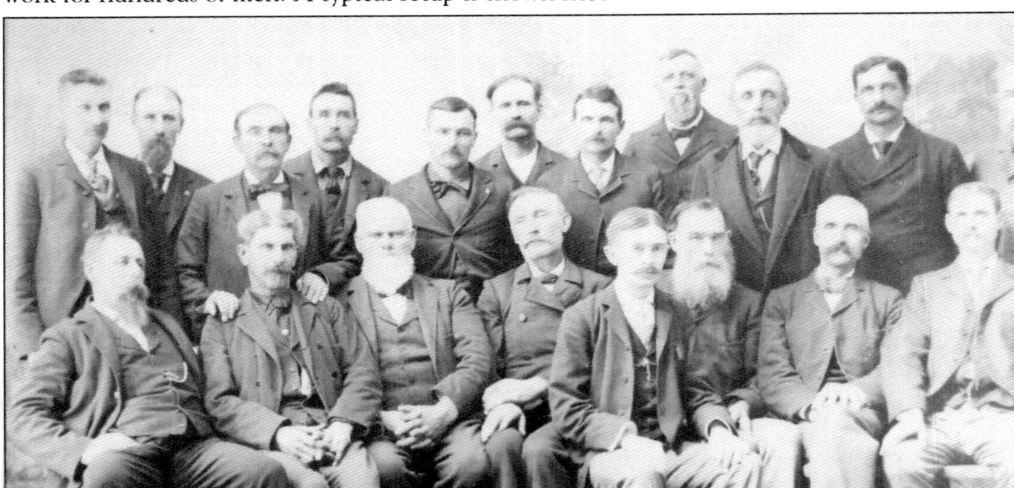

Grand Jury, October 1895. From left to right are as follows: (seated) foreman George Black of Deer Isle, A.J. Pettee of Sullivan, J.S.A. Perkins of Penobscot, J.C. Hammond of Gouldsboro, A.S. Lowell of Bucksport, O.S. Hanscom of Sedgewick, and A.G. Jellison of Ellsworth; (in front) E.S. Clark, county attorney of Eden; (first standing row) Seth N. Rich of Ellsworth, G.R. Lowell of Ellsworth, J.S. Condon of Brooksville, W.W. Norwood of Tremont, E. Parker of Brooklin, H.H. McIntire of Blue Hill, and E.G. Marks of Orland; (back row) J.J. Hibbert of Castine, J.N. Stratton of Hancock, M.G. Saunders of Surry, and J.J. Somes of Mt. Desert.

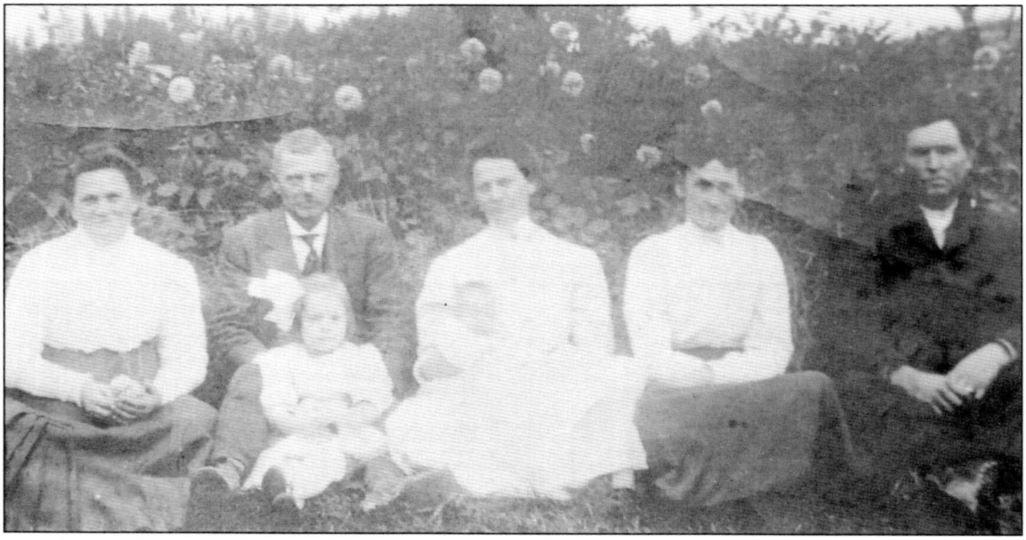

An Ellsworth Falls Family, c. 1908. On the lawn of their gracious home at the Falls are Priscilla (Fox) Davis, George Davis (holding Priscilla Scott), Annie Maud Scott (holding baby Mary Ellen), and Mary and Joe Fox.

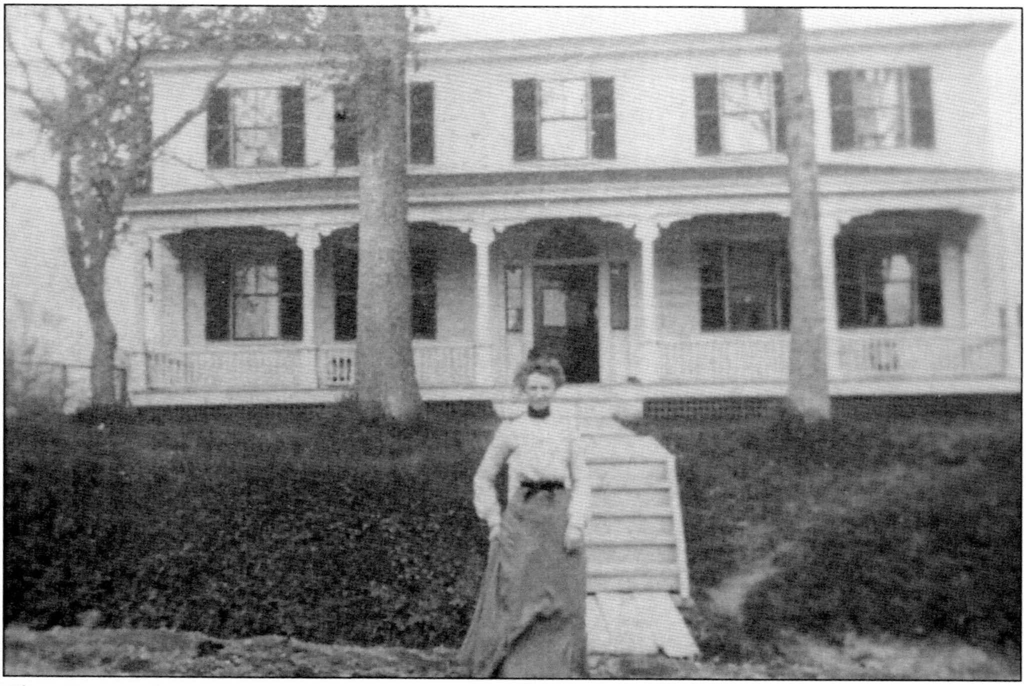

The George Davis Home at Ellsworth Falls. Originally known as the John Chamberlain homestead, the family of expert Union River lumberman George Davis lived here for many years. It now belongs to Dr. Richard Whitney. Davis began working at the age of fifteen for Seth Tisdale, a longtime lumber manufacturer, and worked his way up to superintendent. Later, he was superintendent for Whitcomb, Haynes and Whitney for fifty years. Born at the Falls in 1853, the son of Horace and Susan (Keyes), he married in 1893. He died in 1922, three years after his wife passed away.

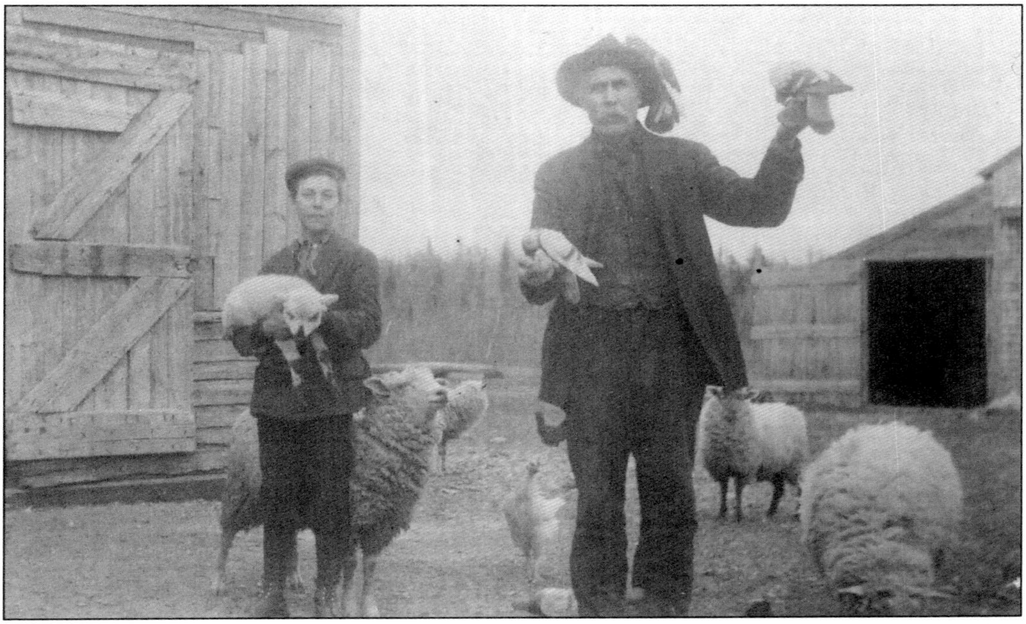

A Balancing Act at Fletcher's Landing, *c.* 1910. Howard Caldwell Fletcher shows his skill in handing pigeons. Perhaps he put some seed in his hat and his hands to entice them? Apparently animals and birds trusted this gentle man and his young son Ernest.

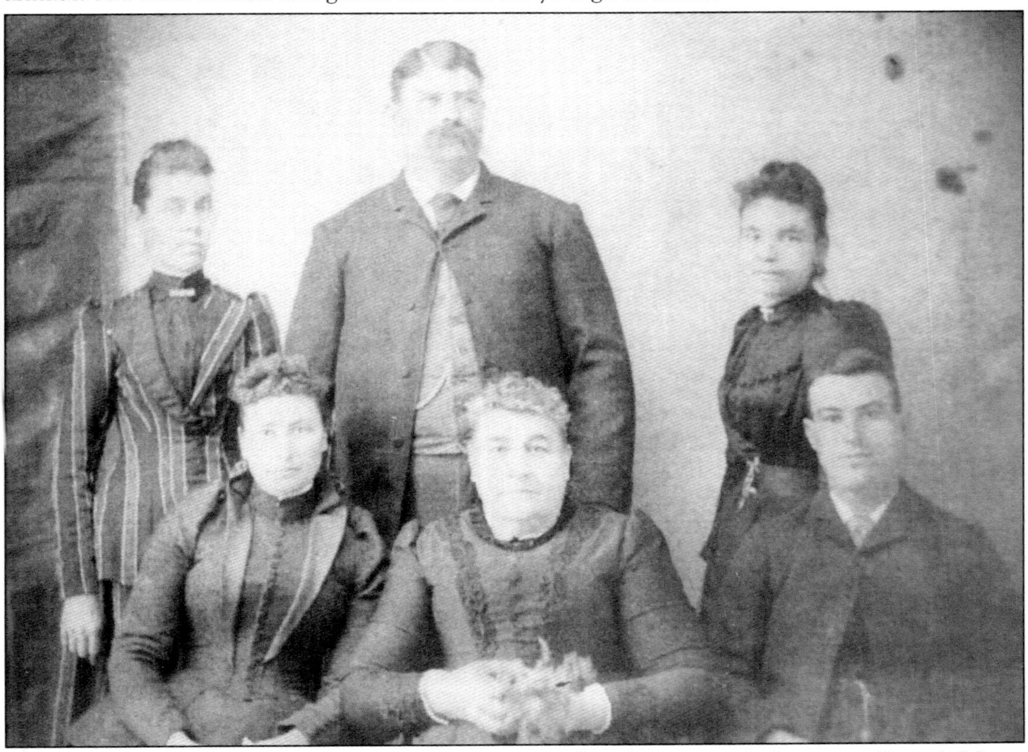

McGown-Salsbury's, *c.* 1880s. Ann Salsbury is seated in the center with some of her children. Elisha, at top center, is the only one identified.

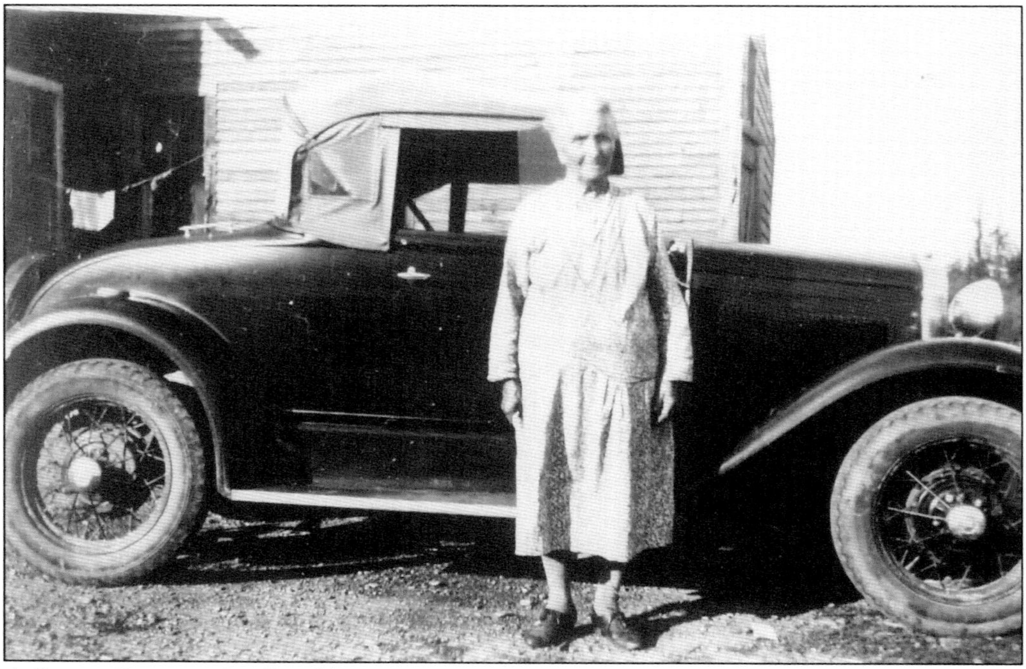

A Snazzy Coupe with a Rumble Seat, c. 1910. Iris Gertrude Goodell (1853–1934), the wife of Howard Fletcher, stands proudly beside the family automobile.

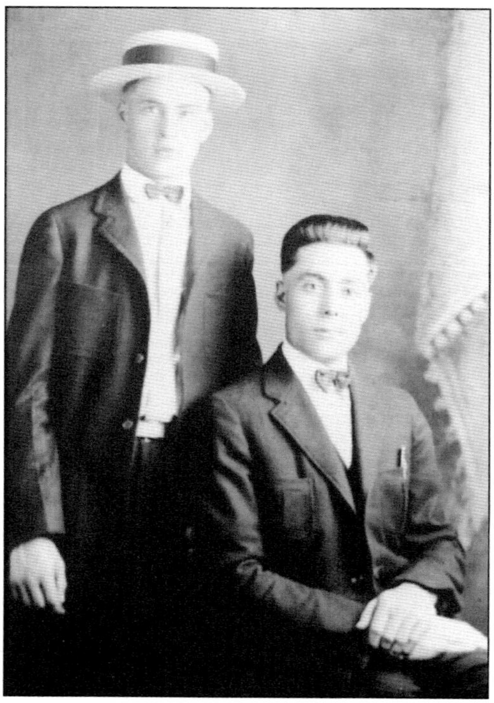

A High School Graduation? Joseph Whitmore (the son of Leslie and Daisy Whitmore) and Ernest Fletcher (seated, the son of Howard and Iris Fletcher) pose for the camera dressed in identical suits, looking the world squarely in the eye.

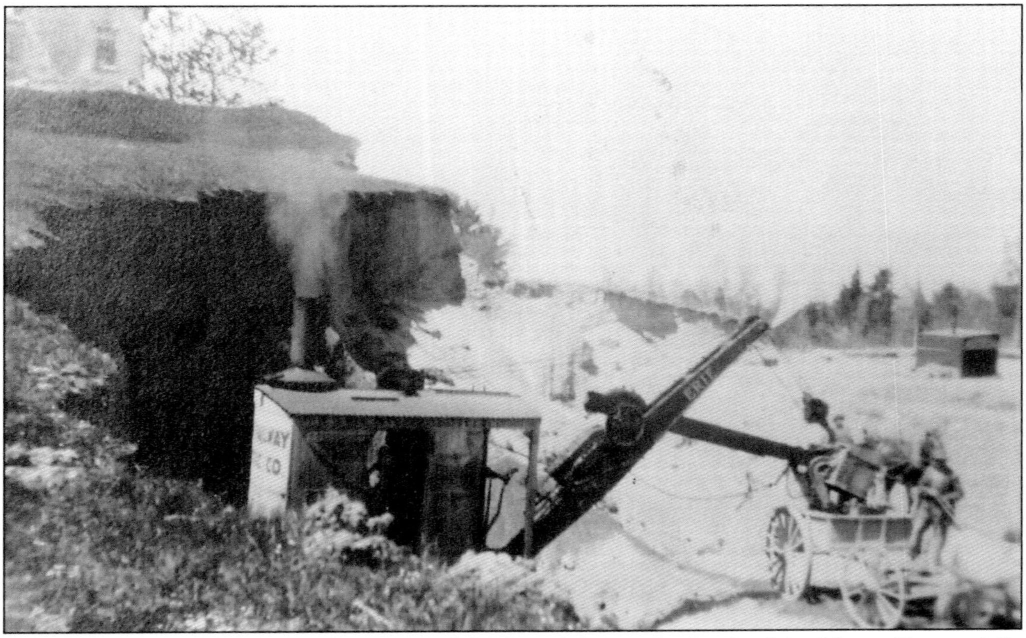

Zelotus Fletcher's Home. The house stands high and dry on the bank of the Union River while the machines work below digging sand. Since the photograph was taken, the entire bank has been harvested.

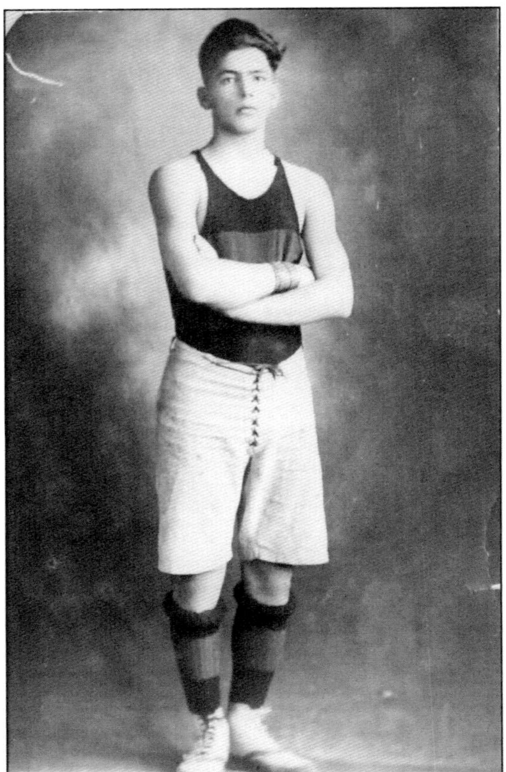

An Ellsworth Boxer, *c.* 1915. Frank Whitehouse Anderson Sr. was a crackerjack boxer in his day and continued to "punch a bag" hung up in his garage until the late 1980s. He was born in North Woodstock, NH, in 1895, to Hollis Anderson and his wife, at a logging camp where Hollis worked as the chief cook. Frank died in 1985 at the age of ninety after a distinguished career in the state legislature and local politics.

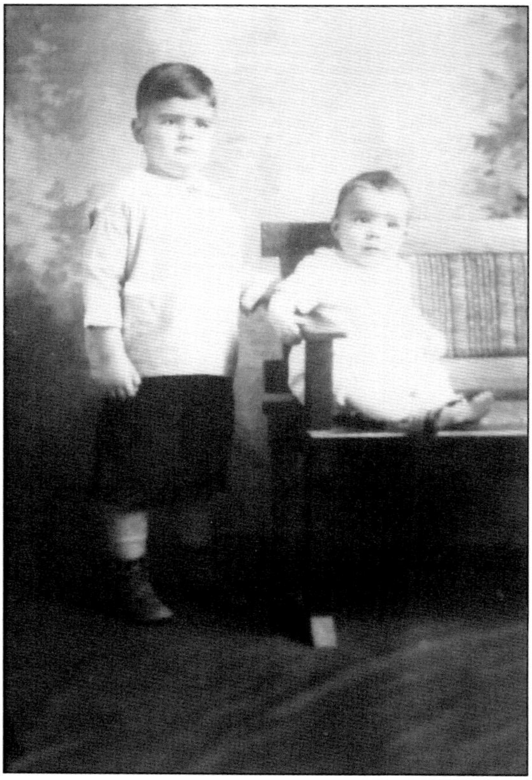

Anderson Brothers, *c.* 1926. Frank Anderson Jr. and his brother George were the sons of Frank and Marion (Coughlin) of Ellsworth. Frank served in the Marine Corp in World War II and entered the game warden service when he returned home. He owned and ran the Amherst General Store in that town for a number of years. George served in the Navy and entered New England Tel & Tel after getting out of the service. He retired from that career and lives on the Surry Road in Ellsworth.

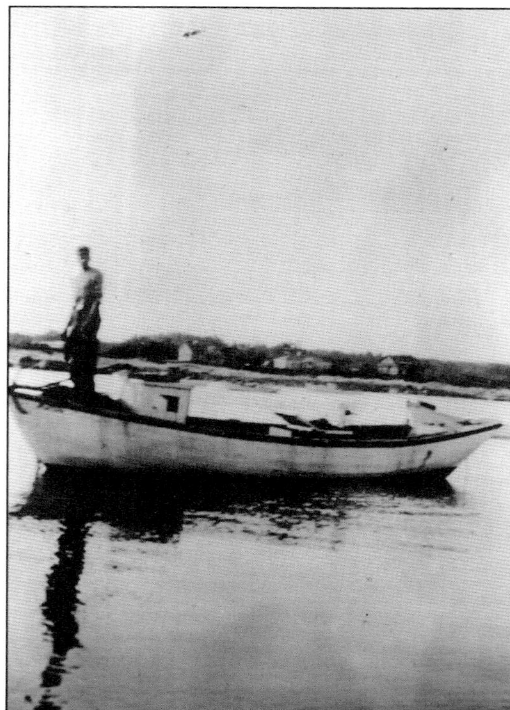

A Work Boat, Ellsworth Falls. The young lad is about to drop anchor in Union River just above Lower Falls Dam, *c.* 1898. Resembling a dory, this type of boat was a necessary tool during log drives.

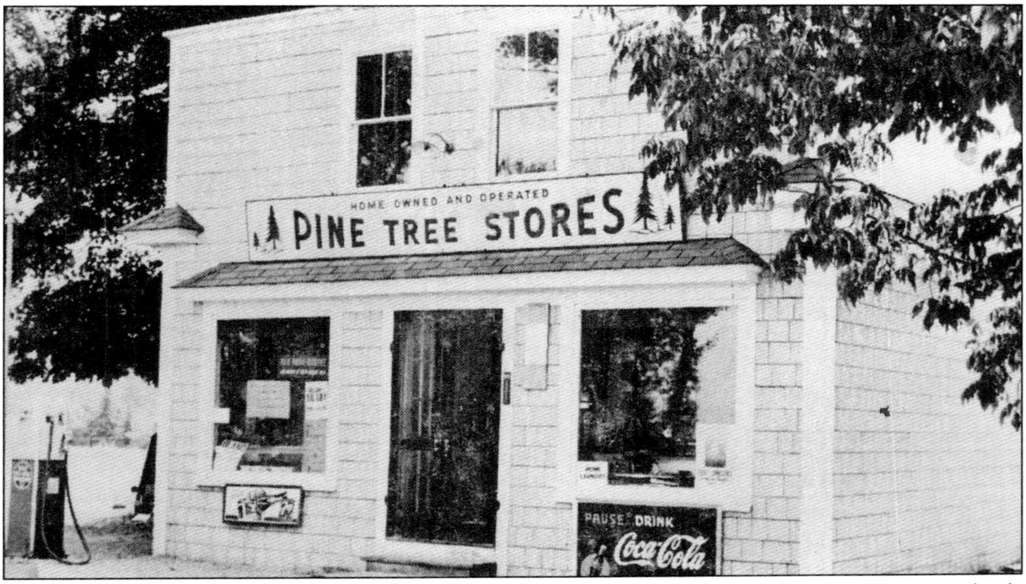

The Otis General Store Celebrates Sixty Years. The original Salsbury's General Store was built 1936–37 and was located across the highway from its present site in Otis. It was a small building at first, perhaps 15 by 20 feet, but soon expanded business demanded a larger structure. In January of 1945, Roland Jr. remembers his father boarding in the floor of this second store. Roland Jr. had tended the store since he was twelve or fourteen years of age, but he entered the military in 1945. The third store was the basis for the one now supplying the tri-towns and vacationers to Beech Hill Pond.

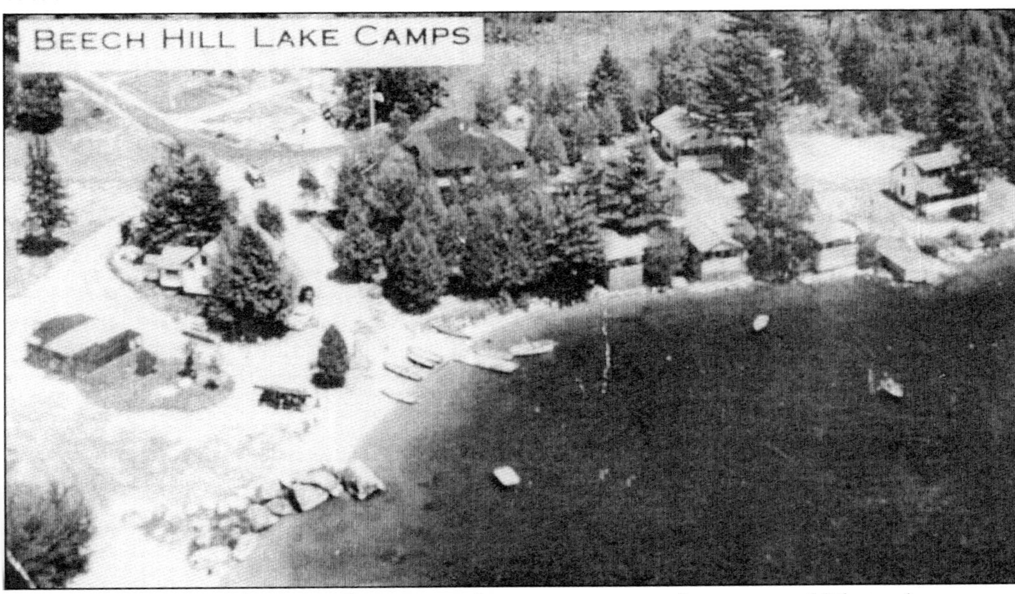

The Beech Pond Settlement. This group of camps was once the center of life in the town of New Trenton, now Otis, as early as 1840. The original 10,000 acres purchased by Jabez Salsbury of Mount Desert Island encompassed both pond and settlement. Charles Watts, shown here landing near his brother Frank's cabin, served meals here to the public and ran a store in the basement of the dining hall (center).

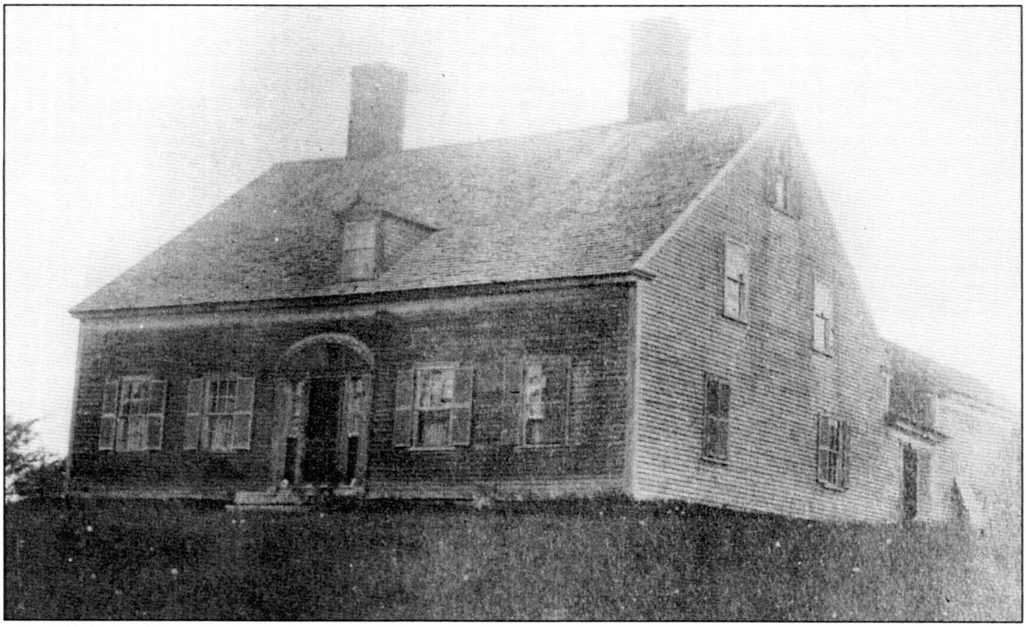

The Old Settler's Homestead. Built *c.* 1850, this was the home of Charles Otis, a brother to first settler Joseph, for whom the town was named. Located on Gary Moore Road, this house was eventually torn down; the home of Dwight and Joan Tate has been built on the old foundation.

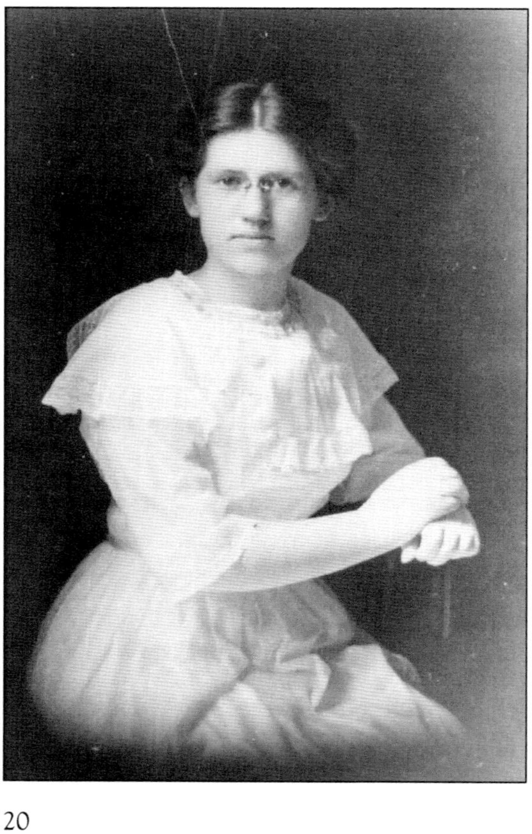

A Graduate of the Eastern Maine Conference Seminary at Bucksport. Erma Evelyn Jordan (1894–1986) married Roland Salsbury Sr. and they celebrated their 50th wedding anniversary before his death in 1964. They were the owners and operators of the Otis General Store for many years. Both were active in local, state, and national Patrons of Husbandry. Erma was president of the St. Croix District Garden Club and founded the Tri-Town Garden Club at Otis. For many years, her radio program, "Coming through the Garden-Gate," was a favorite in the county.

Two

North on Route 180:
Otis, Mariaville, Amherst

Otis was first settled in 1805 by Isaac Frazier, Nathaniel Jellison, James Gilpatrick, and Alan Milliken, who came from Trenton, Maine. It was named for two well-loved citizens, Esquire Joseph Otis and his wife Fanny. Both died in that town, in 1856 and 1861 respectively. Mariaville was called "Tilden" for its largest land owner, Joseph Tilden. Parts of Mariaville, incorporated in 1836, are now the towns of Aurora, Waltham, and Amherst. First settlers were John Fabrique, Seth Orcutt, B. and D. Epps, James Hapworth, and Elisha Goodwin; Emerson Orcutt and Zelotus Grover were among the first permanent settlers.

Amherst was called North Mariaville but was "set off" in 1822 and incorporated in 1831. First settlers were Jesse Giles, John Barker, Thomas Hapworth, Mr. Graves, and Captain Goodell Silsby. The Foster, Chick, Grover, and Fletcher families came in 1810, the men being drawn to the work provided at the mill and dam in Mariaville and the tannery set up in Amherst.

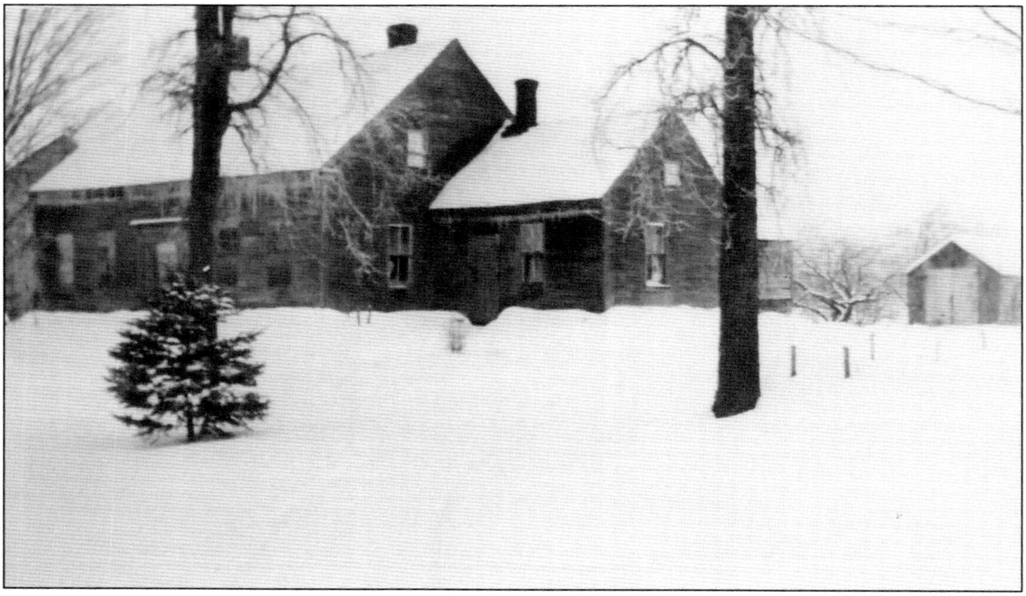

The James Brimmer Homestead. Built as early as 1840, this architecture was typical of homes built throughout the Union River Valley.

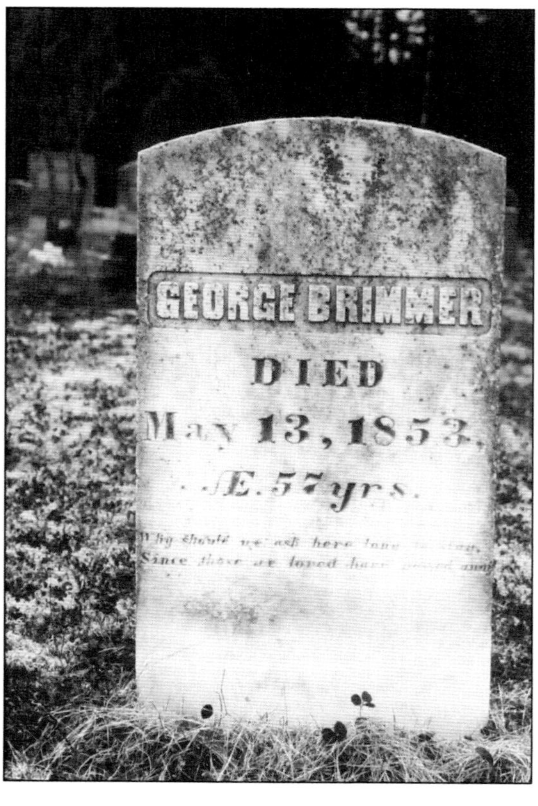

George Brimmer's Headstone. When Brimmer died on May 13, 1853, at the age of fifty-seven, he was buried in the cemetery he gave to the town. "Why should we ask here long to stay, Since those we loved have passed away."

Mariaville, *c.* 1890. Ida DeBeck married Frank Frost, the son of Thomas Frost and Louisa (Smith). Both of these families were early settlers to Mariaville from New Hampshire.

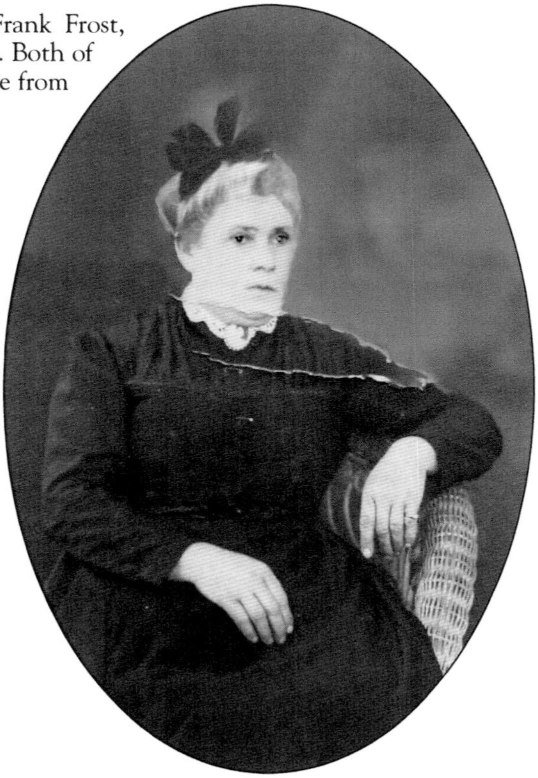

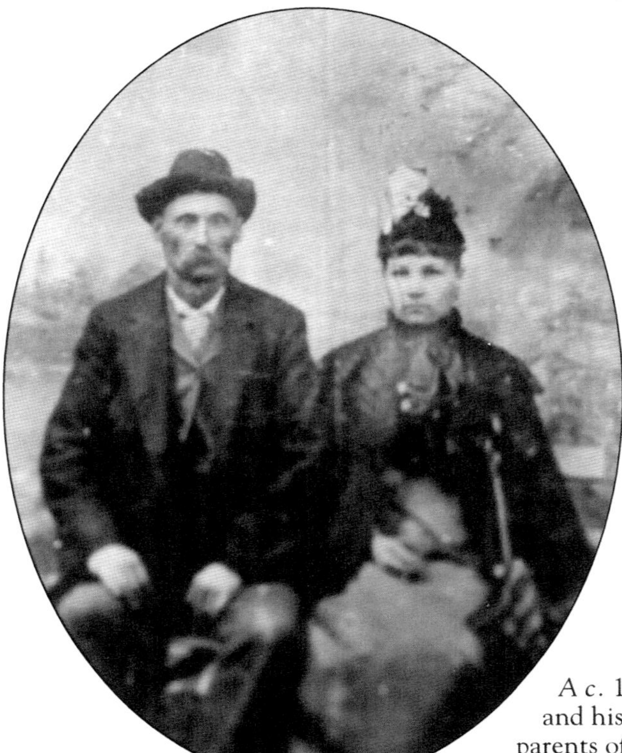

A *c.* 1870s Tintype. William DeBeck and his wife, Elizabeth Kidd, were the parents of Ida DeBeck, who married Frank Frost of Mariaville.

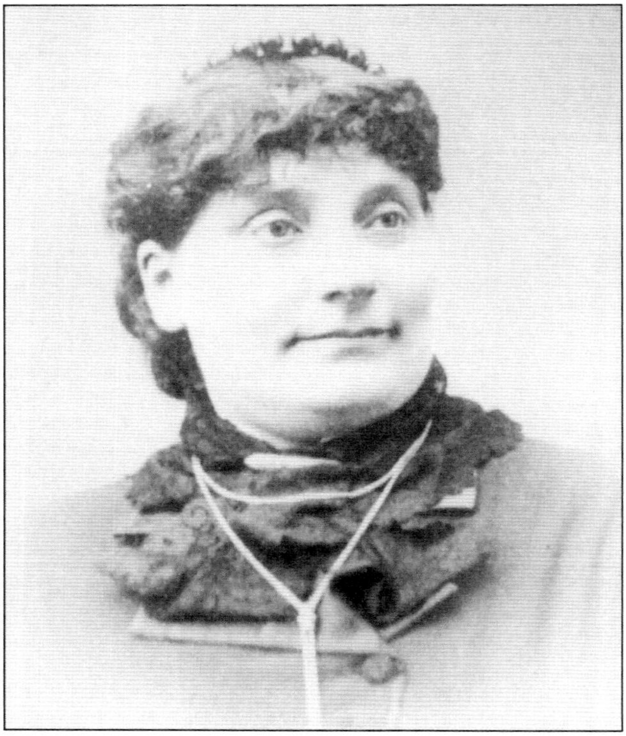

Perfenda Ruby Dority. Perfenda married John Dougherty, and the couple lived at Dedham and early Trenton before moving to Mariaville. Their name was later spelled "Dority."

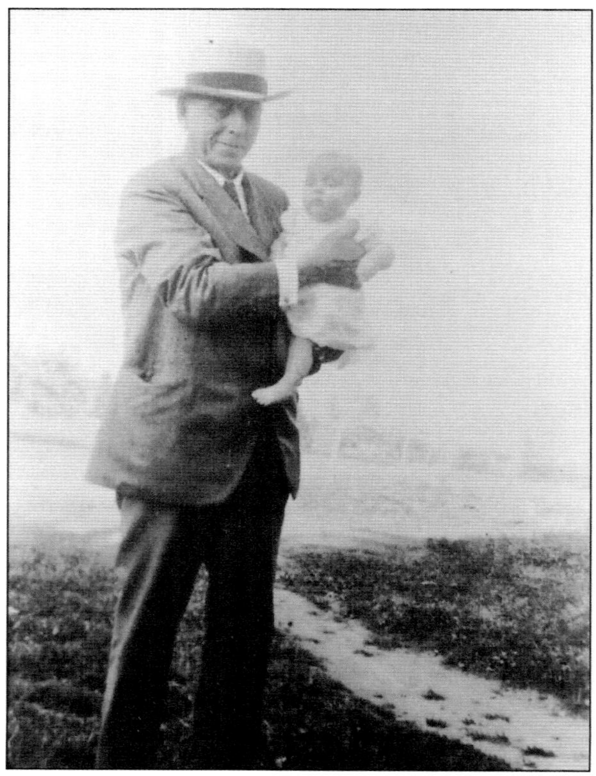

Noted Area Physician Dr. Charles Carr Morrison. Born on July 12, 1856, at Mariaville, Charles was the son of John Tinker Morrison and Lucy Jordan Carr. He married Ida M. Conners originally; after she died in 1917, he remarried to Harriet Roberts. The Morrison family was in Ellsworth as early as 1782 and settled in what became known as "The Morrison District." Joseph Morrison moved from Ellsworth to Mariaville in 1809 into a log cabin on Emery's land. He married Tamah Haslam and they had twelve children. Of the twelve, Dr. Charles descended from John (b. 1804), and married first to Mary Tinker and then to Lucy Jordan Carr, *c.* 1841, who was the mother of his nine children.

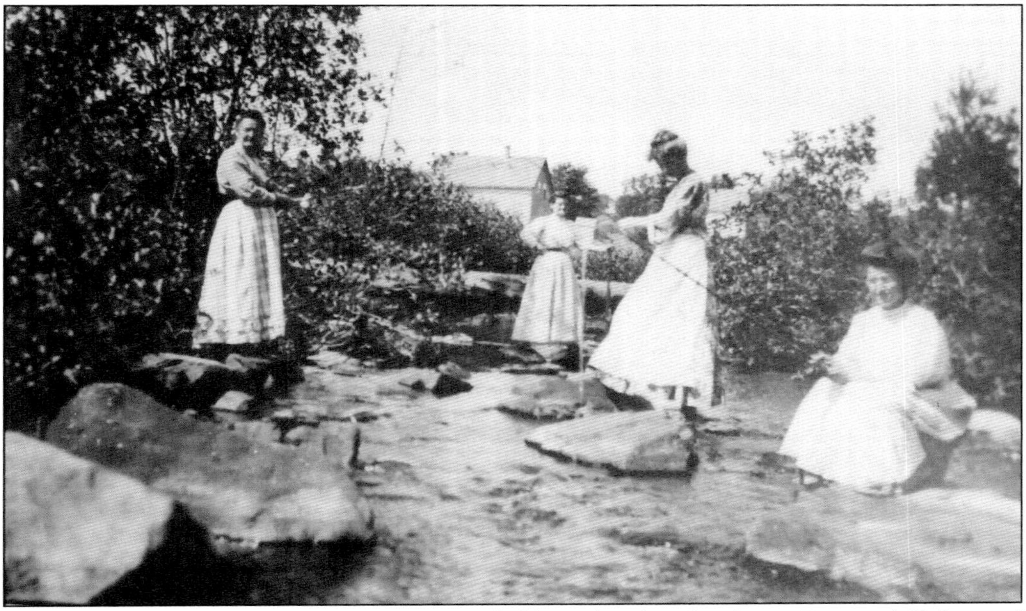

Mariaville, 1909. Hannah Jordan Hanscom (left) teaches her daughters Cora and Helen and her daughter-in-law Clara how to reel in a trout from Tannery Brook.

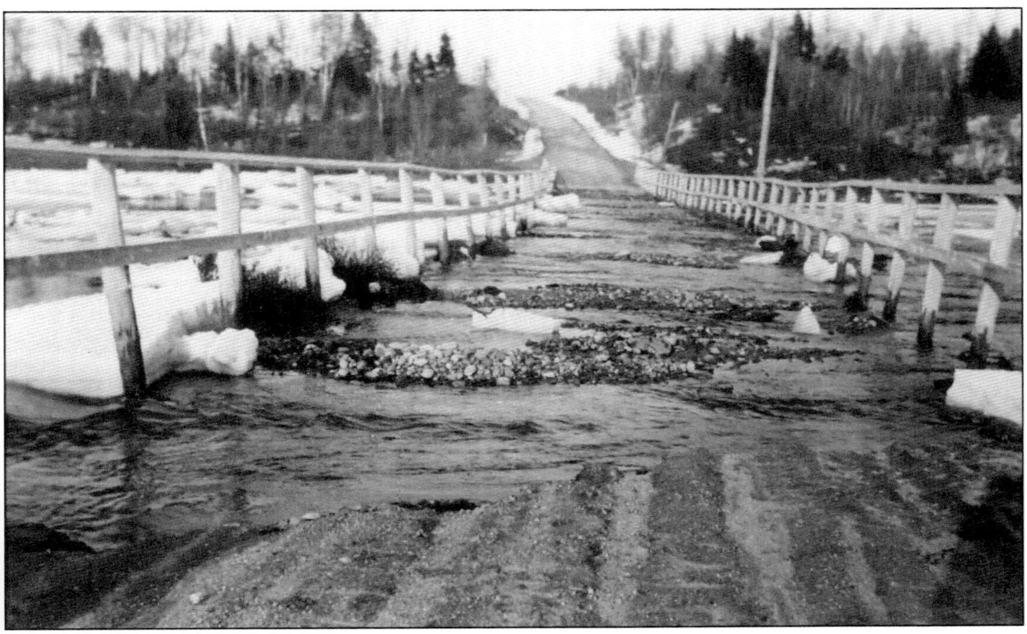

Goodwin's Bridge on Union River, *c.* 1937. It is certain that this bridge over the Union River at Mariaville was not the first one, but it was built very early. The first was built by Elisha Goodwin perhaps near the date 1820 when settlers began moving further and further into North Mariaville. The roadway connected Amherst to the settlement at Mariaville Falls. Before the bridge was raised above the yearly floods, this scene was often repeated.

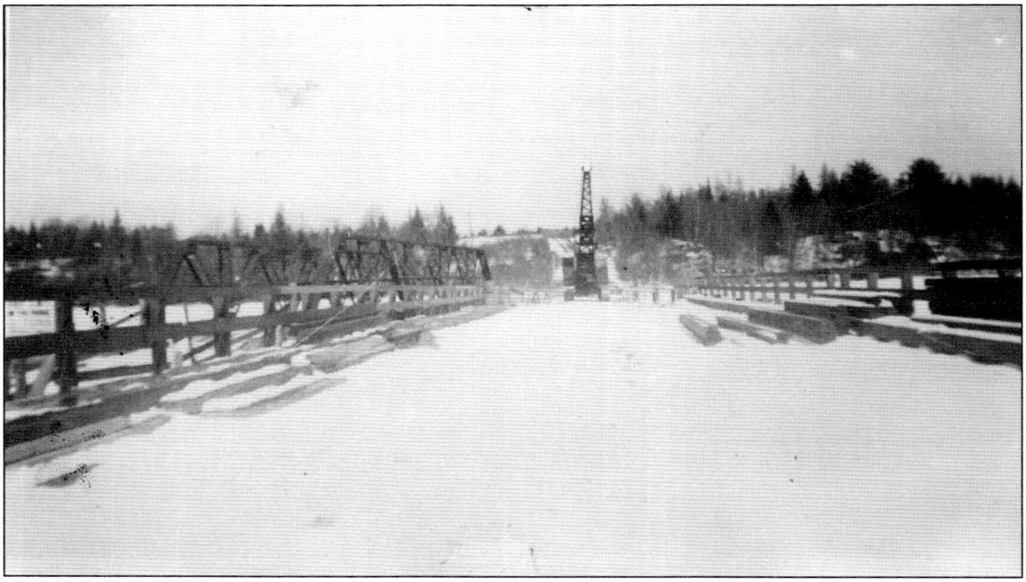

Another Bridge over the West Branch. The wooden bridge, which had replaced a stone and wood structure, was torn down before 1948. Les Frost's family remembers this effort provided a weekly pay check for him and many other men in the community.

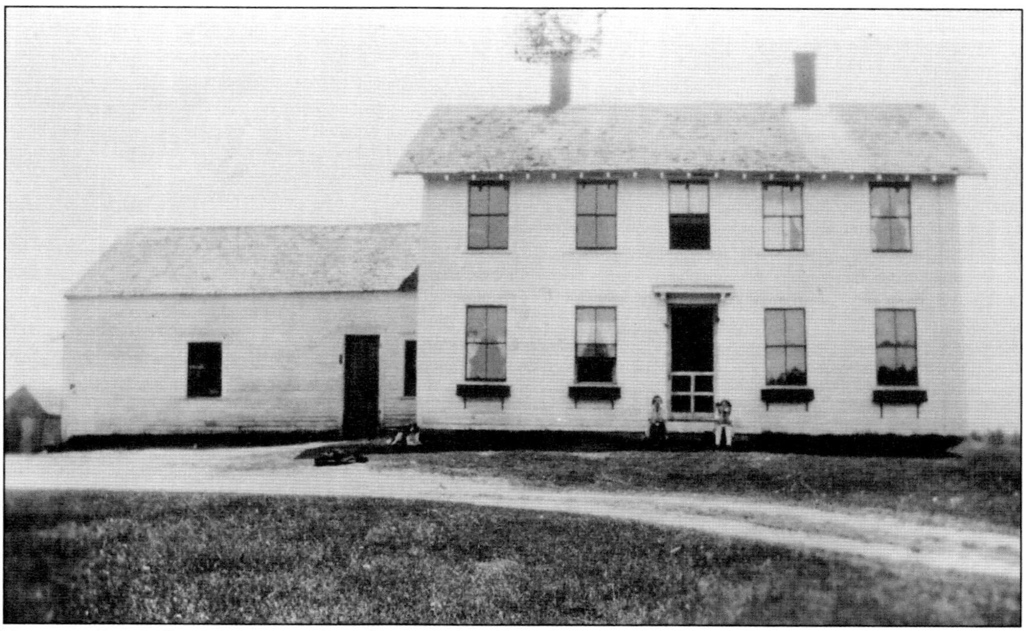

Prior to the 1950s in Mariaville. The Goodwin homestead stood tall and elegant on a rise above Goodwin's bridge for many years until it burned in the 1950s.

A Beloved Citizen, *c.* 1870. Nathan C. Jordan was photographed on his Mariaville farm, his face wreathed in a well-known smile. Upon his death a friend wrote: "A man above the average, with broad, optimistic mind; Noble, faithful father with charity for all mankind."

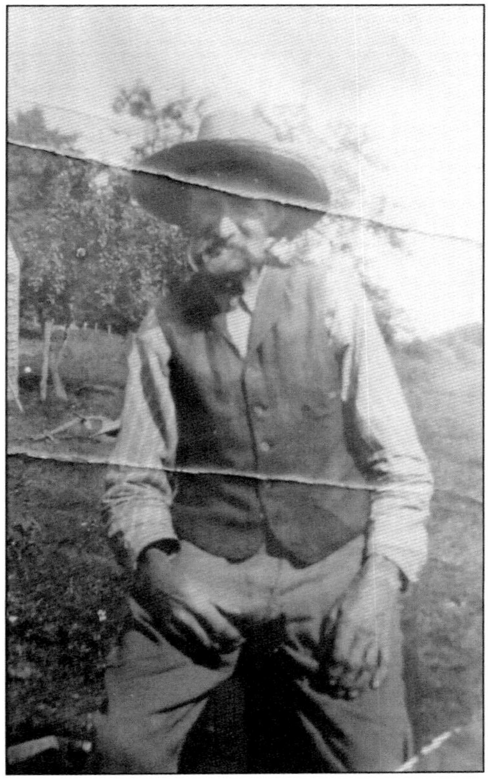

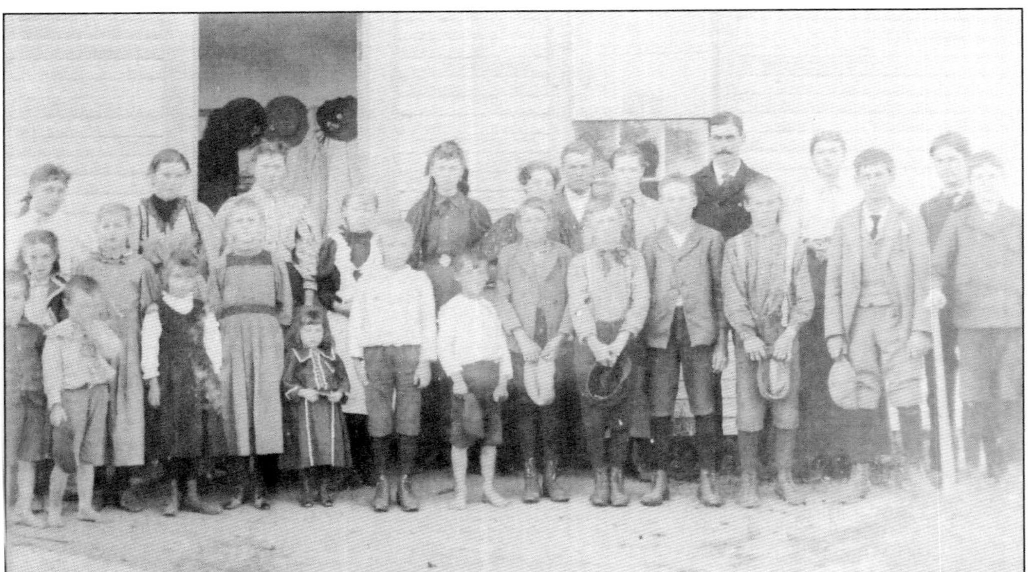

The Mariaville School, *c.* 1899. Known as school #1, this building stood near where the present town office is today. The only children identified are Fred Dority (third from right) and Helen Hanscom (the smallest child in the front row). They would later marry and raise a large family. The teacher is Elwyn C. Lord.

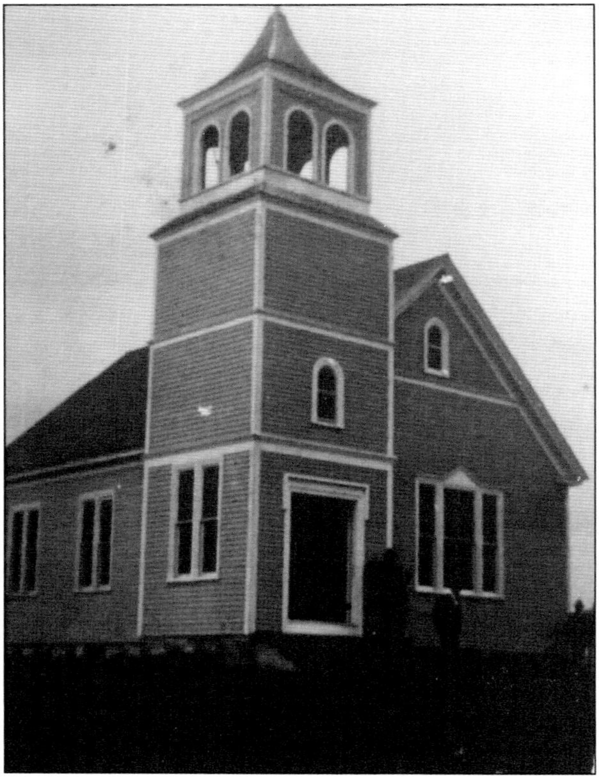

The Baptist Church, *c.* 1910. A busy place at one time, this church was up for sale several years ago. Its bell tower and arched windows still stand today, but the church corporation has closed.

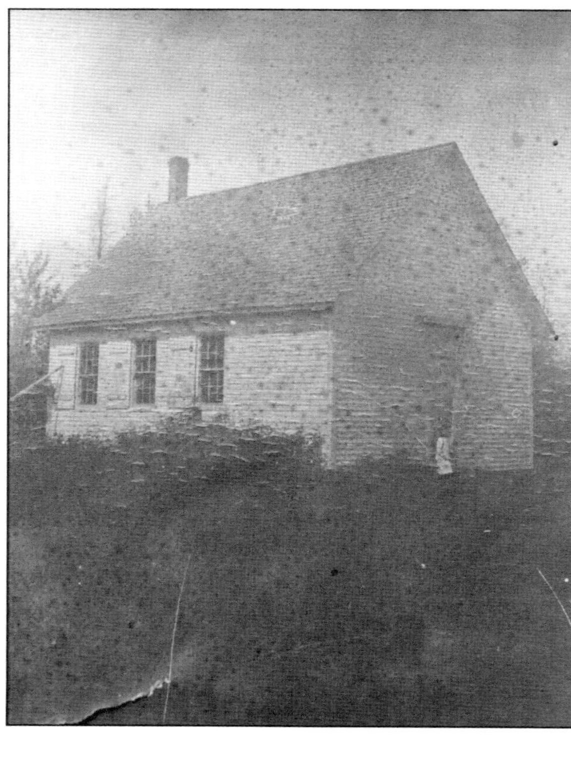

The Mariaville Upper School, *c.* 1913. Located near the Edgecomb Homestead, this was one of the town's earliest schools. Leslie and Willa Frost stand by the front steps.

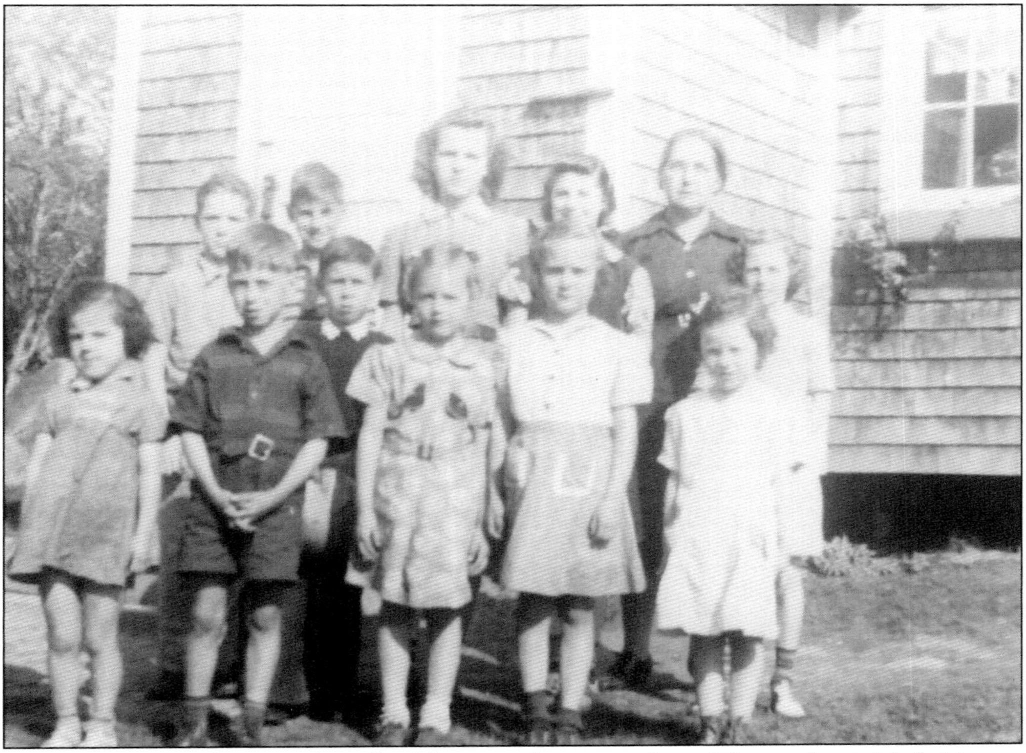

Washington School, 1941. This school has since been torn down. The teacher is Merle Norton Foster. From left to right are as follows: (front row) Norma Awalt, Clyde Frost, Robert Goodreau, Geneva Frost, Harriet Frost, and Corace Frost; (back row) Harold Frost, Maurice Frost, Eva Frost, Hilda Frost, Mrs. Foster, and Ida Frost.

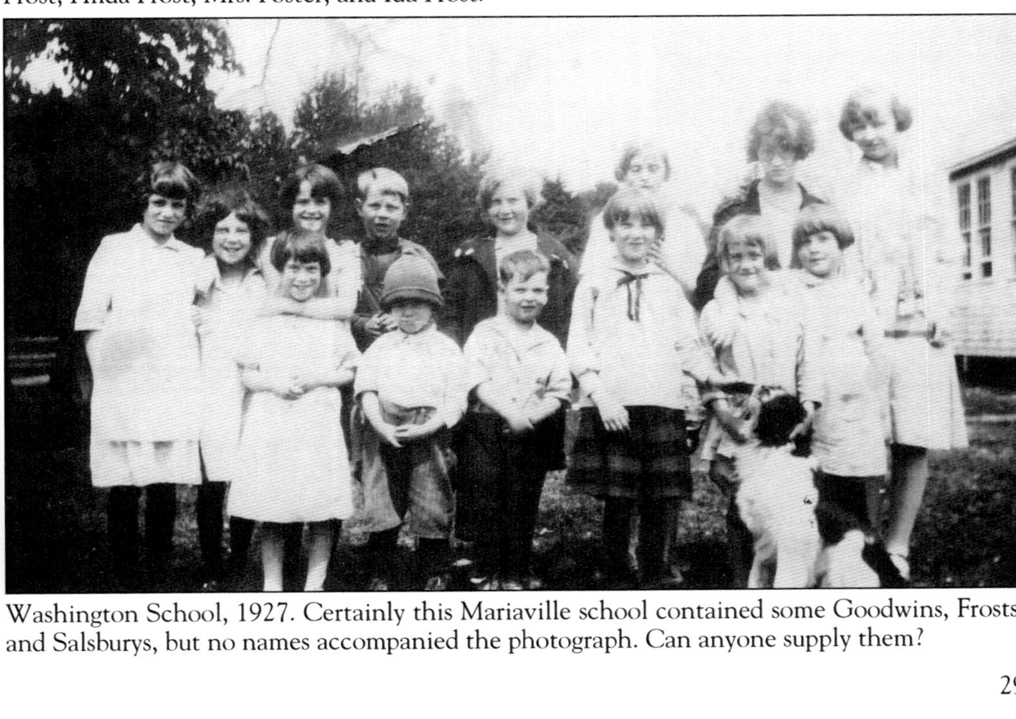

Washington School, 1927. Certainly this Mariaville school contained some Goodwins, Frosts, and Salsburys, but no names accompanied the photograph. Can anyone supply them?

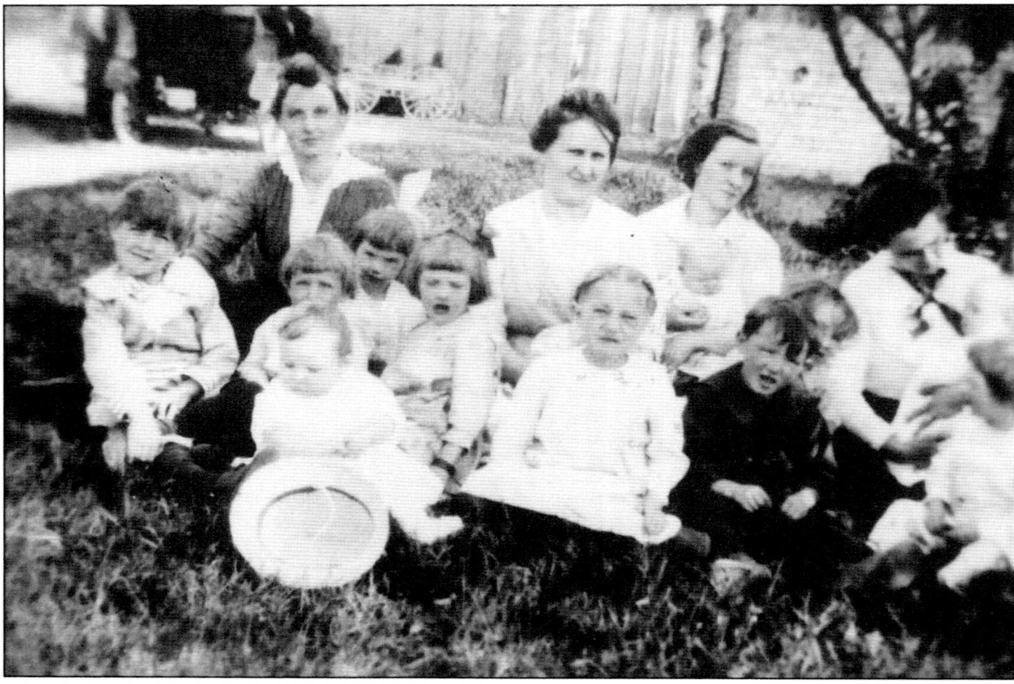

Tiny Tots in Mariaville. Some of the tots do not appear to be "happy campers." Perhaps they were told lunch would be later. From left to right are as follows: (front row, going to the far right) Edward Frost, Vera Frost, Thelma Foster, Phyllis Frost, and Ida (Frost) Tate; (back row, beginning behind Vera Frost) Lura Frost, Mattie (Frost) Foster, Ella Frost, and Isabelle Frost.

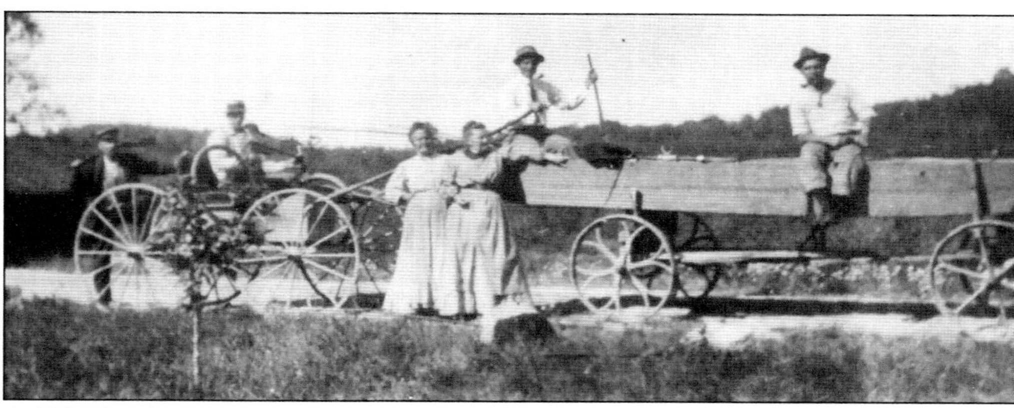

A 1909 Family Outing in Slow Gear. Elwood Silsby is driving the carriage on the left; Cora Hanscom Silsby, his wife, and a friend, Mrs. Harriman, are at center; and Vernon Hanscom is holding the carriage shaft behind them. The man at the far left is perhaps Manley Bailey.

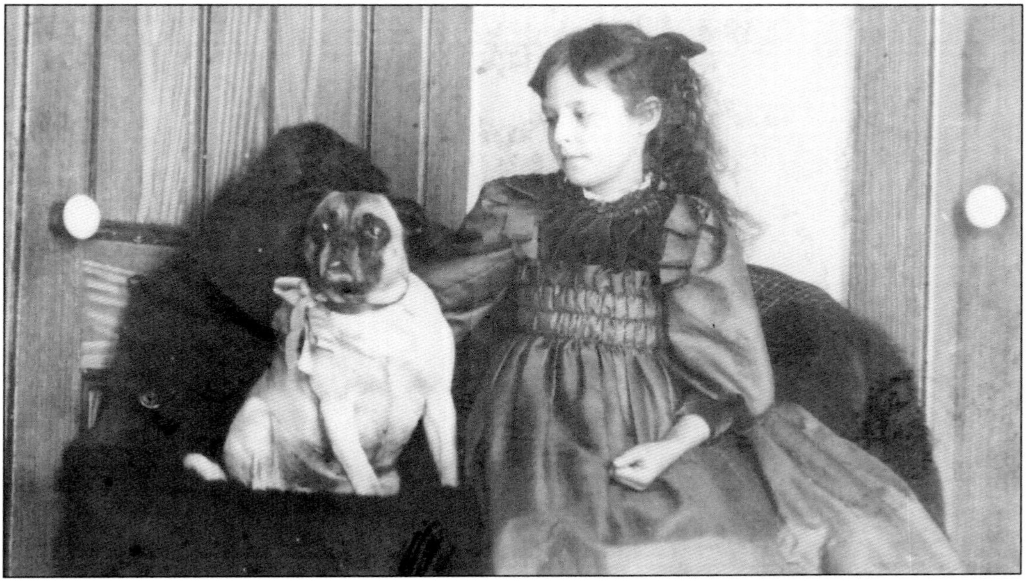

Helen Church Hanscom. Born at Mariaville in 1887, the daughter of Thomas Oren Hanscom and Hannah (Jordan), Helen is shown here with the family pet, "Tiger." Helen left the family farm and graduated from Castine Normal School before her marriage to Fred Dority.

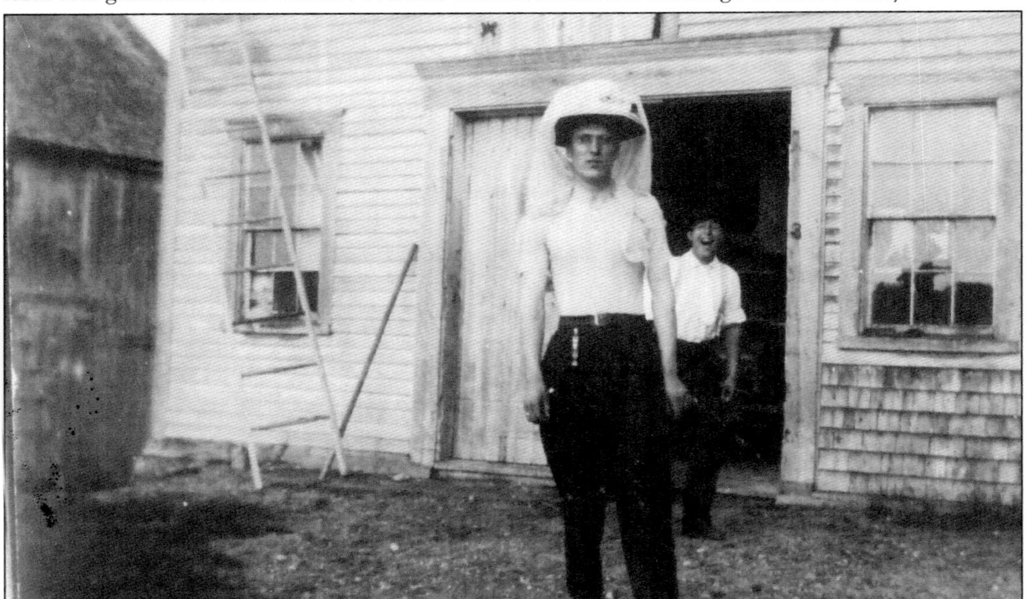

Harry Judson Silsby. A native of Amherst, Harry was the son of Elwood and Cora (Hanscom). After working for the Winchester Arms Company in New Haven, CT, he enlisted to serve in the Army during World War I. He saw action in France with the 102nd Infantry Regiment, for which he was awarded the Croix de Guerre by the French government and a Purple Heart with three oak leaf clusters for wounds in battle. Following the war, he served as an instructor at Fort Devens, MA, and later worked for Dupont. He is shown here enjoying a few carefree moments before going overseas; his headgear is a beekeeper's hood worn while "gathering" a migrating swarm and putting it into a new hive.

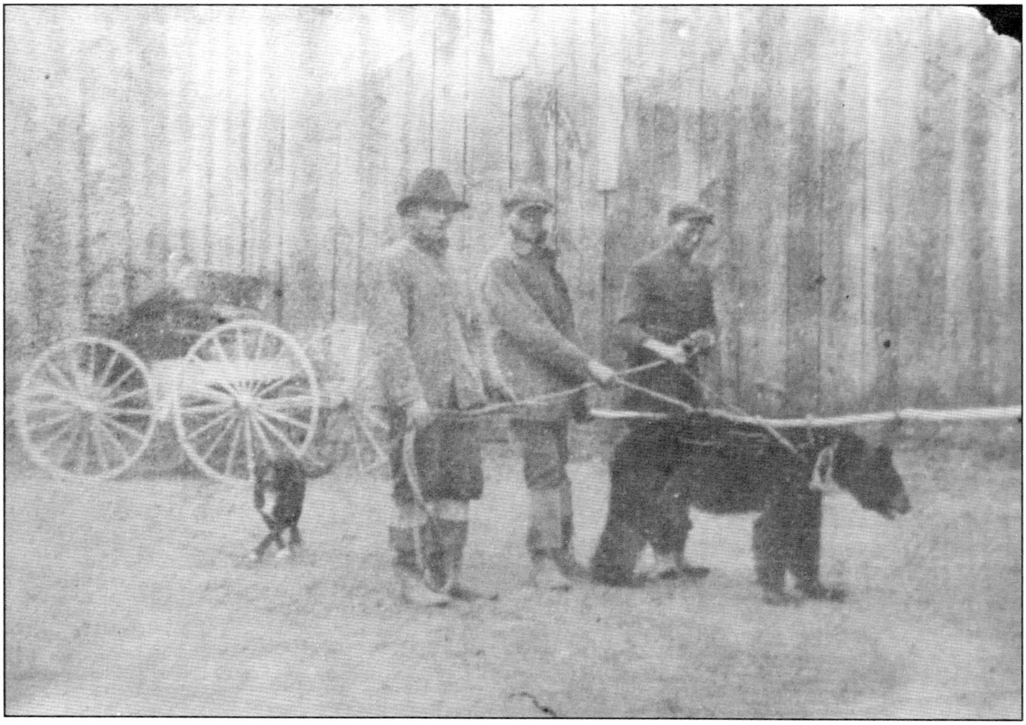

Having a Little Sport before They Let Him Go Again. This small bear was found on the blueberry barrens one year and the Frost cousins hitched it up for the photographer. Leslie remarked when he was older that if he caught one of his boys doing the same thing he'd tan their britches. From left to right are Albert, Leslie, and Elwood Frost.

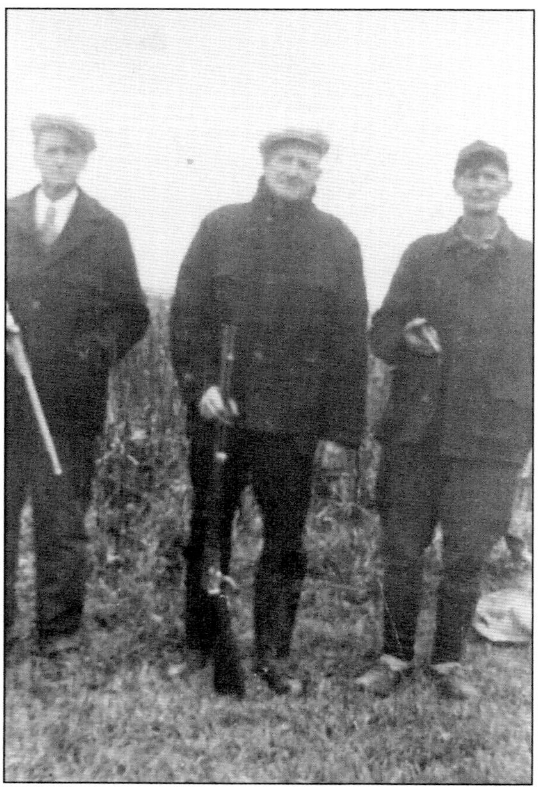

Bird Hunters at Mariaville. Lush fields of grass and abundant water produce game birds in Hancock County, as these oldtimers know. From left to right are Alvin Wilbur, Reuben Rankin, and Martin Moore.

Hunters Drawn to Eastern Maine. Dr. Fred Wheaton, a longtime friend of the Frost family, came each year to try his hand at rabbit and bird hunting. Here he is about 1919 with shot gun, shells, and two of Les Frost's hounds.

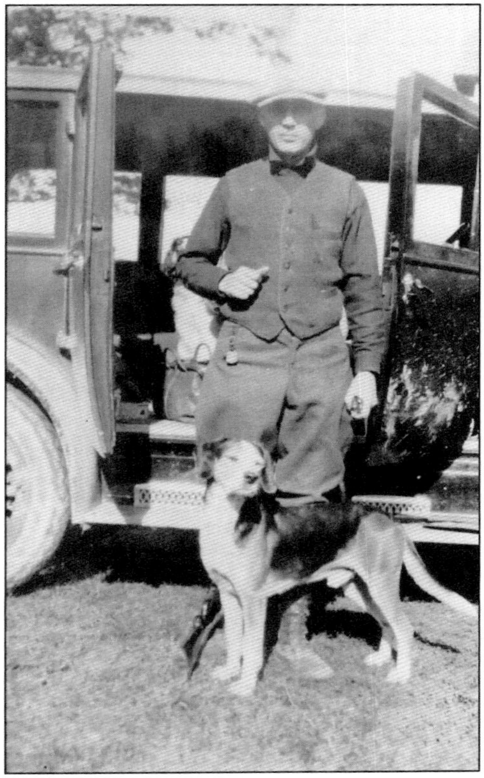

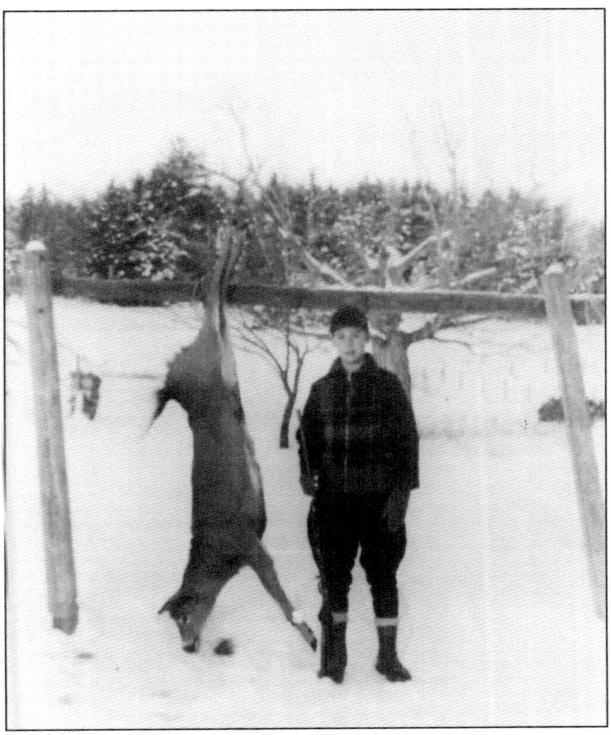

That Was a Very Good Year. Thirteen-year-old Arthur Dority of Mariaville proudly stands with his trophy deer about 1930. Not only was the hunt successful, but it insured there would be plenty of mincemeat for pies at Thanksgiving and Christmas, as well as venison in place of the usual beef.

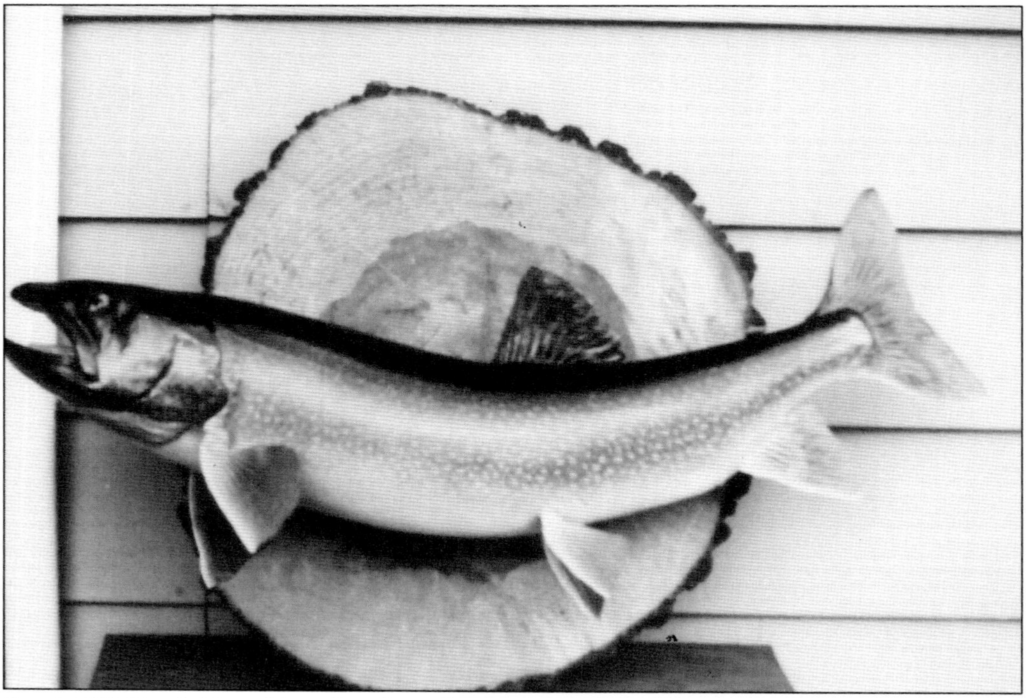

Beech Hill Pond Gives Up a Big One. Caught by Sheldon Dority of Mariaville in 1989, this 23-pound togue may not have set the record but it was a darn good catch. The largest togue from the pond was that caught by Hollis Grindle of Ellsworth, weighing 31 pounds 8 ounces.

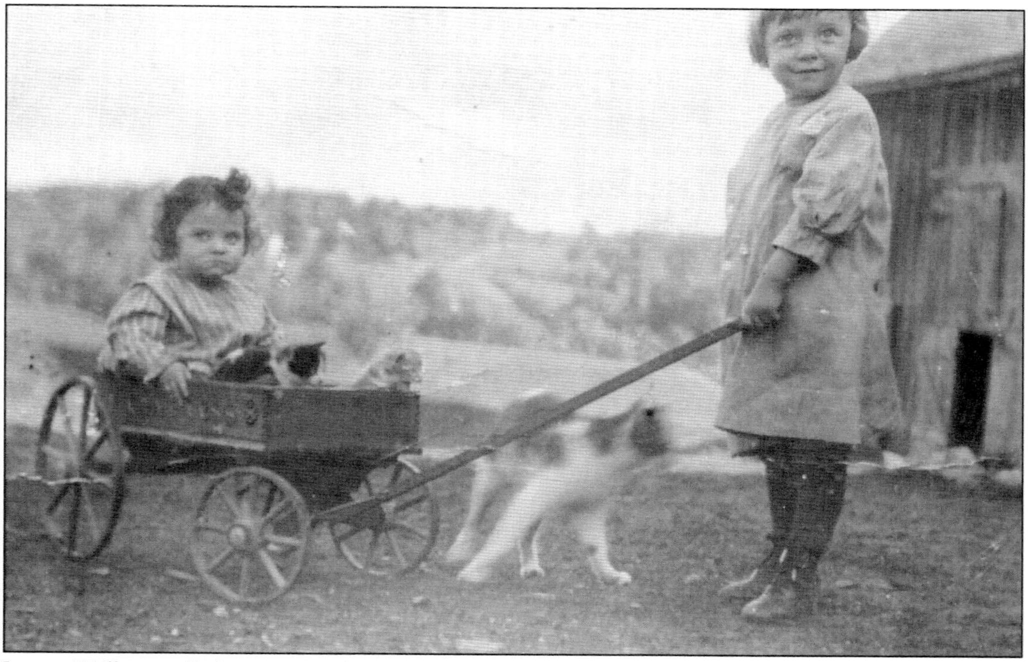

Laura Wilbur pulls her sister Oliver Wilbur and a new litter of kittens in her little red wagon in Ellsworth.

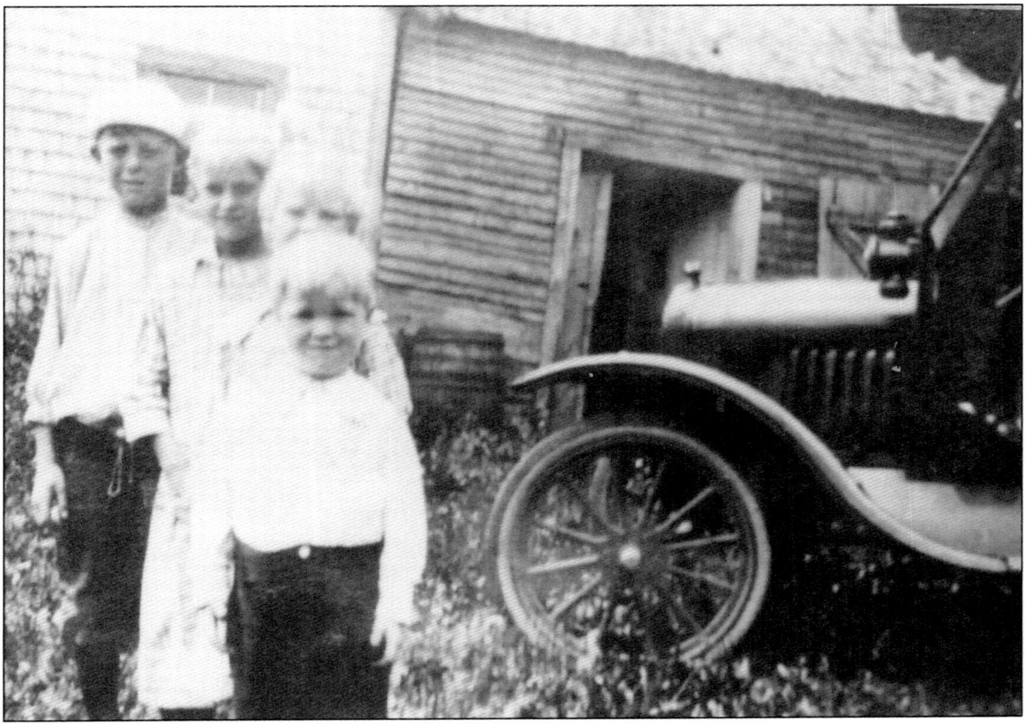

Little Moores All in a Row, *c*. 1930s. Frank (with the sailor hat), Nettie, Esther, and Everett Moore are shown here at the old homestead in Mariaville.

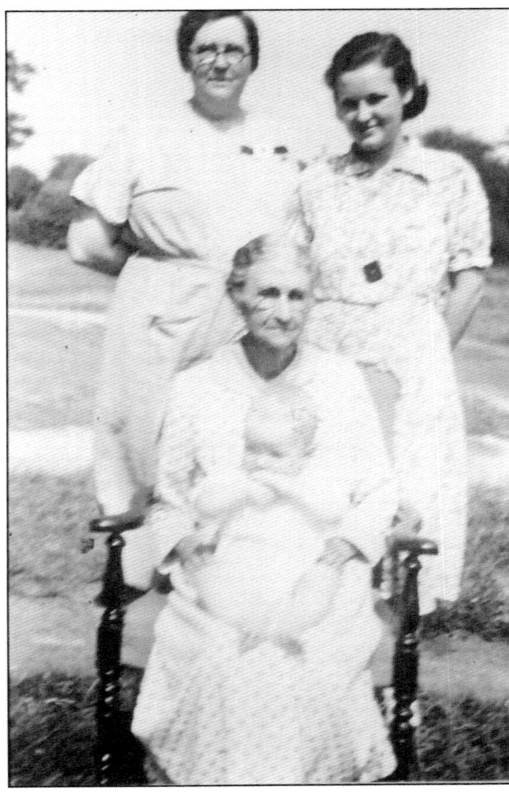

Four Generations of the Austin-Moore Family. Gathered for an historic photograph in the mid-1930s are four generations of the Austin-Moore family. In the front is great-grandmother Marsh Moore holding Bobby Austin, while Lillian Moore Gray and daughter Mary Gray Austin are in the back.

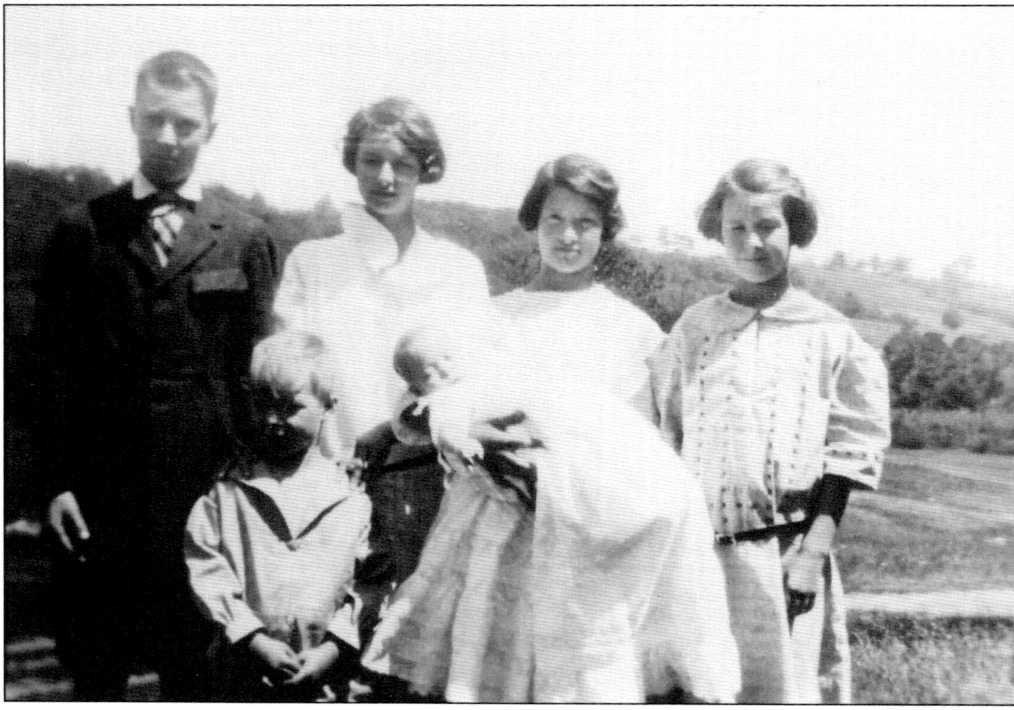

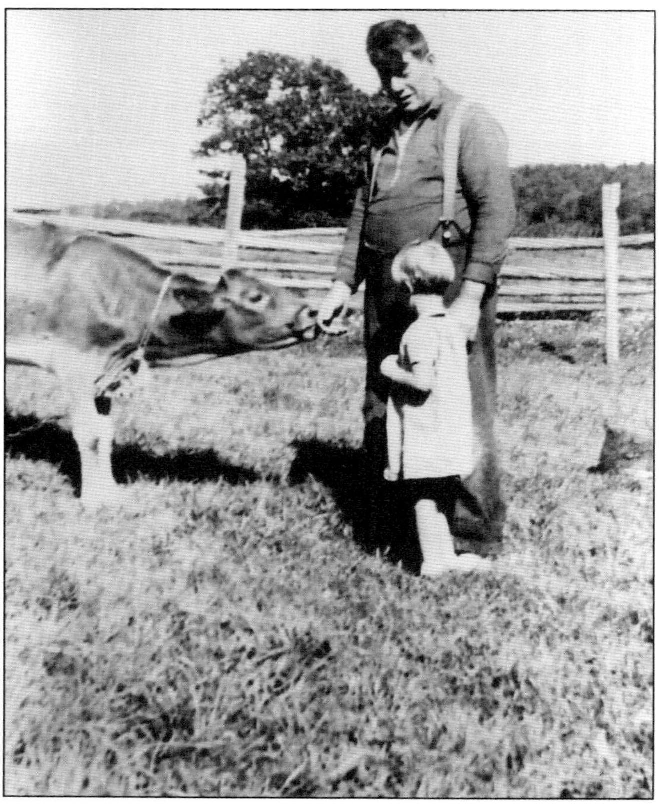

Baby Sister on Christening Day. Descendants of Alanson and Hannah (Haslam) Jordan pose on the front lawn of their Jordan ancestors' home, built in 1834 in what is now Mariaville. The children are those of Fred and Helen (Hanscom) Dority; they are, from left to right, Erland, Erva, Audrey, Mathel, Millard, and Baby Agnes.

She Won't Bite You, *c.* 1938. Leslie Frost of Mariaville introduces the newest member of the herd to his little daughter Geneva.

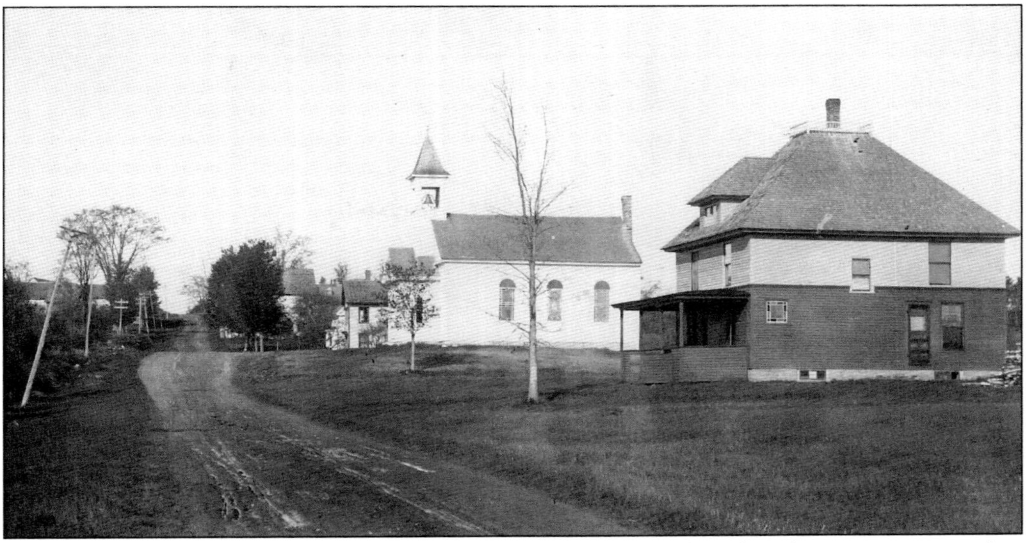

The Amherst-Aurora Congregational Church. Congregationalist church meetings were first held beginning September 14, 1830, in Aurora at the home of Samuel Silsby. There being no house of worship at the time, it was decided after holding several years of worship at the town hall in Amherst to call the church the Amherst-Aurora Church. Between 1842 and 1844, Captain Elisha Chick, one of the first settlers of that town, gave the land on which the church now stands. He also donated forty days of labor, and was given his own pew in return for his generosity. Mr. George C. White was the contractor and builder of the church, which was completed in 1844, and Benjamin Silsby was the first deacon.

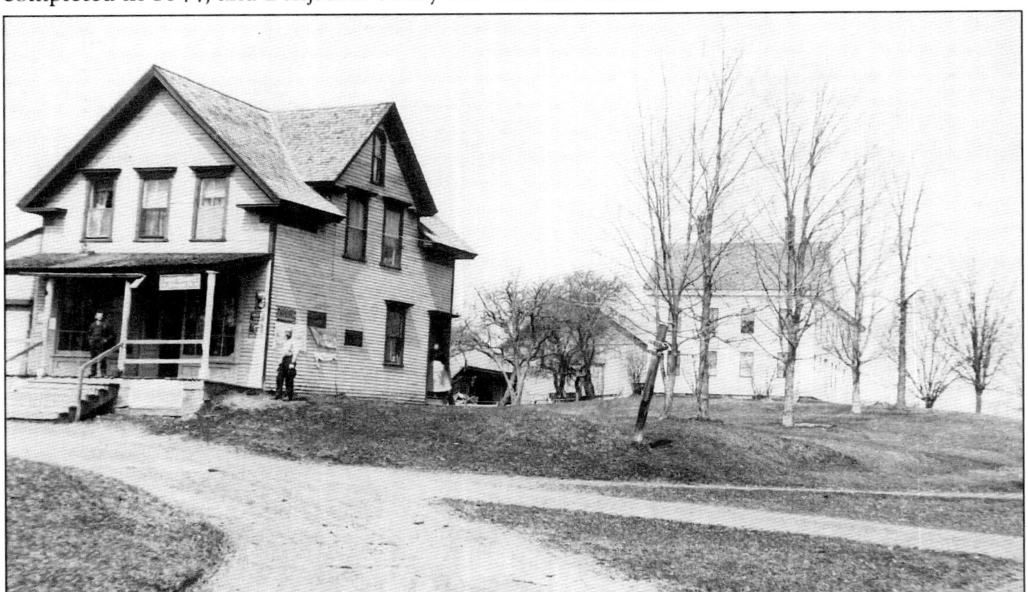

The J.G. Dunham Store, *c.* 1860. Parts of this building still stand at the four corners in Amherst on the Airline Road originally built by Dunham. He and his wife are shown to the right and left of the store. Behind is the Amherst Hotel, and it, too, is still standing. Part of this house, certainly the land, was the home of first settler Judah West. Here the American flag was raised each Fourth of July by town patriots.

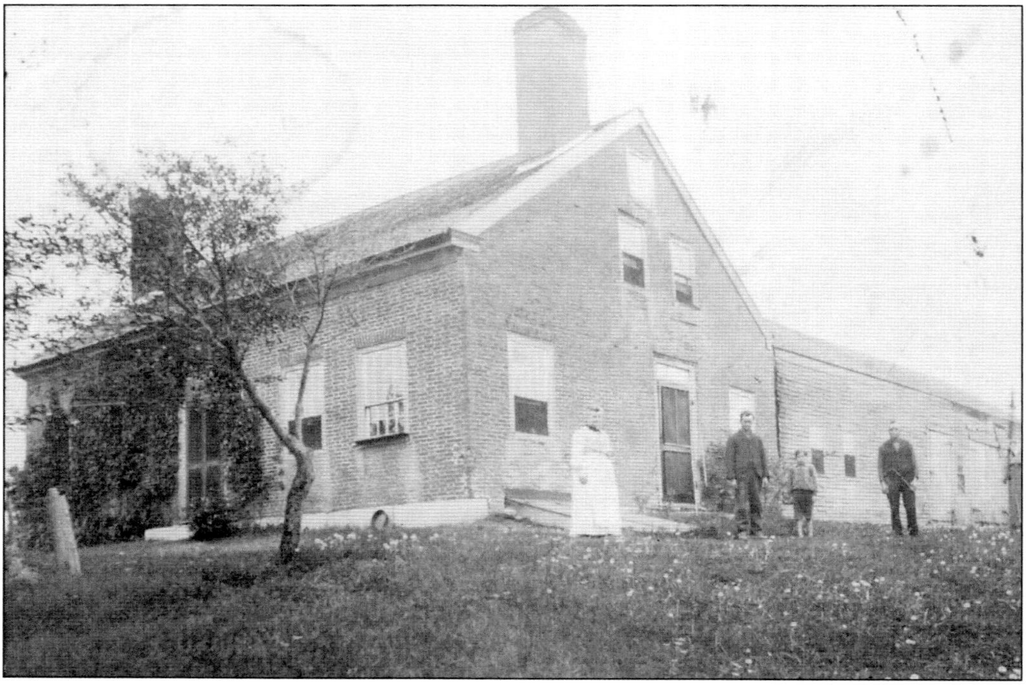

The Smith Homestead, Built in the 1860s. Charles and Elmira stand before their palatial home built of bricks made on their own property. The clay was dug from the banks of nearby Chick Brook. The home still stands today but shows the effects of many owners and declining prosperity.

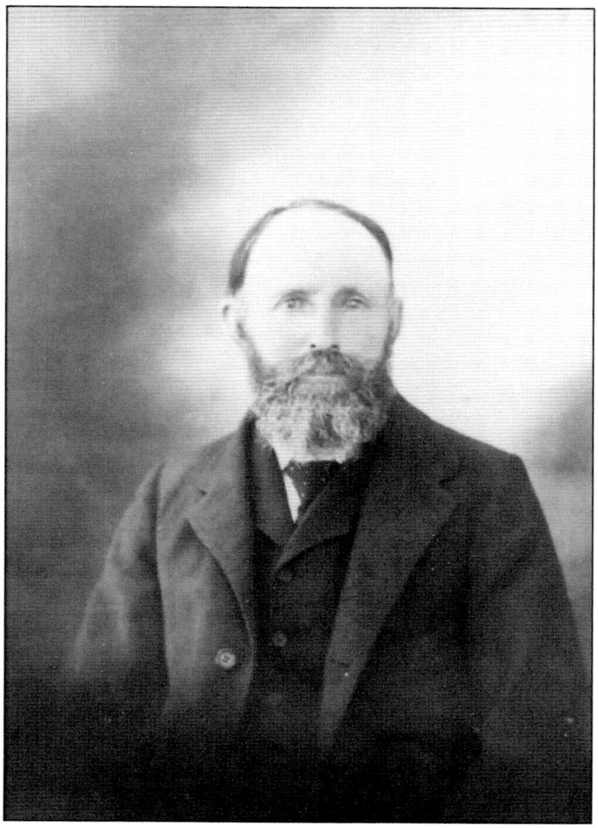

The Deacon of the Amherst Congregational Church. Charles Smith passed away in June 1927 at the age of eighty, having been a resident of the town for seventy-three years. Born in Orrington, he came to Amherst as a blacksmith apprentice. After serving his apprenticeship, he married Almira Rankins. Townspeople recalled him as "beloved by all his fellow citizens and making a place for himself in the community which will be hard for another to fill."

An Amherst Native Who Served the Nation Well. Nathaniel Chick, born in 1812 in Amherst to Moses Chick and Lucy (Pillsbury), worked in the woods logging before enlisting to aid his country. He married Betsy Williams on November 14, 1835 and fathered six children, but lost his wife to consumption in 1849. In 1850 he married again, to Mary Chatterly, and had seven more offspring. After serving in the 30th Maine Regiment in Baton Rouge, LA, he came home with "chronic diarrhea." On September 18, 1864, he died.

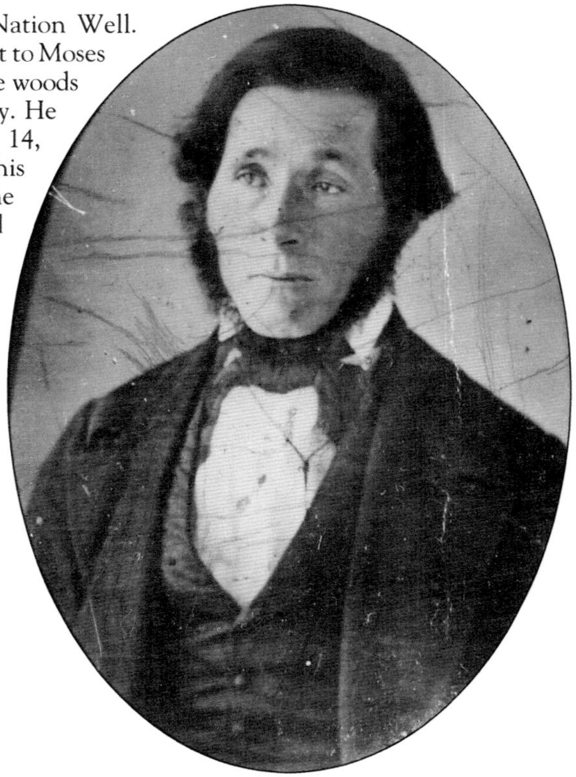

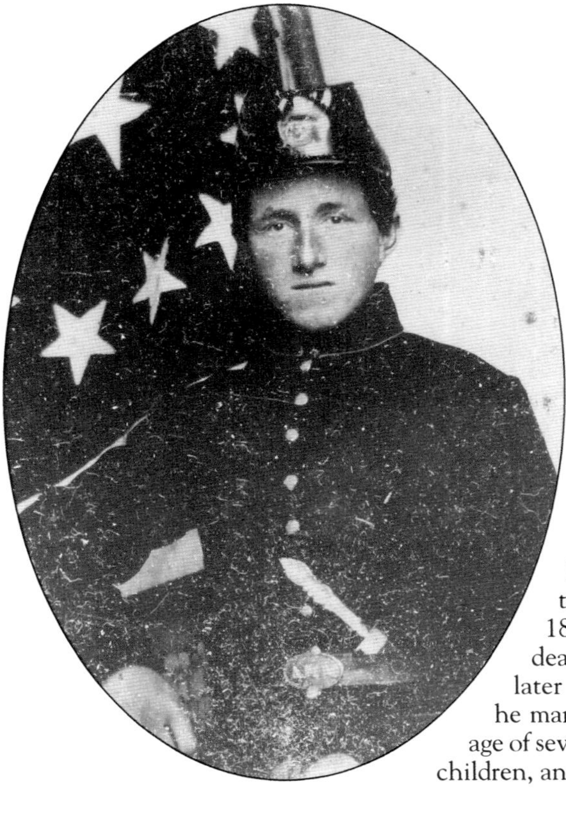

A Civil War Soldier from Great Pond. George Wilson Chick was born on March 18, 1840, in Aurora, the son of Nathaniel and Betsy (Williams). He entered the Civil War when he was twenty-one and served for four years. In 1866, he married Mary Freeze, and after her death, he went west to Minneapolis, MN. He later settled in Iowa and on October 20, 1887, he married Hattie Jayne. He died in 1918 at the age of seventy-eight, surrounded by his widow, three children, and nine grandchildren.

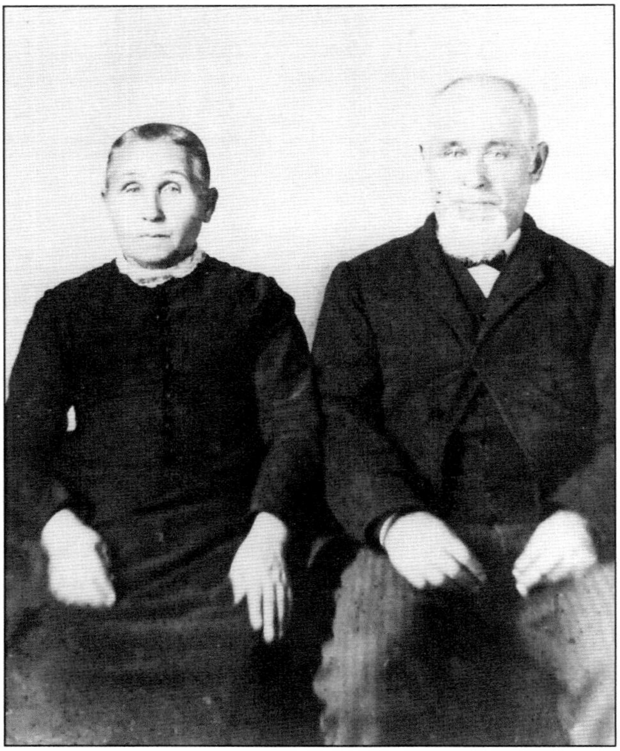

Twins Wed Brothers. Sumner twins Rosetta and Lucetta married brothers Peter Nourse Giles and Eben Giles. Life in our frontier towns became a land of double cousins and one dared not speak badly of anyone for fear of insulting a relative. Lucetta and Peter Giles are shown here on the left; on the right are Rosetta and Eben Giles.

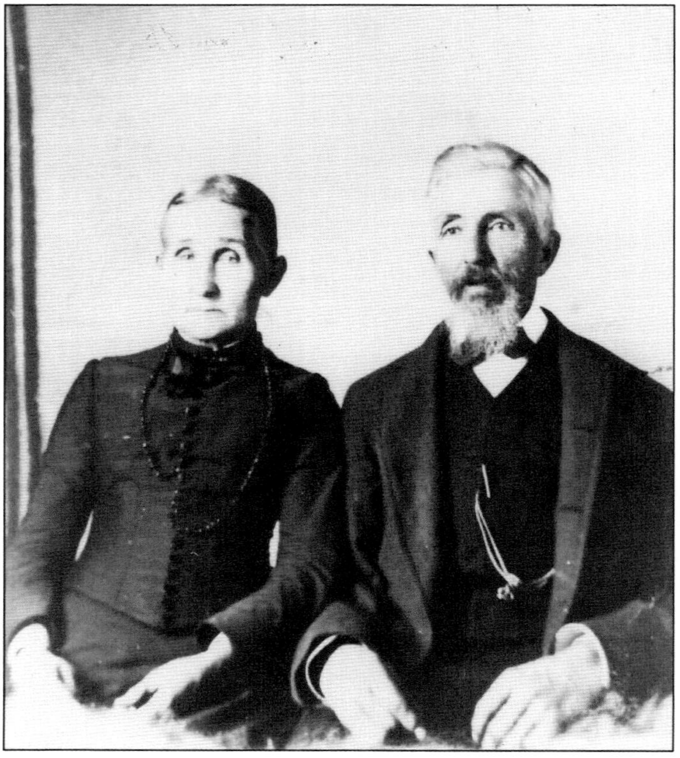

A Young Married Couple in 1886. Luther Giles married Georgianna Gusha in 1886, but they had a short wedded life because she died in 1893. Some years the town clerk wrote to the county registry "no marriage this year as we are all too poor." Those that did tie the knot often died young due to the hardships of living in rural Maine at that time.

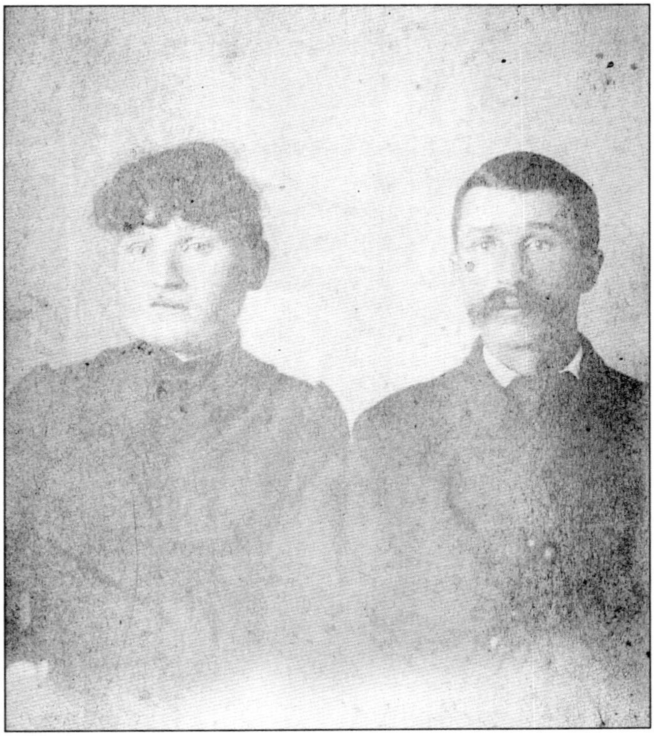

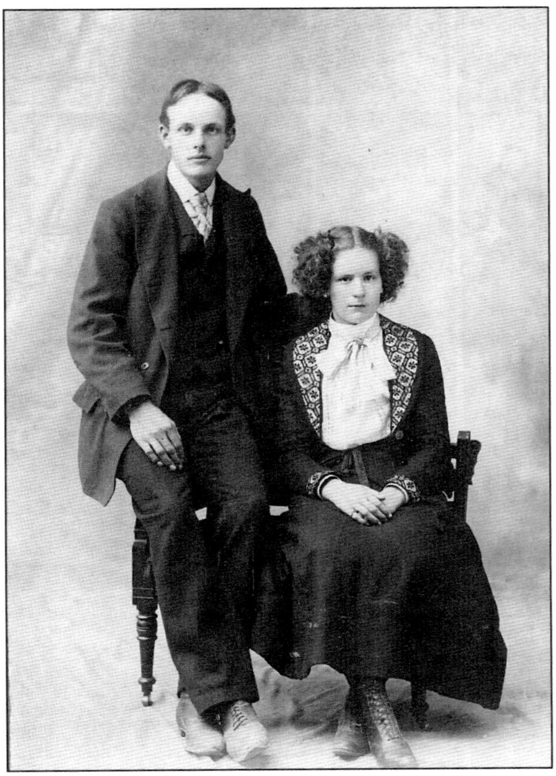

Two Early Settler Families Unite. Herbert Nickerson Jr. wed Eva MacDonald at Amherst (the dates are unknown). One is consistently impressed with the beauty of costumes in the days of our grandparents.

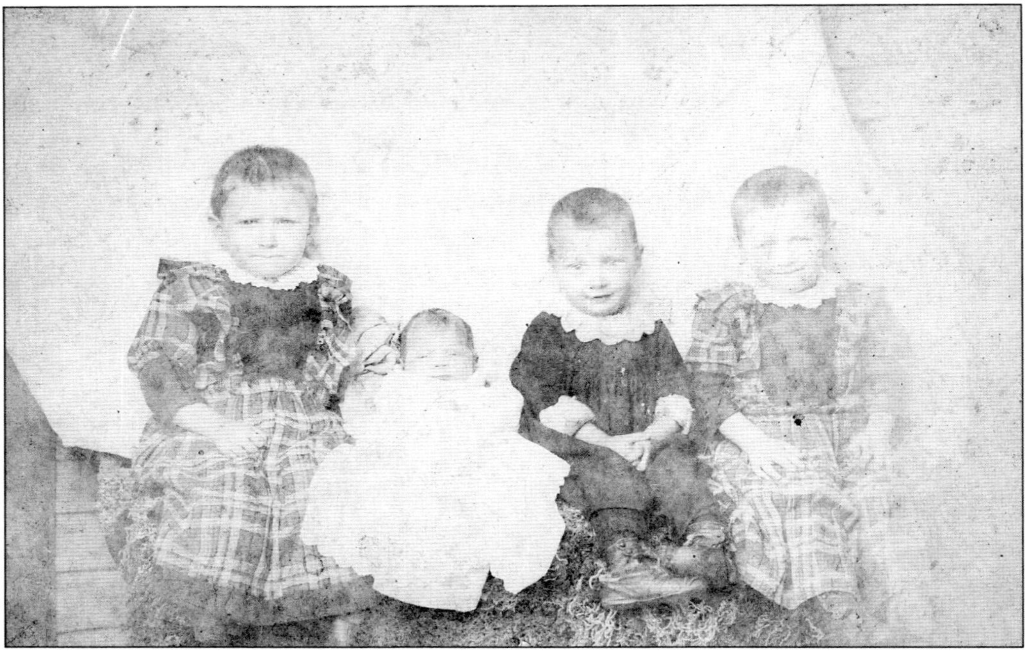

The Orcutt Children, *c.* 1905. From left to right are Ida May (b. 1891), John Herbert (b. 1888), Mabel Francis (b. 1890), and baby Leroy (b. 1905), the children of Frank Tilden Orcutt and Effie M. (Gusha). Frank settled in Carmel, ME.

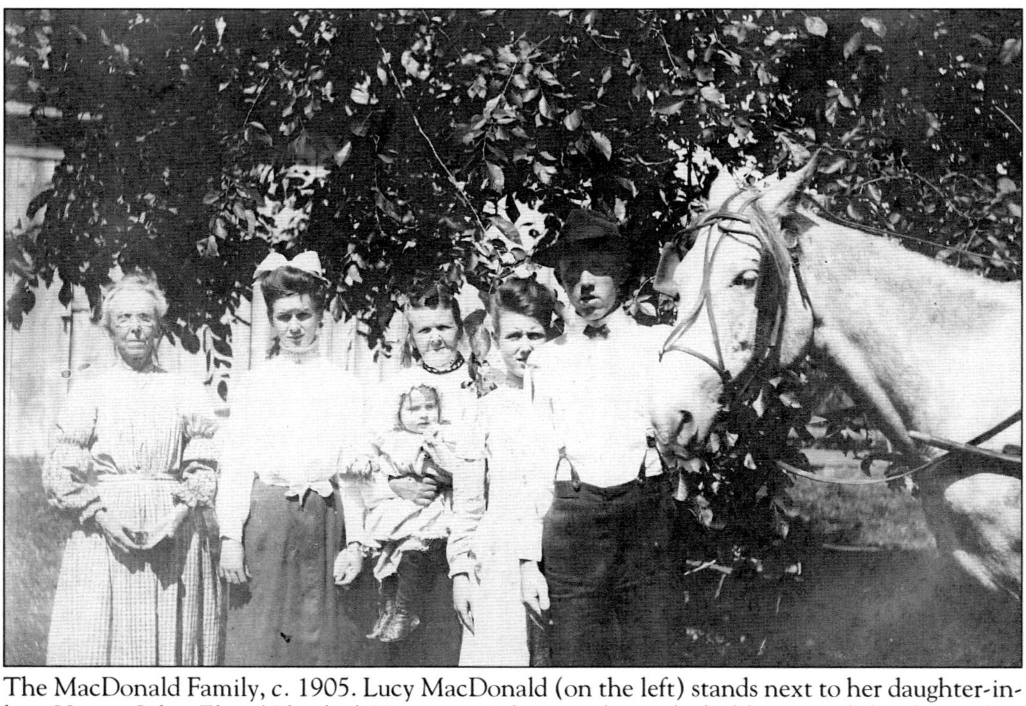

The MacDonald Family, *c.* 1905. Lucy MacDonald (on the left) stands next to her daughter-in-law, Hattie Giles; Eliza (Clewley) Hanscom-Giles is on her right holding grand-daughter Alice Campbell; next is Lucy (Watts) Rivers just in back of Adelbert MacDonald.

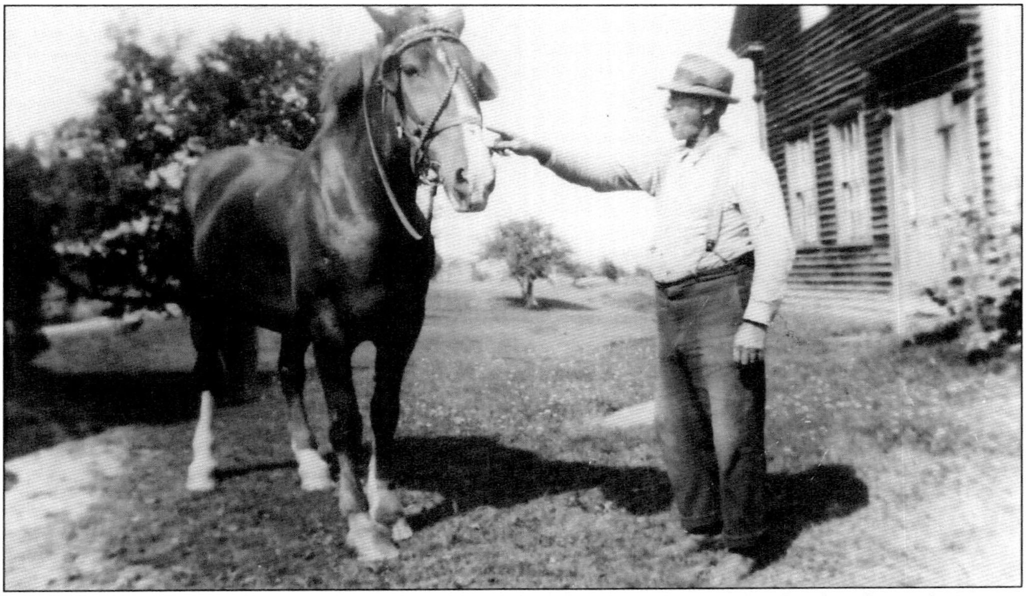

A Great Horsemanship Display. Erving Roberts was perhaps one of the fondest horse lovers in the town of Amherst. He was a quiet, gentle man and here shows how he could control even the largest work horse with just his voice.

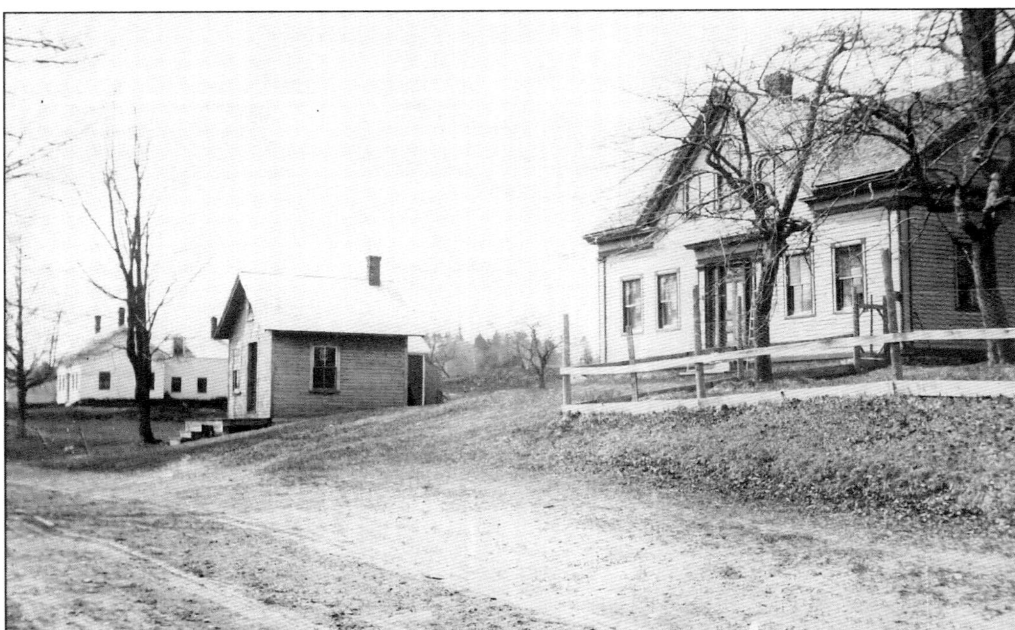

The Amherst Cheese House, *c*. 1921–22. The little building in the middle of the photograph is all that was left for many years of the cheese-making industry in town. It was later converted to a town library by Mrs. George Orcutt. The building to the right, built by Peter Sumner after his service in the Civil War, is still standing.

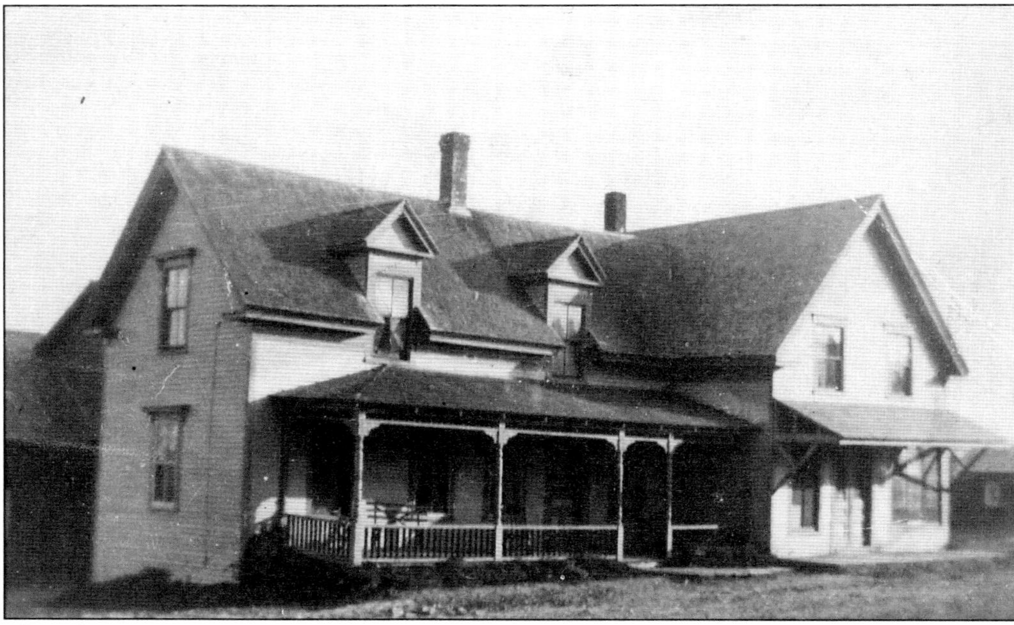

The Johnston Homestead, *c.* 1860s. This home in Amherst is no longer standing but for many years it housed a large family belonging to Atcheson and Elizabeth Johnston, one of the town's Irish immigrant families. The family operated a variety store at the four corners of the town as well as the post office and a millinery store. Before the Buzzell Tannery burned, life was good in the town.

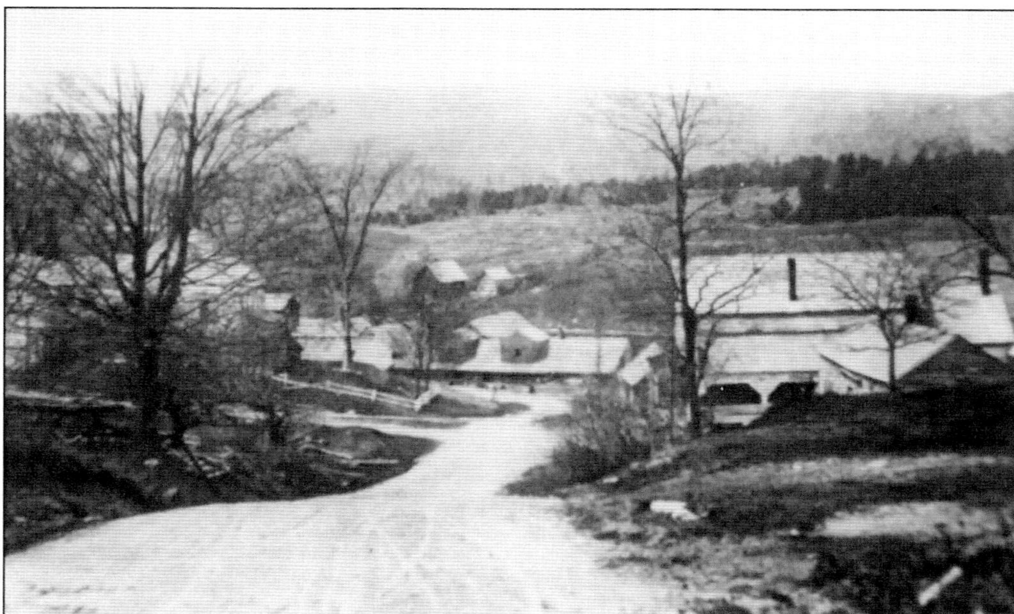

The Tannery District in Amherst, 1898. These large and prosperous homes which seem to march up Tannery Hill were built during the boom years at Amherst. The tannery burned in 1903, and soon this entire district was torn down or burned. Union River, which powered the mill and tannery, lies in the valley below this steep hill.

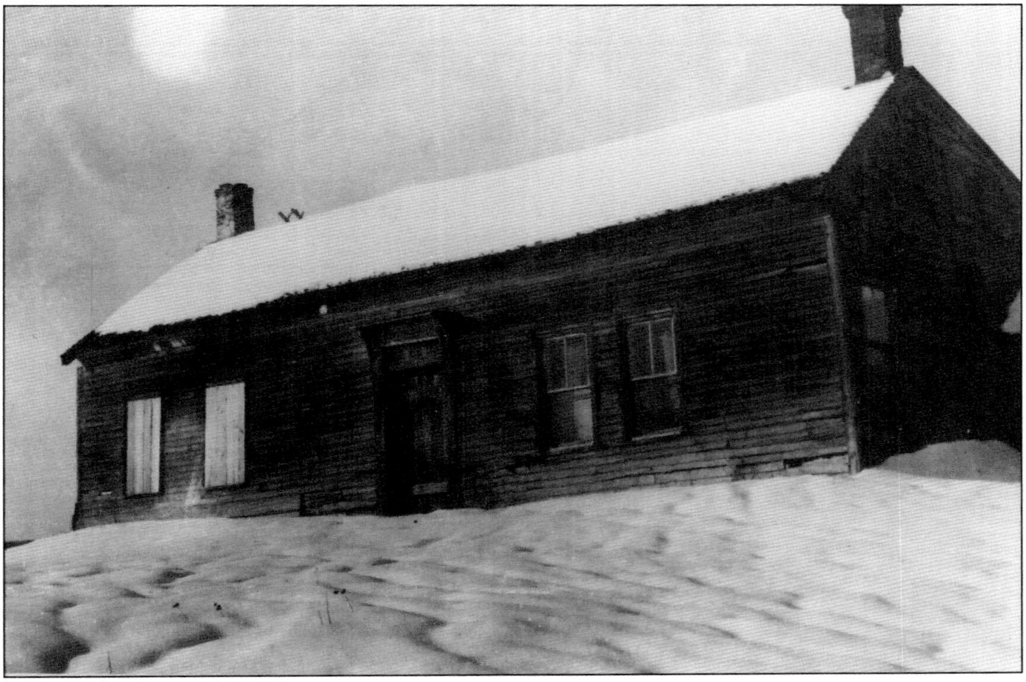

Little Miss Addie Giles (right), *c.* 1879, and the Sumner Homestead (above). Addie Giles, the daughter of Peter and Lucetta (Sumner), married Lewis Albert Sumner on June 24, 1886.

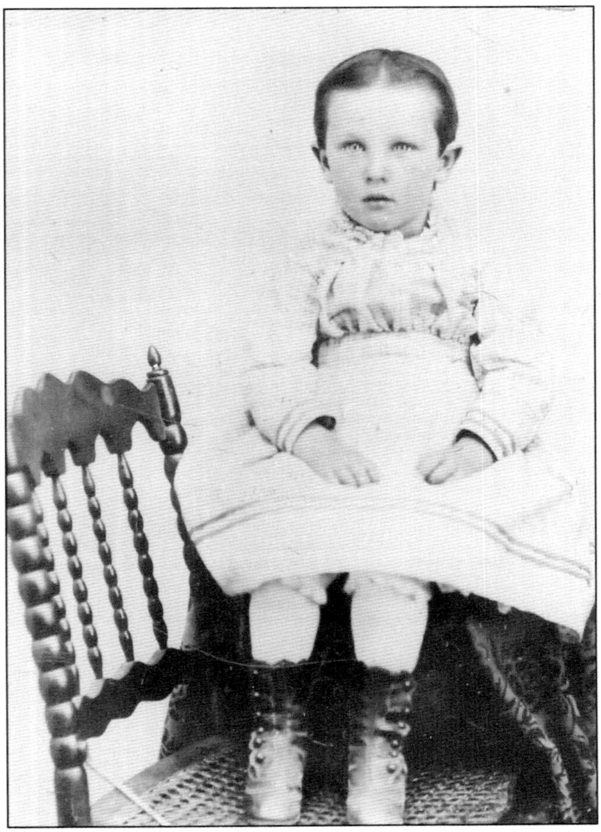

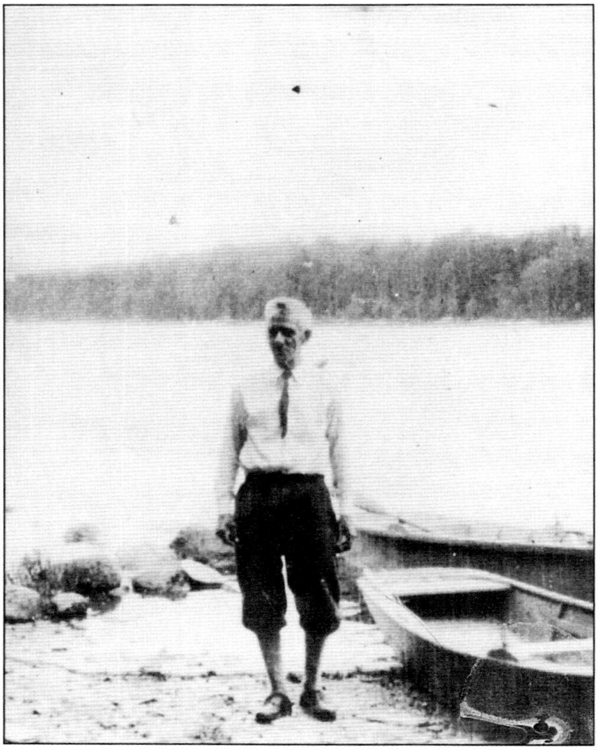

A Woodsman Turned Guide. 1929. Levi Jellison Bragg of Clifton was typical of the Hancock country men who had to turn to other occupations when the lumber mills began to close and the tanneries burned. One of his letters spoke of being "just back from taking my boys into Flood's Pond."

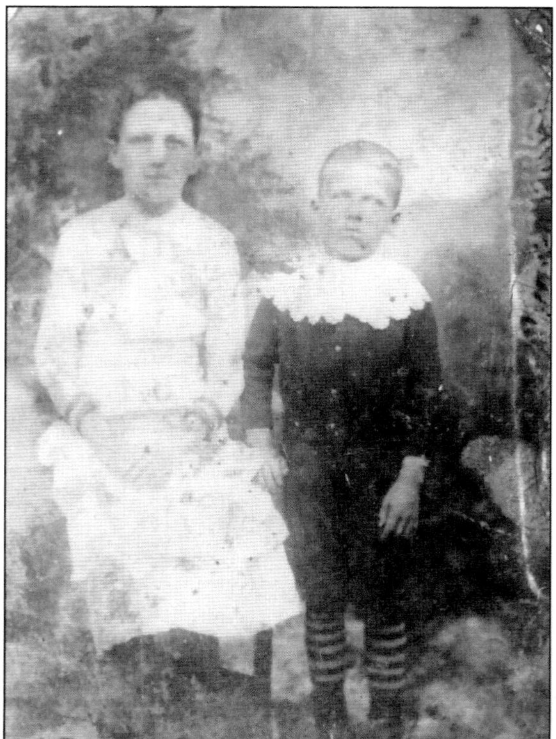

A Somber Pose from an Old Tintype. Vesta Hanscom and her brother, Lafayette Wilson Hanscom, were children of Seth Orcutt Hanscom and Lydia Jane Orcutt of Amherst. They were brought up by their step-grandmother, Liza (Clewley) Hanscom, after their mother died of consumption in 1883.

Brothers of Amherst. Adelbert (left) and his brother Odillion were the sons of Zelotus Fletcher, an early settler in the town. Adelbert married Helen Hanscom and Odillion married Leah Sumner in 1875.

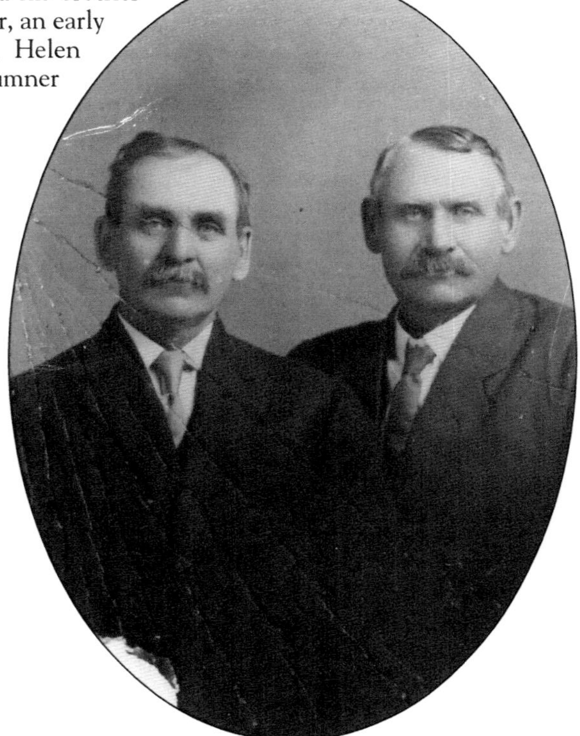

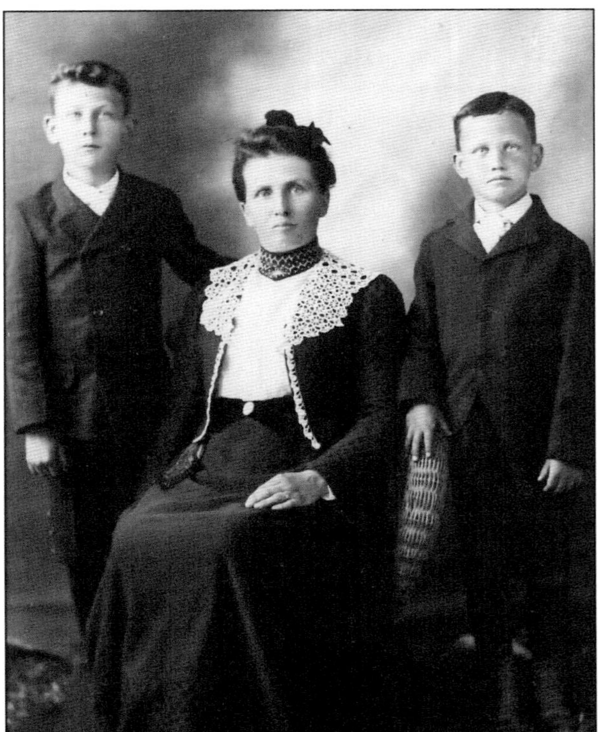

A Dressmaker, Mother, and Homemaker. Helen Sophia Hanscom married Adelbert Fletcher and for most of her life brought in extra money to the family by sewing clothes for the family and locals. She was also one of the first to sew men's pants for Freese's Department Store in Bangor. Her sons, Walter and Martin, are shown here with her, c. 1904.

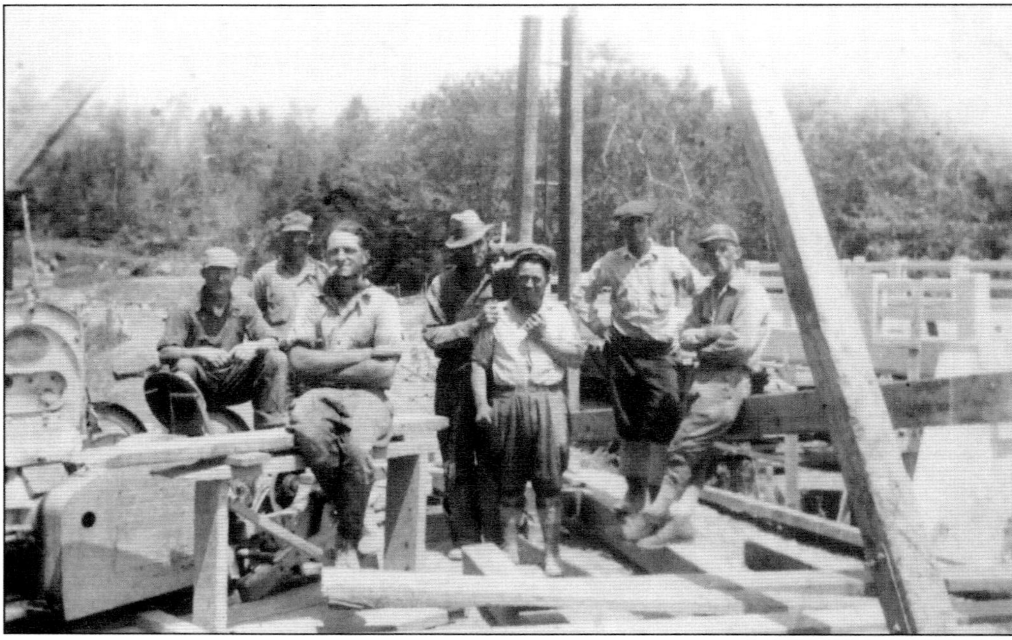

The Jones Bridge, *c.* 1934–36. Some of the men who worked in the county replaced worn-out wooden bridges with the new wonder of the highways, cement. Identified are Albert "Tom" Hanscom (left), and next to him, in front, is his brother-in-law, Levi Bragg Jr. The man on the far right is thought to be Rodell Smith.

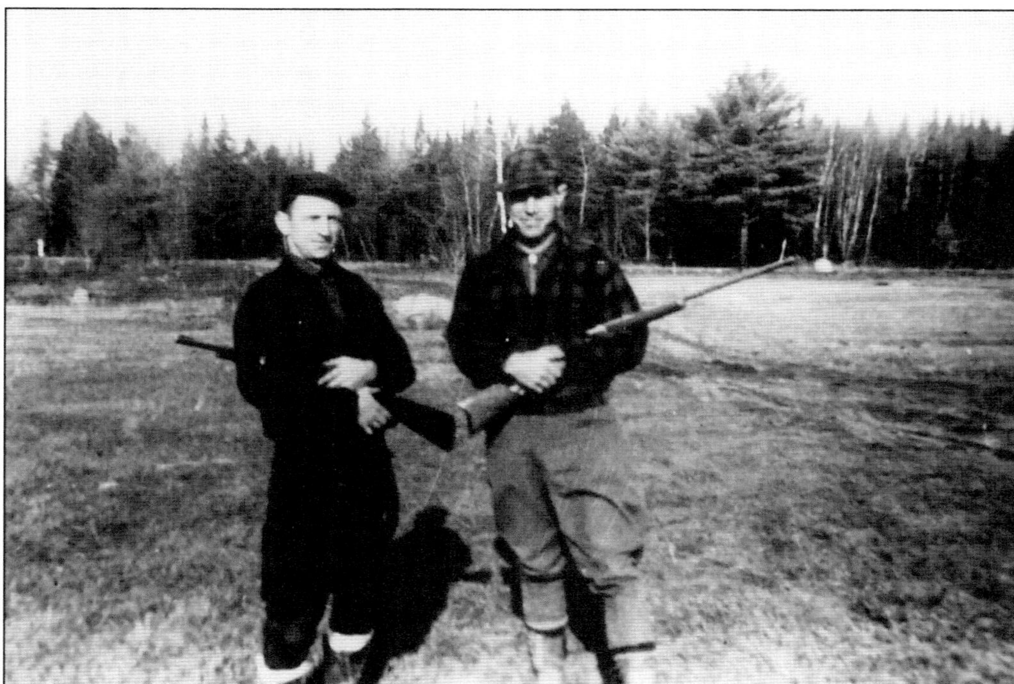

Hunting—Still a Major Sport in the County. Cousins Levi and Robert Bragg show off their prized hunting guns getting ready for early fall deer season at Amherst.

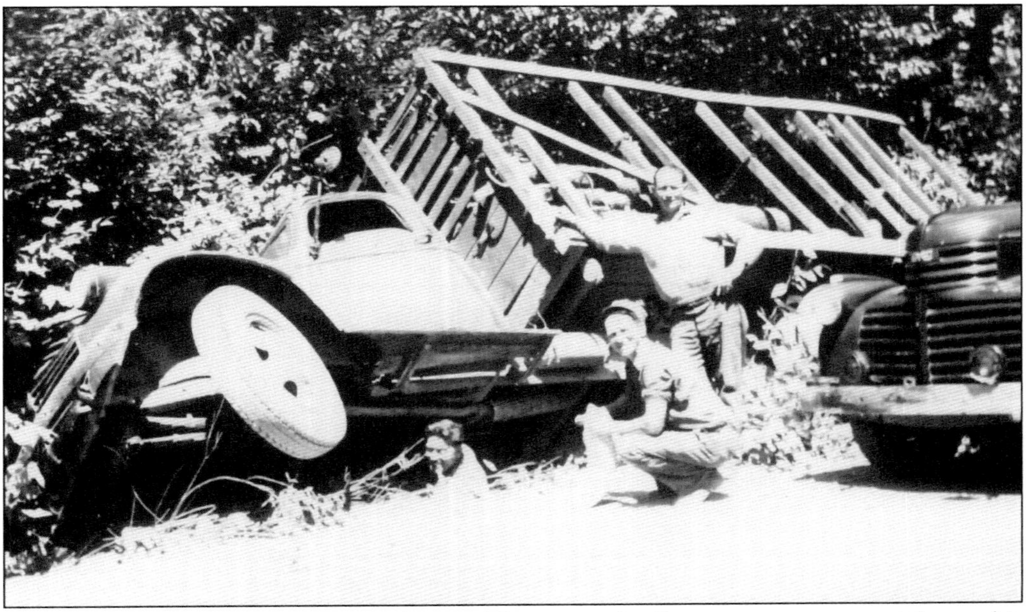

Upset on Birch Ridge, Route 9 near Aurora. This was and still is a not uncommon sight on this stretch of road, known as the Airline, built along the alluvial ridge deposited there by in the last ice age. This particular accident on July 15, 1946, was caused by the universal joint breaking in Levi Bragg Jr.'s truck. A good driver all his life, he couldn't avoid this.

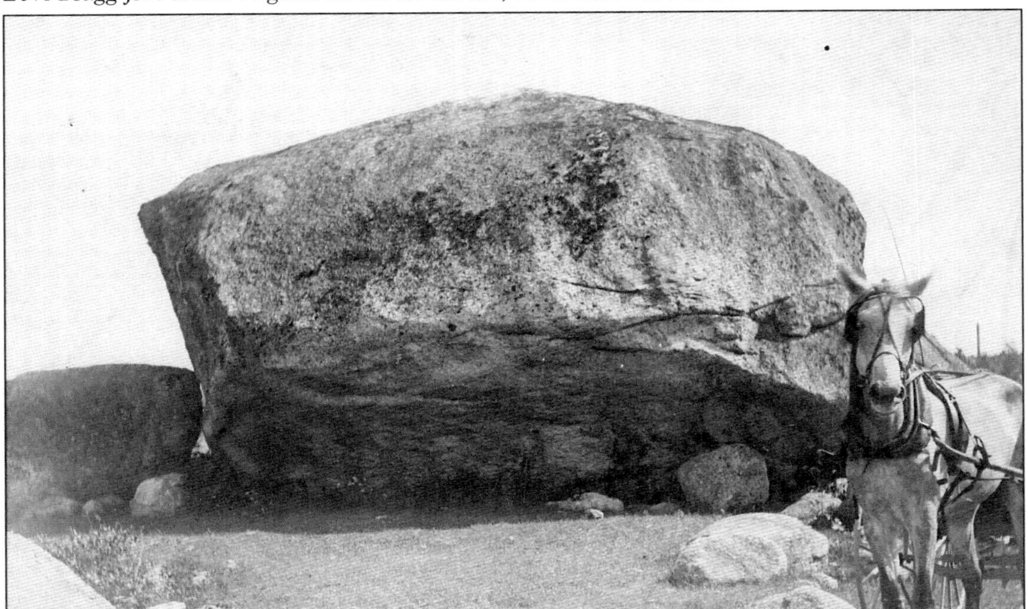

Airline Road Hazards. Called "house rock," this rock is typical of the roadside even today. When the road was pushed through from Bangor to Calais, some of these had to be removed by huge work crews.

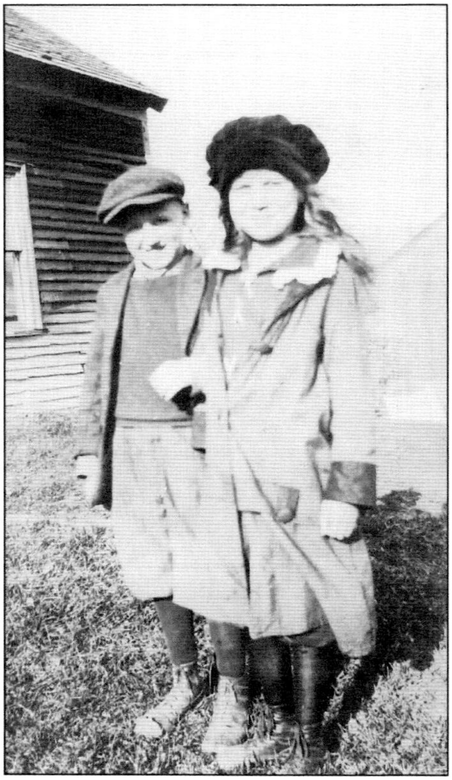

Dressed for the First Day of School. This photograph, taken c. 1910, shows Prescott Sumner and neighbor Alethea Bragg as they pose in front of the Bragg farm on Airline Road.

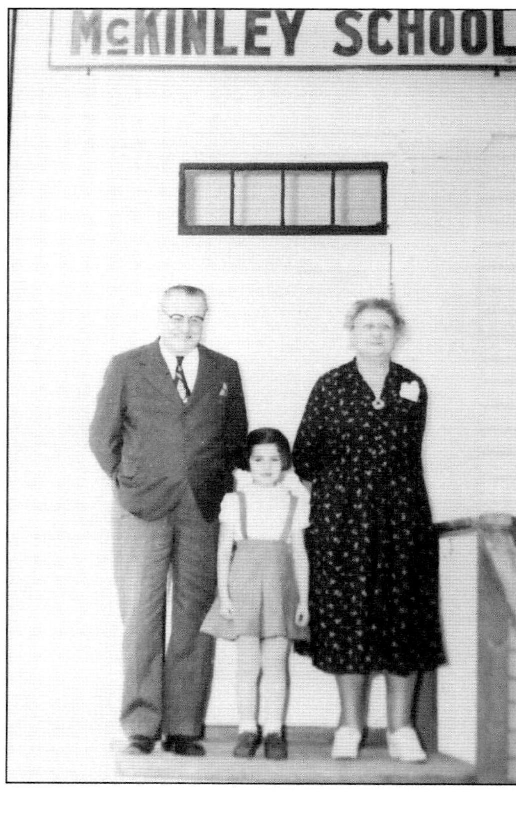

School Days—Good Old Golden Rule Days. Joanne Anderson is shown here with her grandfather, John Morgan Hooper (left), and Miss Phoebe Wessel, a teacher in 1951 at the McKinley School in Amherst. Miss Wessel was the first teacher to both Joanne and Grampy Hooper and the photograph was taken to enter the T.V. show "I've Got a Secret."

Three

North on Route 179:
Osborn, Waltham, Aurora, Great Pond

Osborn was a lottery township laid out in 1784 under the direction of Rufus Putnam for the Commonwealth of Massachusetts. The first settler was Joseph Osborn, who came there in 1807.

Waltham was originally part of Mariaville and was incorporated as a town in 1833. It was named for Waltham, MA, from whence many early settlers immigrated. The river was the "main road" and was known by its Indian name "Tau-ce-wan-neity." Lebbeus Kingman, the first settler, named the town "Timber-brook-ridge," which is still used today.

Aurora was settled in 1805 by four Silsby brothers from New Hampshire, Samuel, Benjamin, David, and Roswell. Samuel Giles was the first white child born in the town. He lived to be ninety-nine years old, "one of the remarkable old men of Hancock county."

Great Pond was first settled by Joshua Williams and his sons Clark and Simeon. Joshua, a veteran of the American Revolution, was paid for his service in lands instead of cash, and he erected a mill on the Great Pond. The largest land owner was Squire Joseph Tilden, who purchased 23,040 acres from the Bingham Millions. It was first surveyed by Benjamin Kimball in 1809.

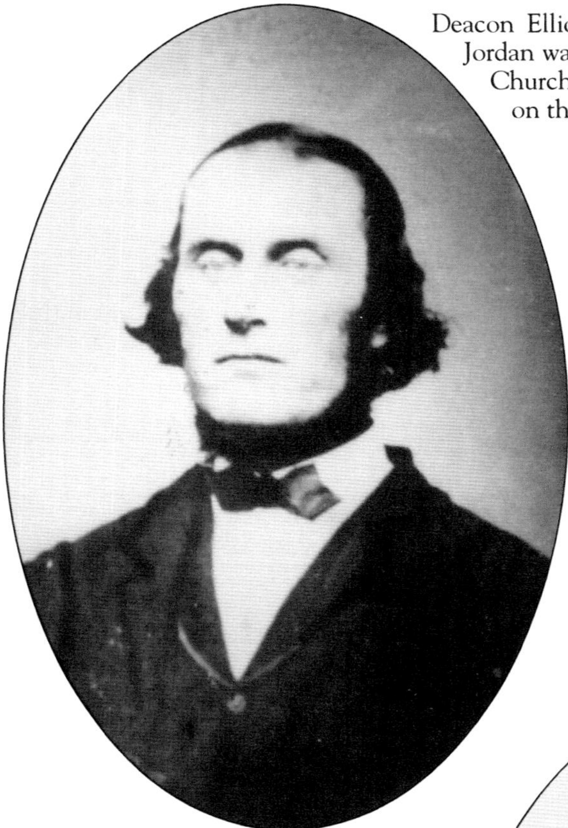

Deacon Elliot Jordan and His Wife, *c.* 1870. Elliot Jordan was the first deacon of the Waltham Baptist Church; his wife, Elizabeth (Parsons) Jordan, is on the right.

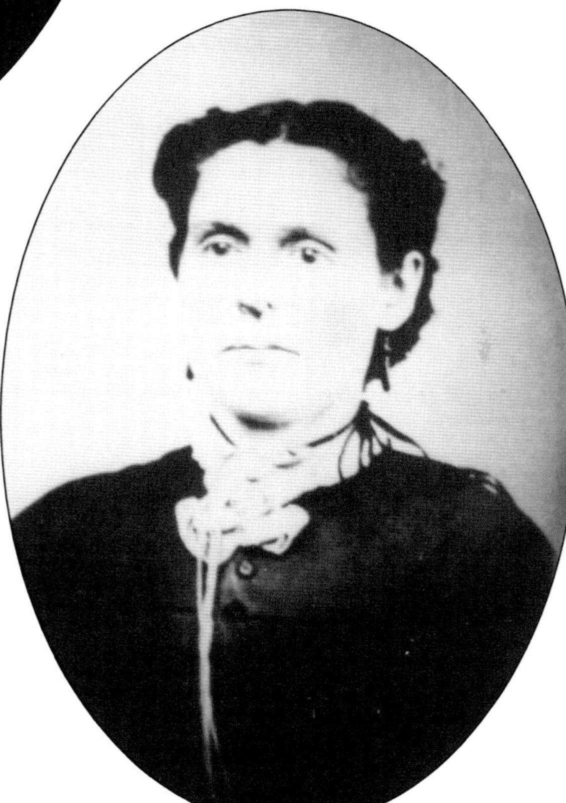

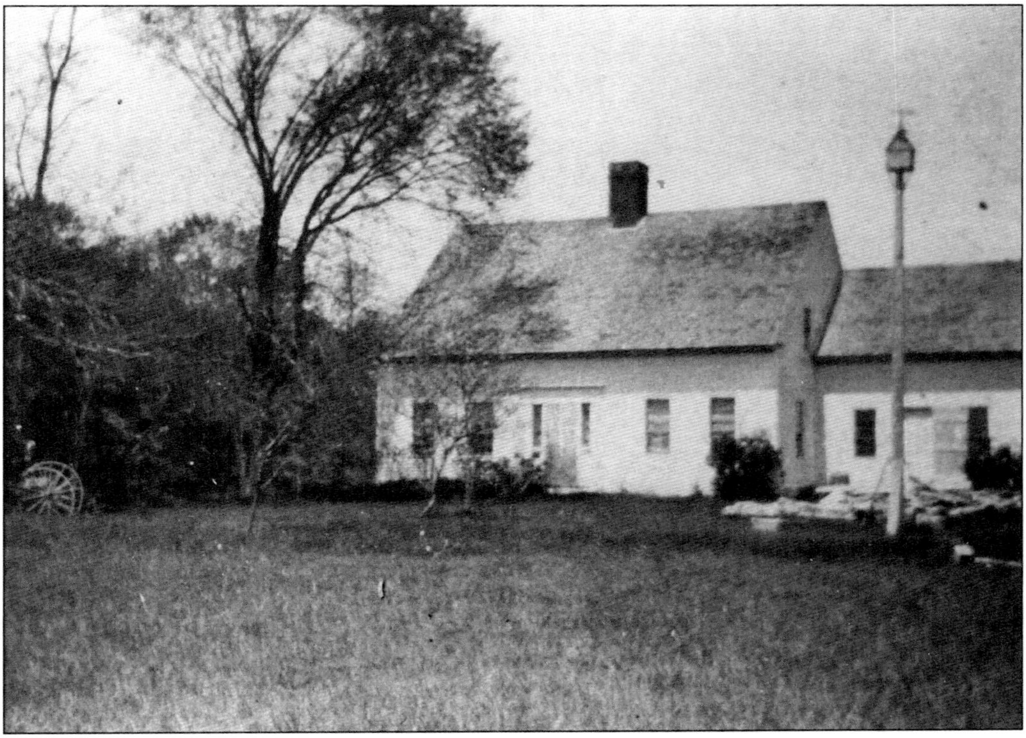

The Deacon Elliot Jordan Home. This cozy little home at Waltham was destroyed by fire in the 1930s. Wood fires, oil lamps, lanterns, and candles were often the cause of these fires.

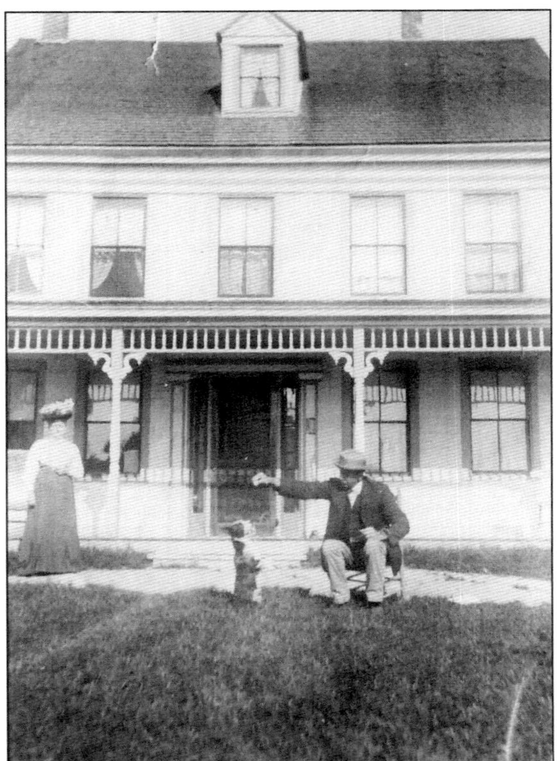

Foxes Hotel, *c.* 1870. Owners William Fox and wife watch their dog do tricks in front of their home and business on Foxes Flat, Waltham.

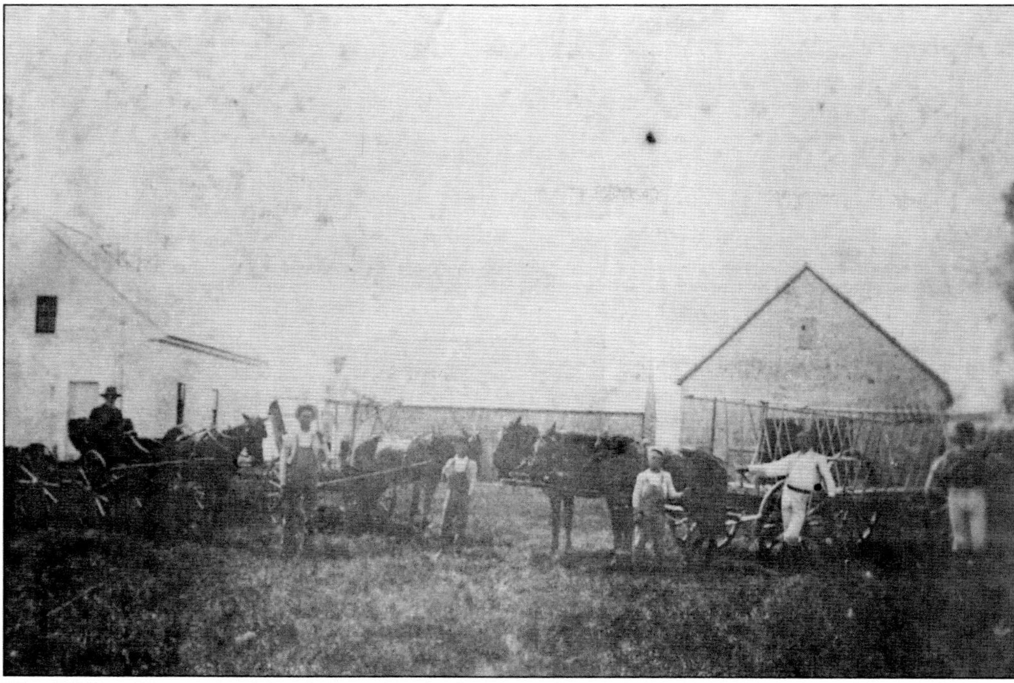

The Wilbur Homestead. Built *c.* 1838, the house still stands today. Mahlon Wilbur and a haying crew are shown here in front of the barn.

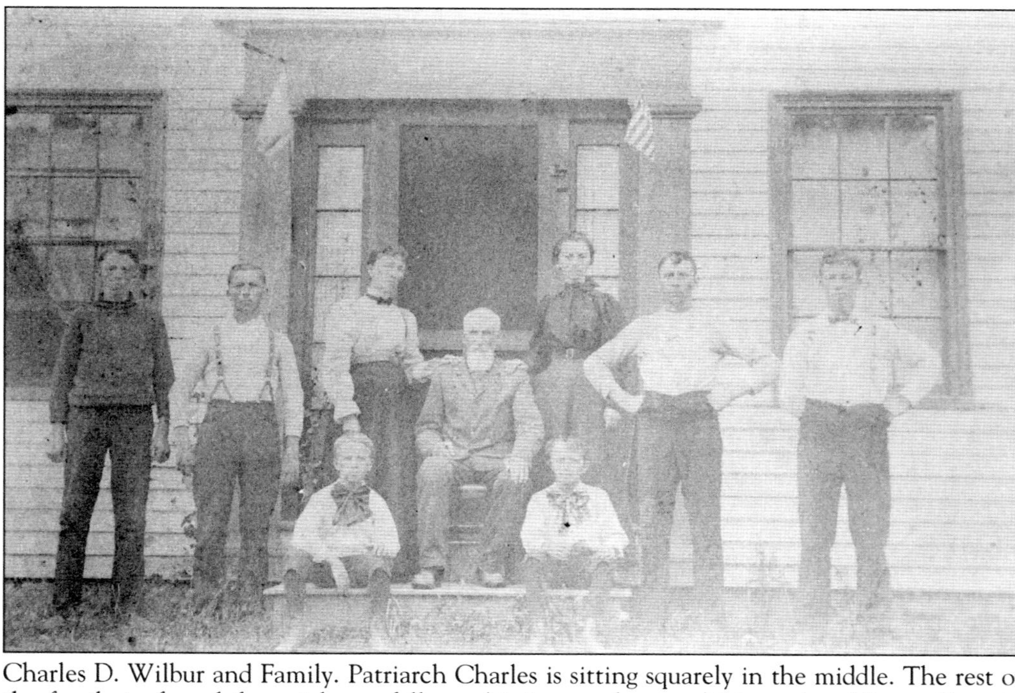

Charles D. Wilbur and Family. Patriarch Charles is sitting squarely in the middle. The rest of the family is, from left to right, as follows: (sitting on the steps) Howard and Jasper Francis; (standing) Ellery, wife Celista, Vida Wilbur, Mahlon, and Leona.

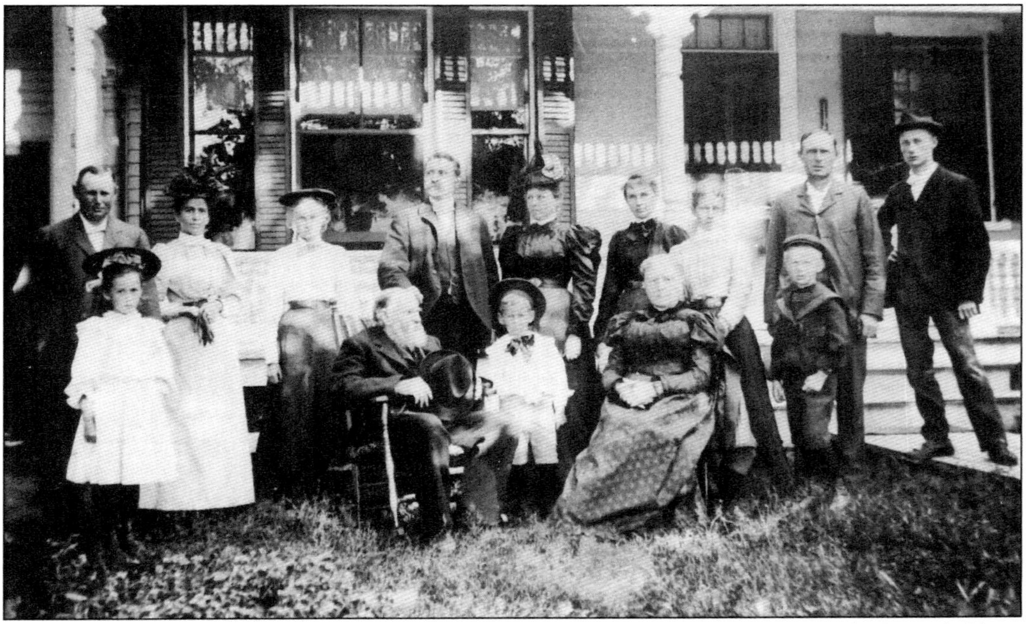

Lamoine Sunday, *c.* 1870s. Francis and Lydia (Wilbur) Hodgkins with pose with their children and grandchildren, dressed in their Sunday best. Corsetted and with at least seven petticoats under their heavy dresses, these women had a right to look stern.

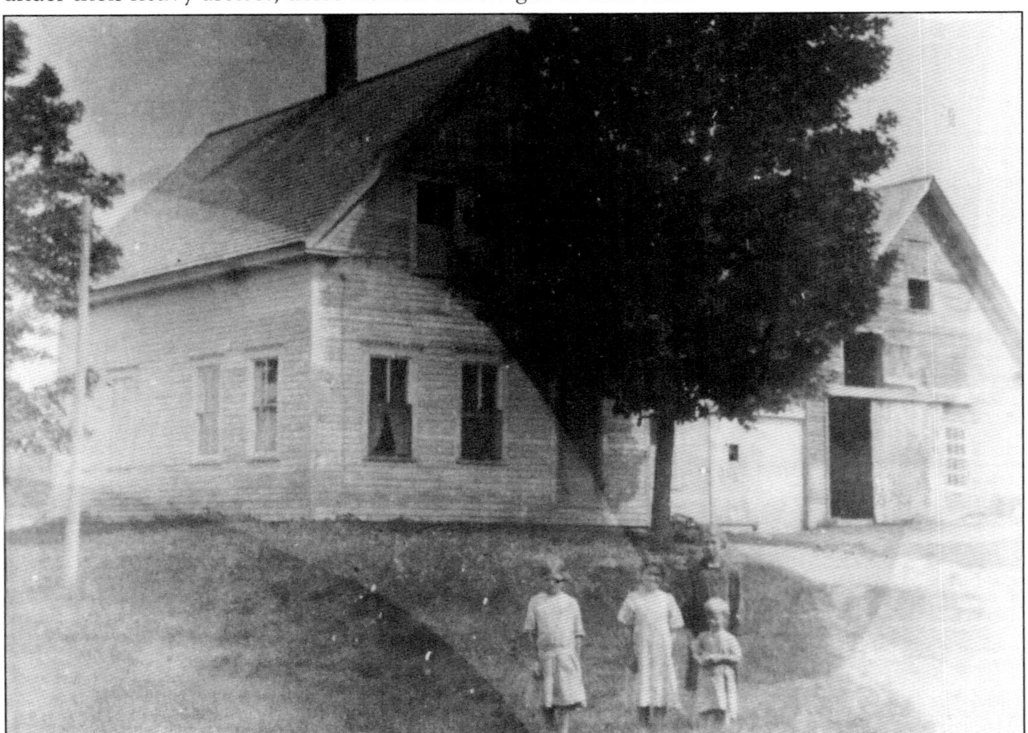

The Bunker Homestead, *c.* 1916. From left to right are Genevieve, Marguerite, Lizzie, and Clyde Bunker.

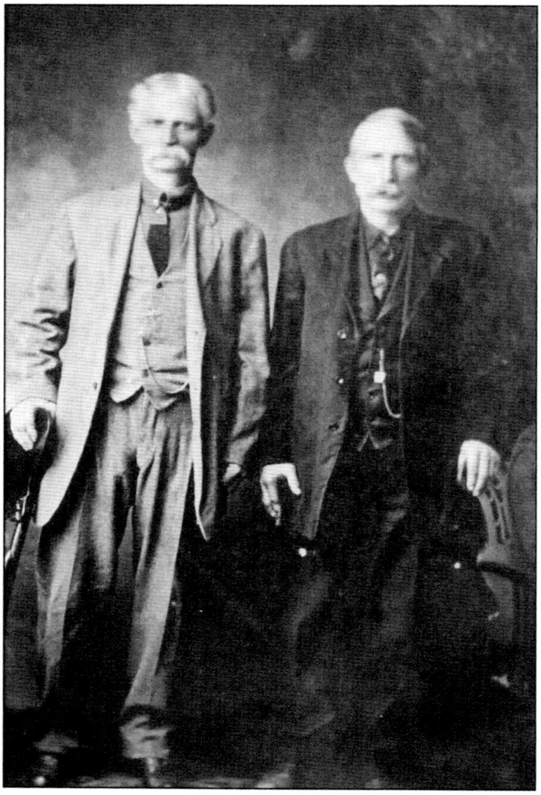

Go West Young Man, and They Did. These two Waltham boys, Francis Albert and Byron Wilbur, went west to seek their fortunes. Francis went to California and Byron went to Michigan, never to return to Maine.

A Waltham Woods Camp, *c.* 1890. This scene was repeated throughout the county and is typical of the construction of that era. Logs were the base, chinked with moss and mud, and the roof was boarded over for extra warmth. Sod was often used for roofing before the advent of tarred paper.

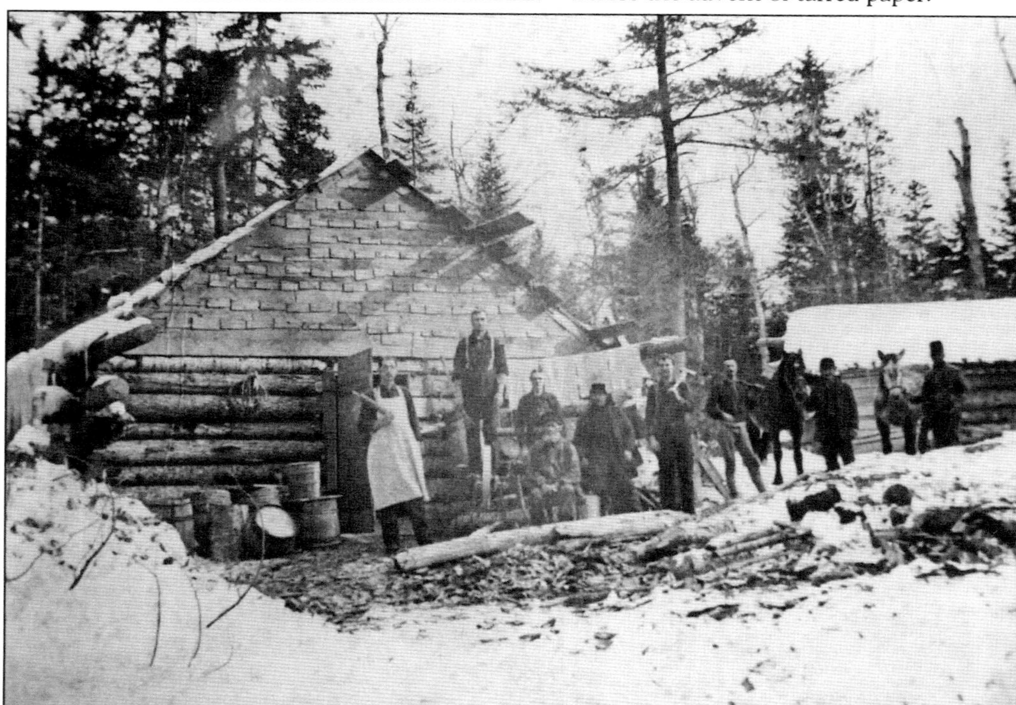

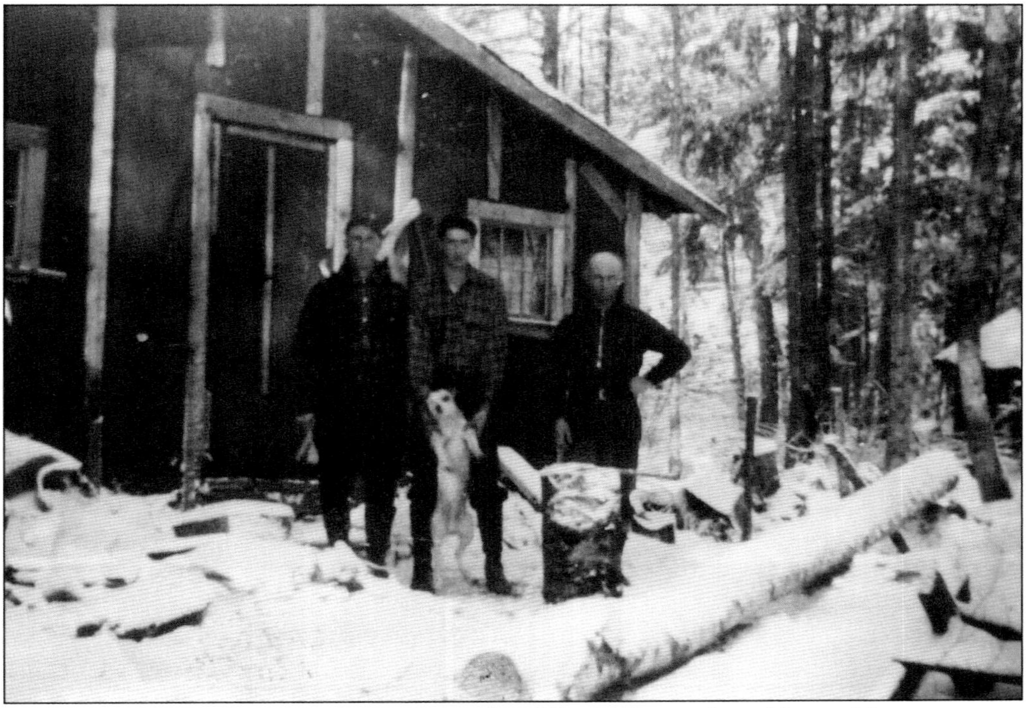

A Log Crew on Union River, 1939. Bernard and Basil Edgecomb and Irving Urann pause at camp while harvesting logs at Mariaville Falls.

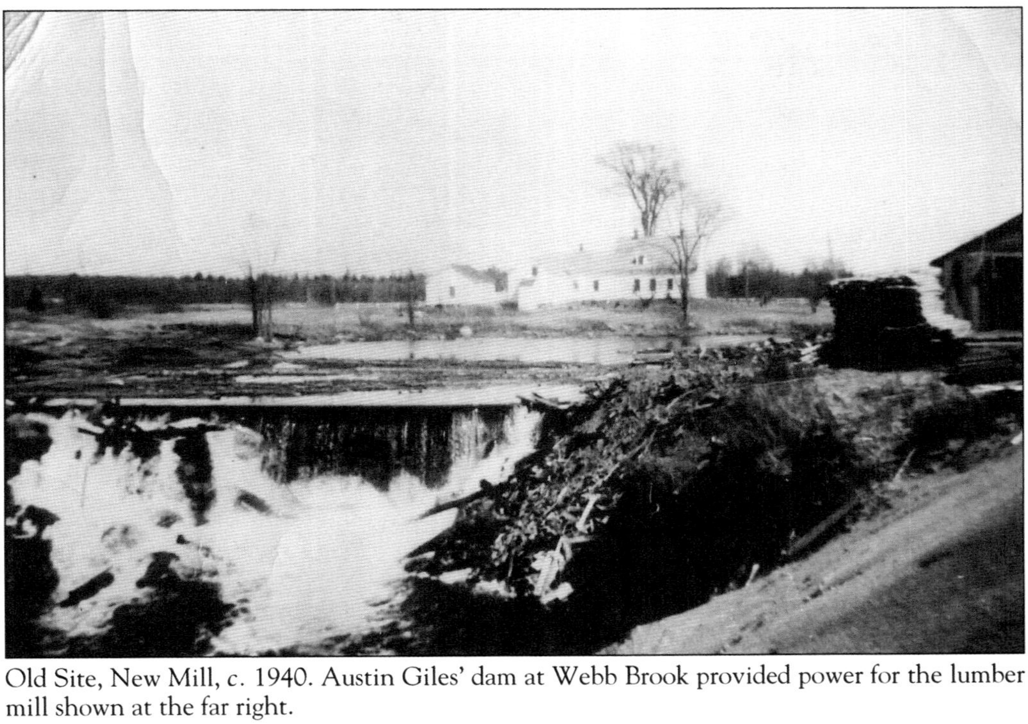

Old Site, New Mill, c. 1940. Austin Giles' dam at Webb Brook provided power for the lumber mill shown at the far right.

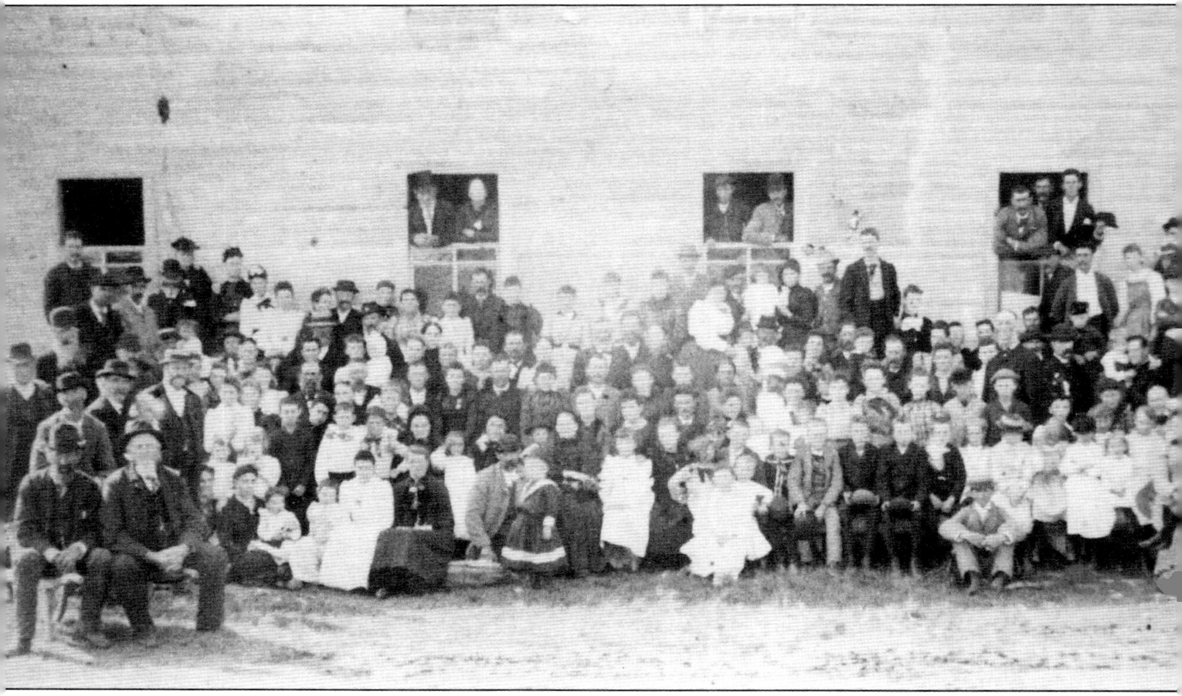

Descendants of Captain George Haslam, *c.* 1890. Taken in front of Waltham Town Hall, the clan was already enormous. Captain George served in the American Revolution while living at Union River Plantation. He married Prudence Wescott. Waltham town records still carry the story of his flight from England near the Tamar River and how he jumped ship as a youngster in America.

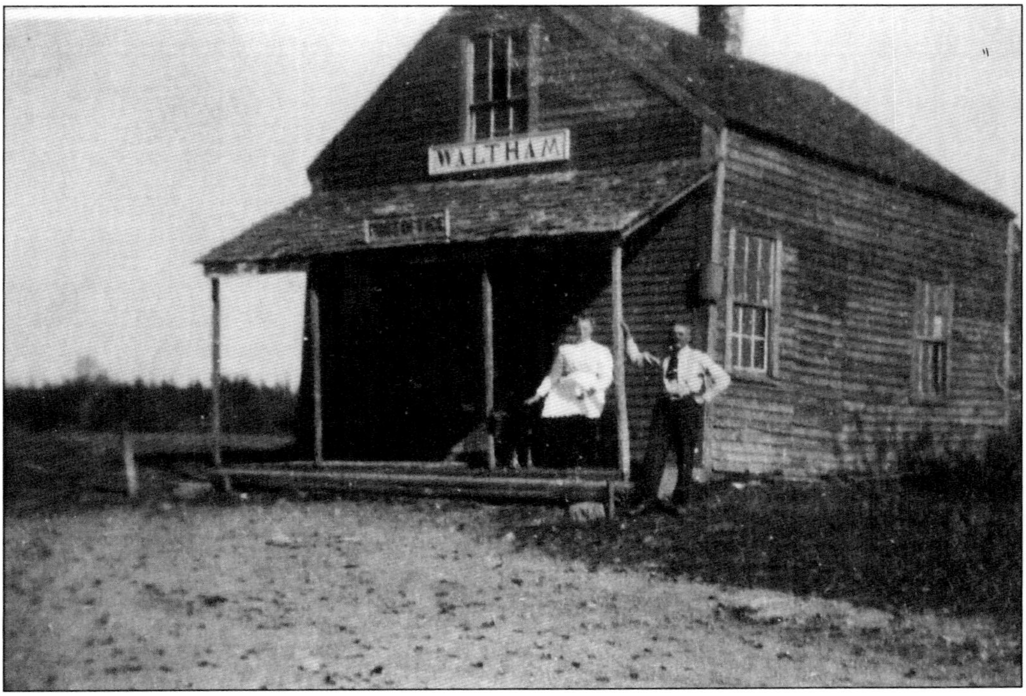

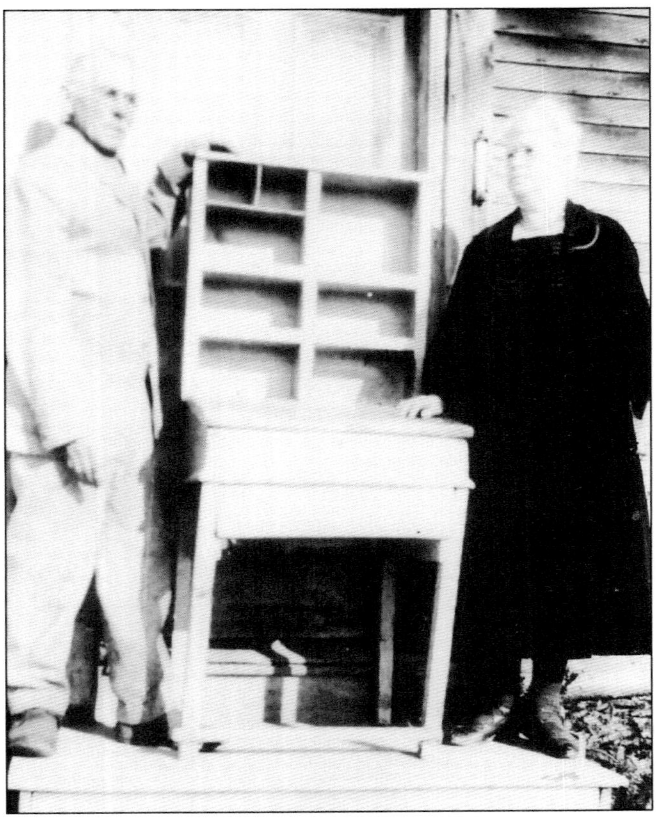

The Waltham Post Office (above) and the Colbys (right). Postmaster Asa Colby and his wife Zella are shown in the top photograph in front of the old post office. It was torn down many years ago and now mail is delivered by RFD. To the right the Colbys show off the quaint holder for letters, newspapers, and packages.

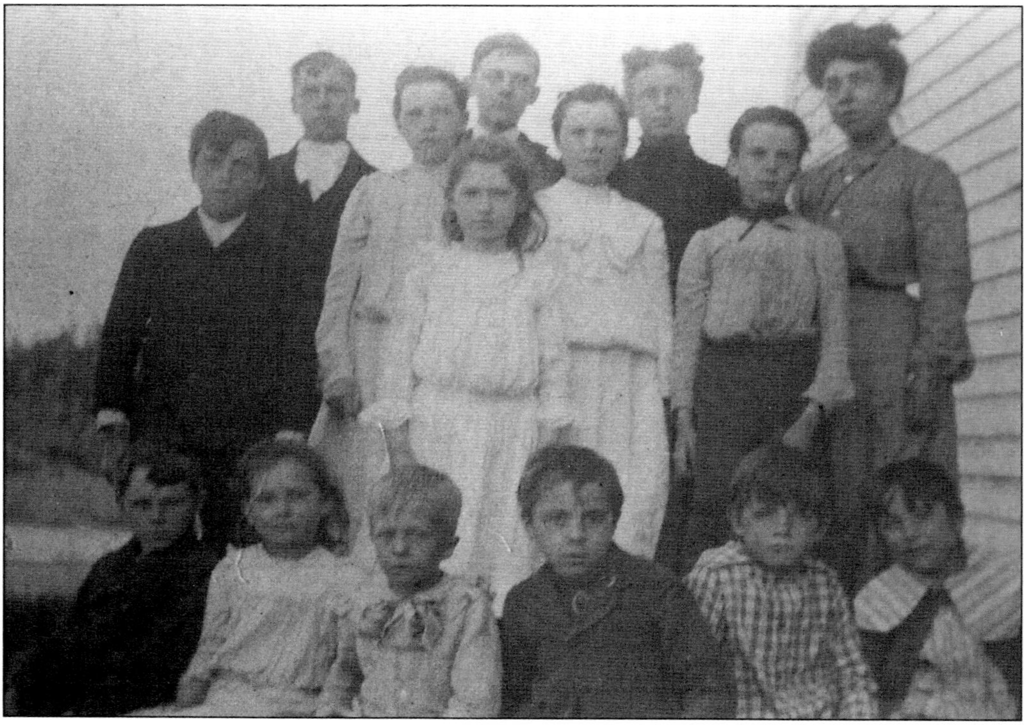

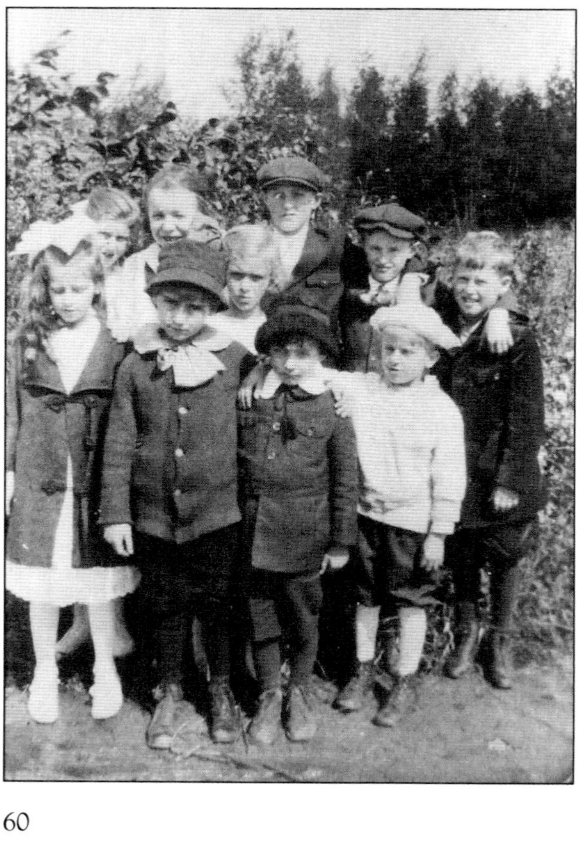

Longfellow School in Waltham. The following students are shown in this June 30, 1904 photograph: (front row) Leon Googins, Madalyn Jordan, Erland Haslam, Wilson Jordan, Leamon Jordan, and Roland Jordan; (back row) Arthur Jordan, Harry Jordan, Bessie Jordan, Harvard Haslam, Erma Jordan, Marion Jordan, and Grace Jordan. Teacher Laura (Weed) Jordan is on the right.

The School Opening, *c.* 1902. Lester Jordan (center back) and Lloyd Jordan (center back on right) are the only two members of this Waltham Grammar School class that have been identified.

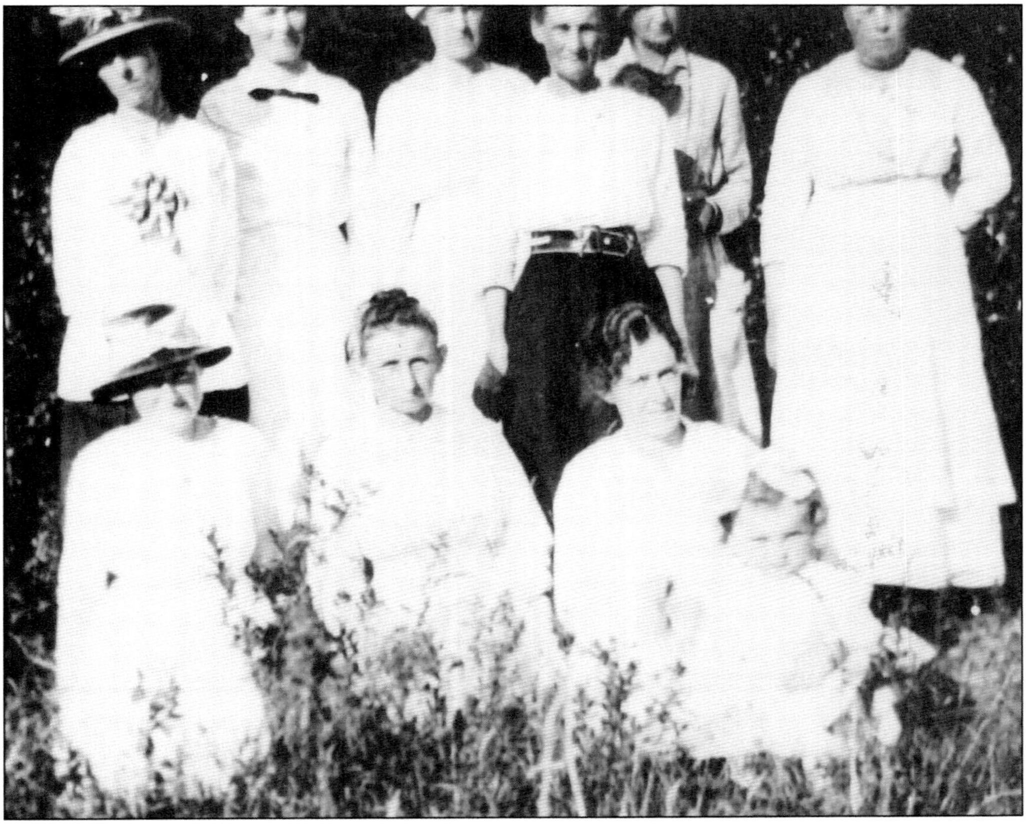

The Help Some How Club, Waltham. It was the fourth anniversary of the club when this photograph was taken on August 4, 1918. The original members of this benevolent organization, which is still going strong, are as follows: Eva Haslam, Alice Jordan, Nora Jordan, Nettie (Jordan) DeBeck, Zella Colby, Mercy (Fox) Hardison, and Lettie (Jordan) Hardison.

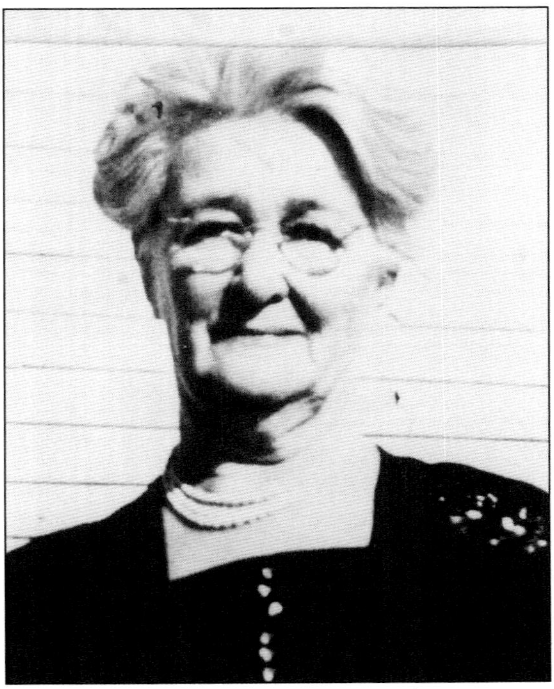

The Founder of the Club at Waltham. Alice (Jordan) Jordan was the founder and president of the Help Some How Club for twenty-two years.

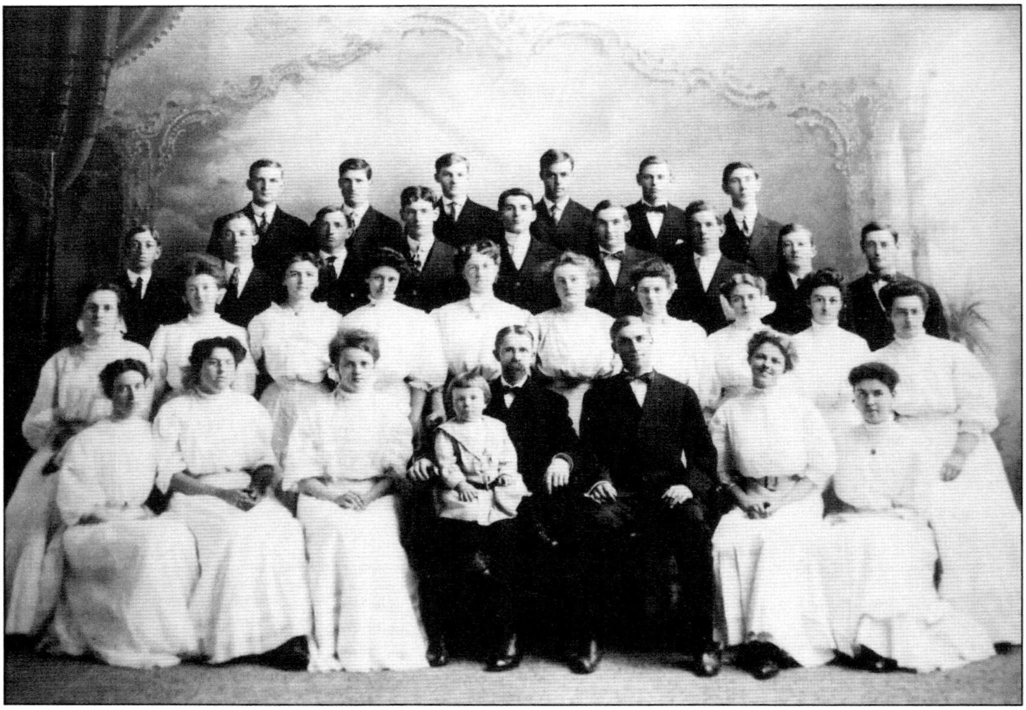

The 1908 Graduates at Pittsfield. This is Flora (Wilbur) Jordan's photograph of her classmates at Maine Central Institute. She is second from the right in the second row.

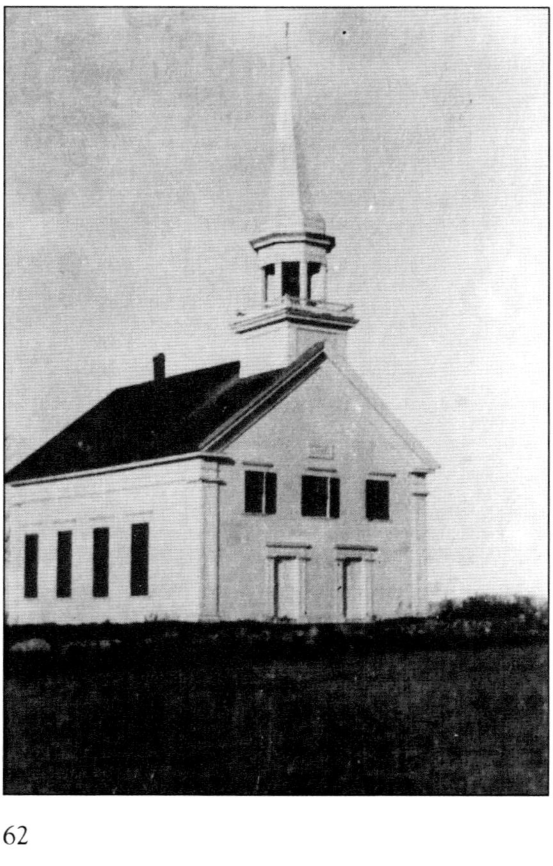

The Waltham Baptist Church, Built in 1853. As the town's population dwindled so did the church's patronage. The building was torn down in 1982. Note the double doors, one for the ladies and one for the gentlemen.

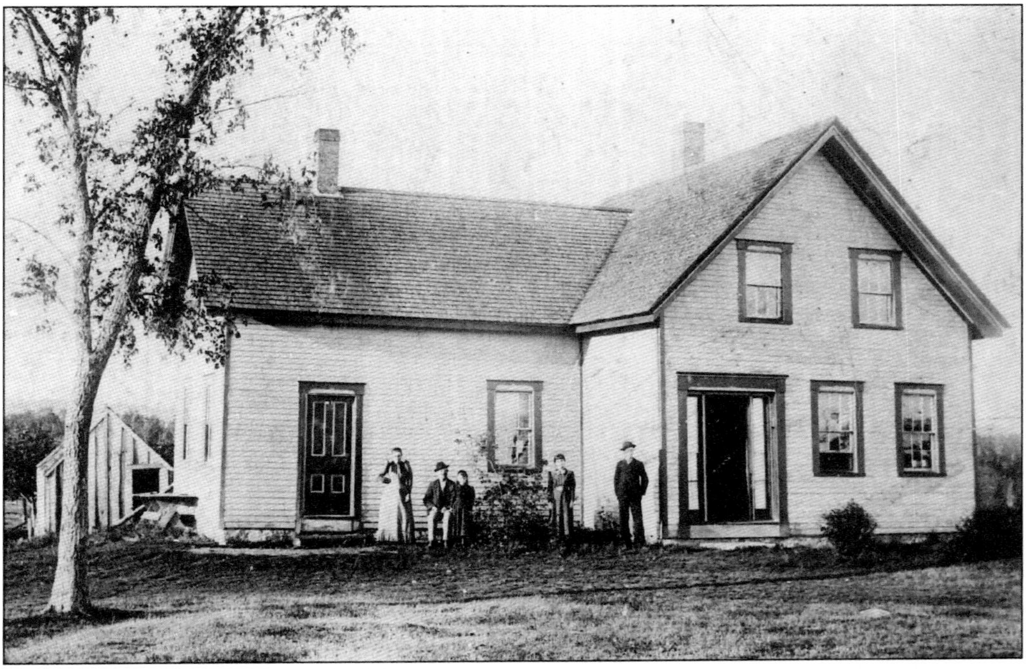

The Waltham Home. Owned by John C. Wilbur, this house was typical of those built in the mid-1800s. Standing in the front yard are Charlotte (Hooper) Wilbur, John C., Flora (Wilbur) Jordan, Mina (Wilbur) Gott, and perhaps David Wilbur. The house was destroyed by fire on May 25, 1941.

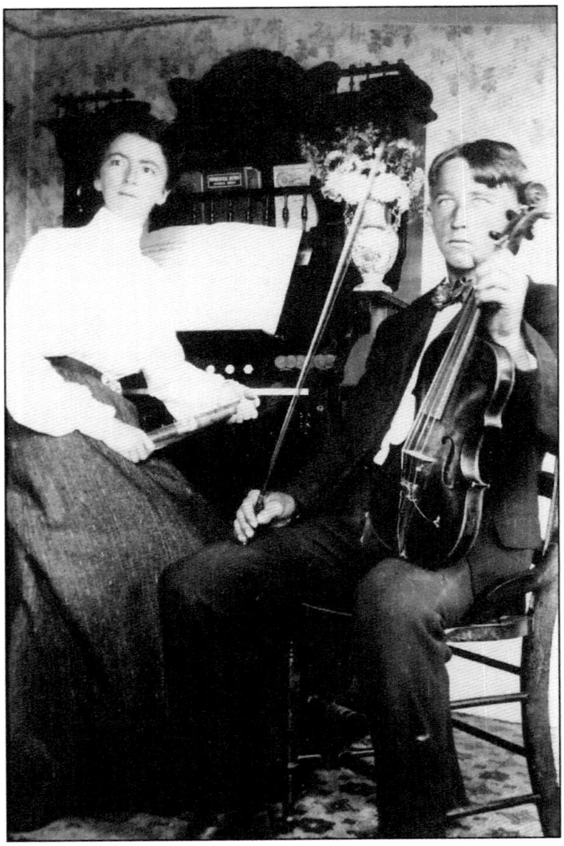

Music, an Important Part of Life. Music and the arts were especially valued in the isolated towns up and down the Union River. Traveling teachers provided enjoyable entertainment. Here are Vida and Howard Wilbur of Eastbrook during America's Victorian Age.

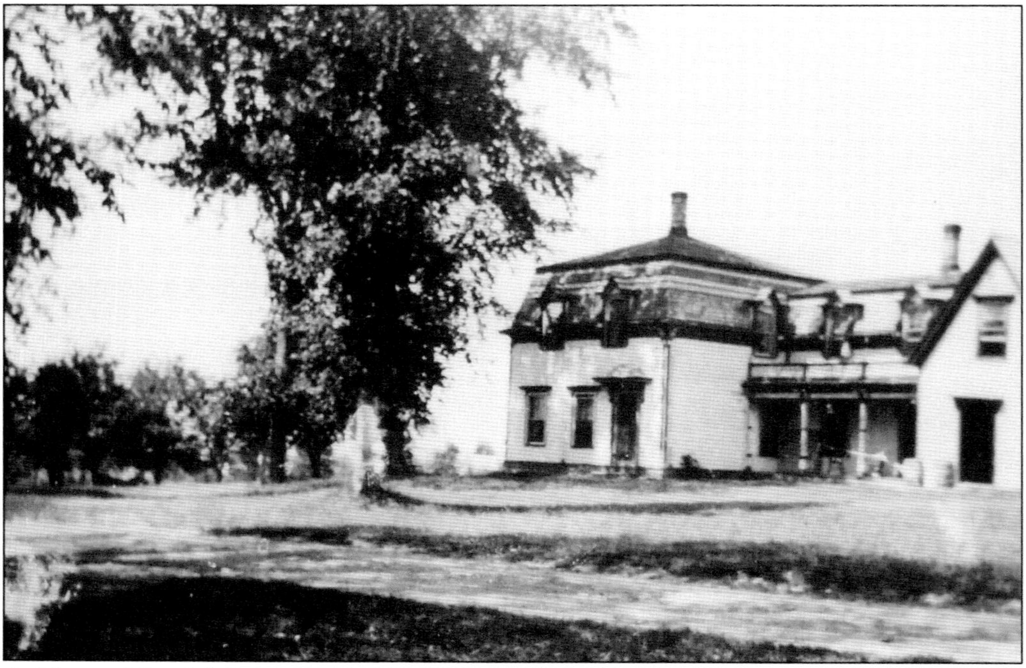

A Mansard-Roofed Beauty with Elms. This style of home, conceived by French architect F. Mansard, quickly became a favorite throughout the county. The trim was often a gaudy color, causing these houses to stand out among the prim white of their neighbors.

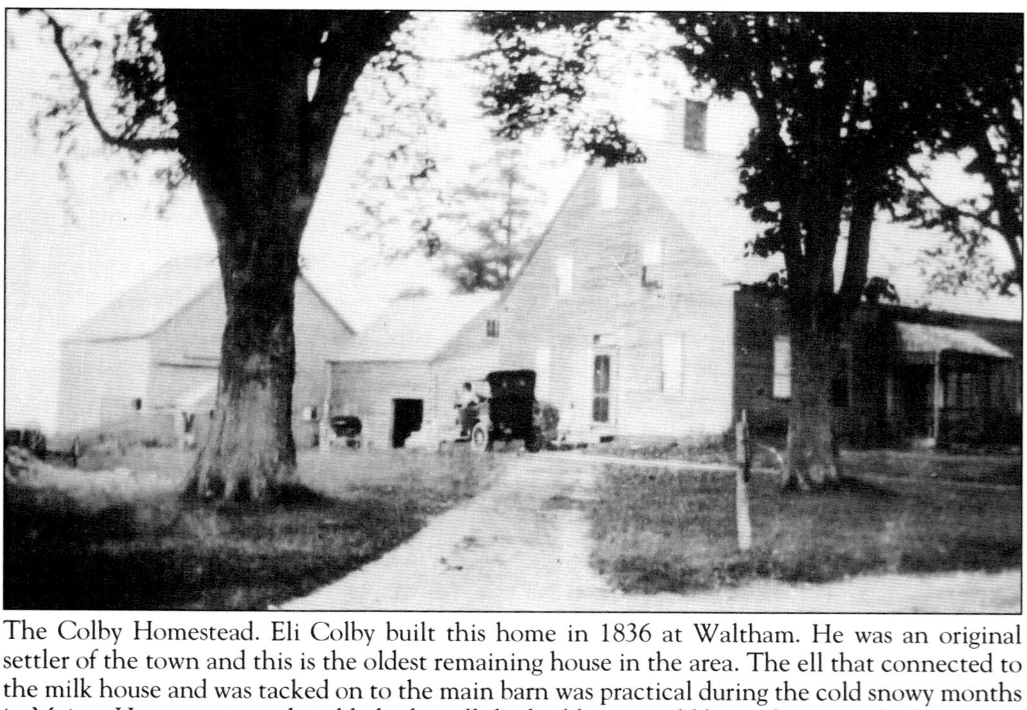

The Colby Homestead. Eli Colby built this home in 1836 at Waltham. He was an original settler of the town and this is the oldest remaining house in the area. The ell that connected to the milk house and was tacked on to the main barn was practical during the cold snowy months in Maine. However, it made it likely that all the buildings would burn if one caught fire.

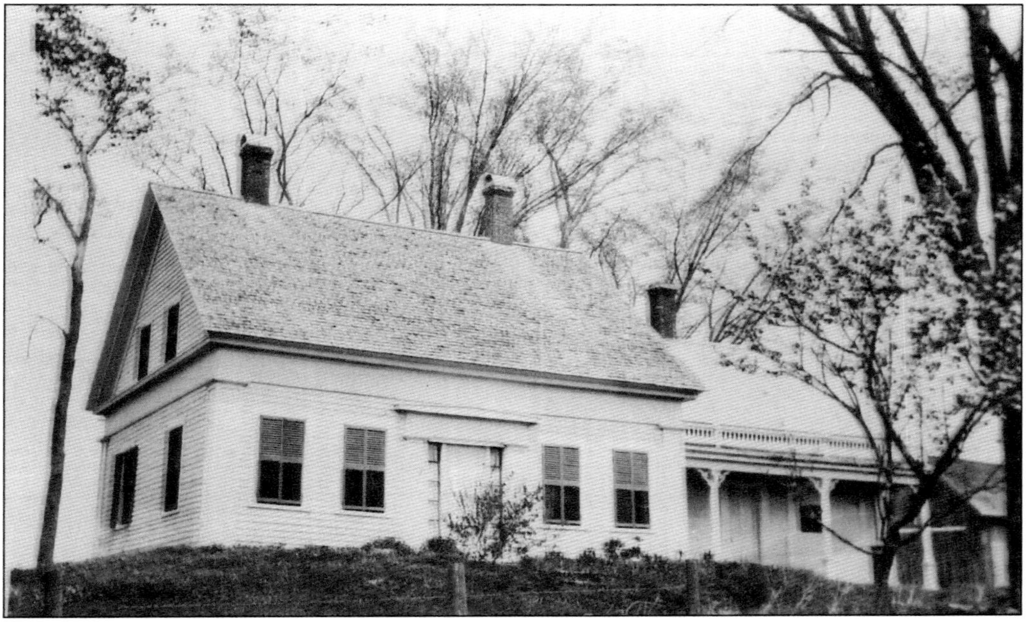

The Haslam House, Built *c.* 1850. Classic Greek-style homes were much loved by early settlers along the river. Wood was used in place of the earlier marble, but the carvings are all in place. The ell was added as a summer kitchen as the family grew in size. This building, the home of Jefferson Haslam, burned in the 1950s.

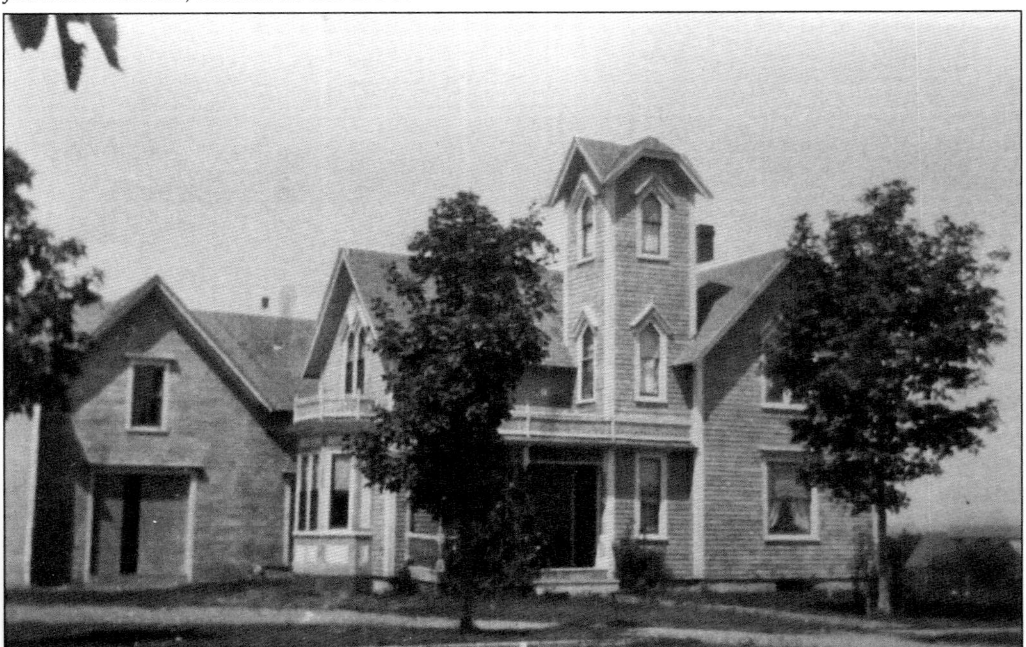

An Unusual Configuration on Webb's Brook. Alvah Haslam built this Victorian-style home and added a tower instead of the commonly used turret. A small porch was put over the bay window and was perhaps used to catch the breeze on hot country days. The home is still planted firmly on the spot it was raised.

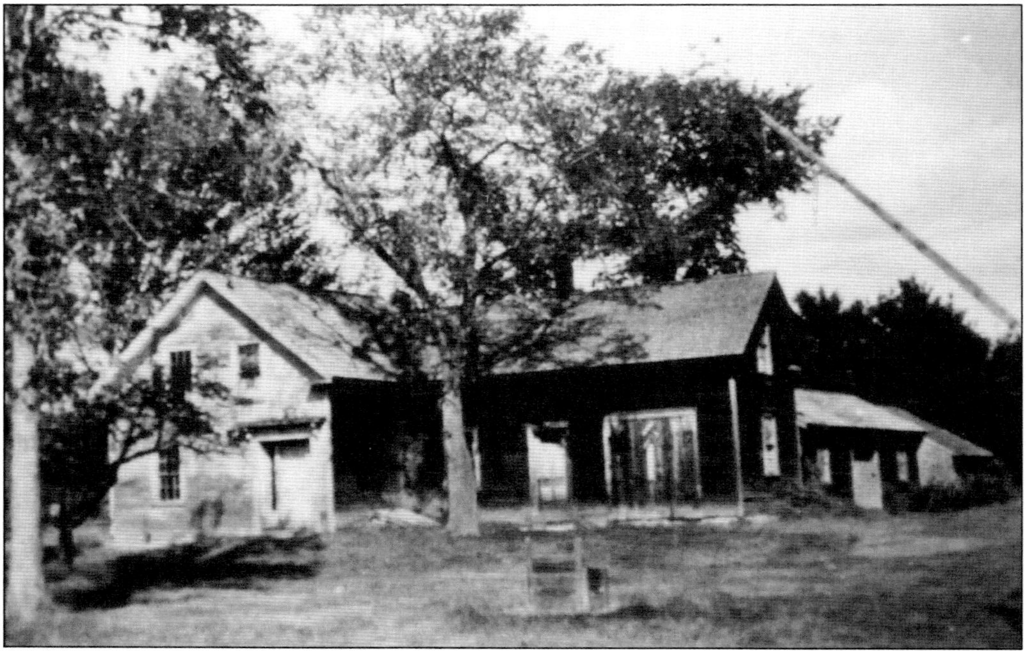

The Kingman House, *c.* 1997. This home stood for a long time near the Waltham cemetery, but is no longer standing.

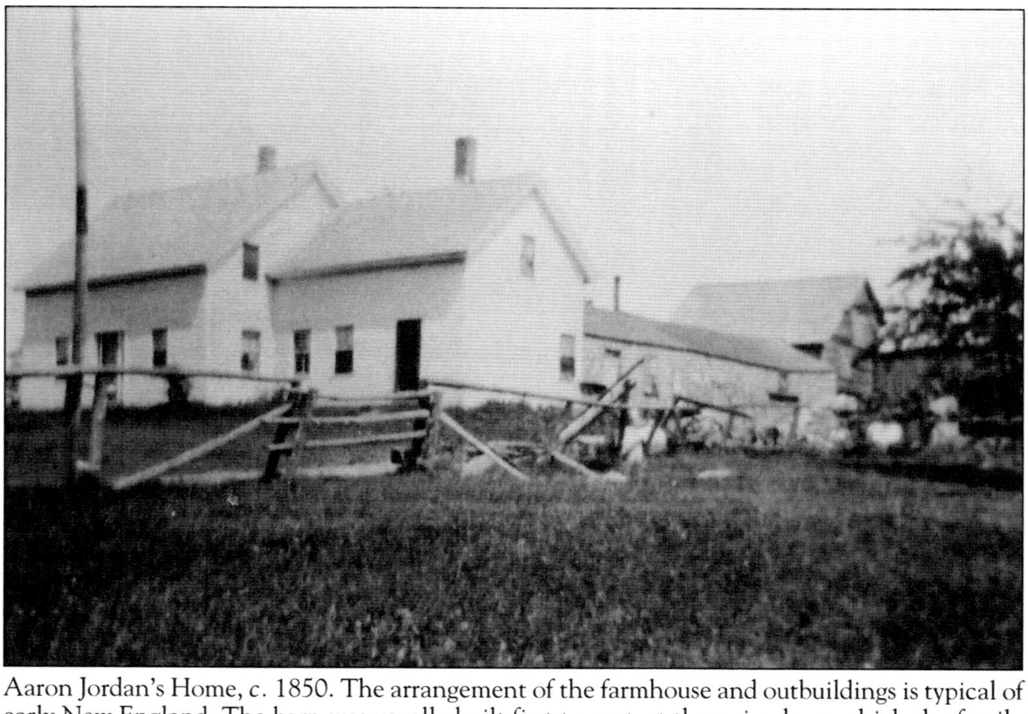

Aaron Jordan's Home, *c.* 1850. The arrangement of the farmhouse and outbuildings is typical of early New England. The barn was usually built first to protect the animals on which the family depended; the main house would be added next, the ell as the family prospered, and the milk room as the family's cow herd grew.

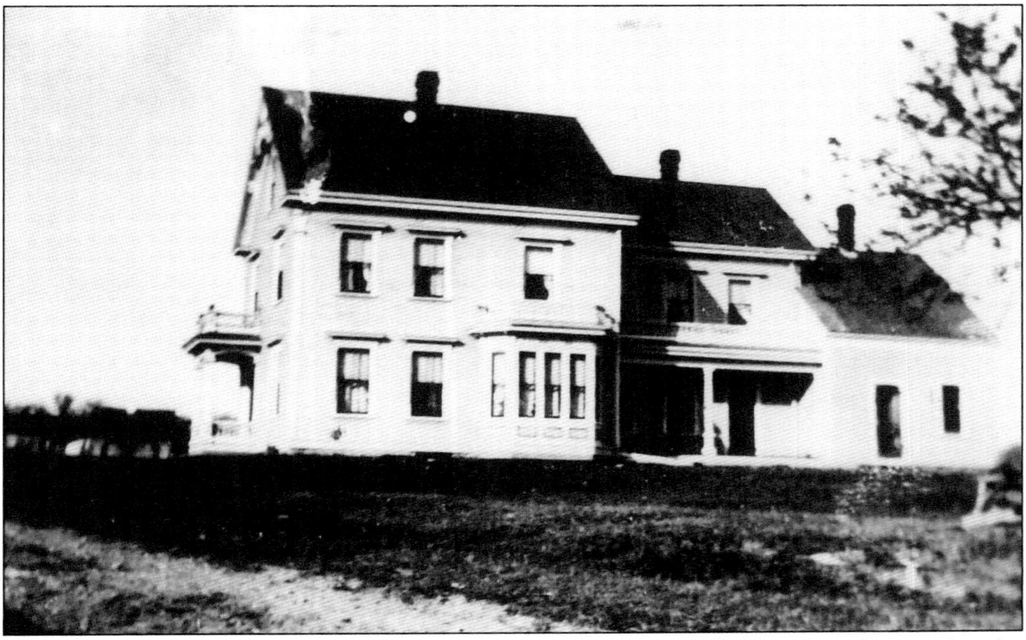

The Jordan Home in Waltham, *c.* 1870. This photograph was probably taken shortly after the home was built, as it is in perfect condition. Complete with bay window and covered front entrance, it was the home of Franklin Jordan.

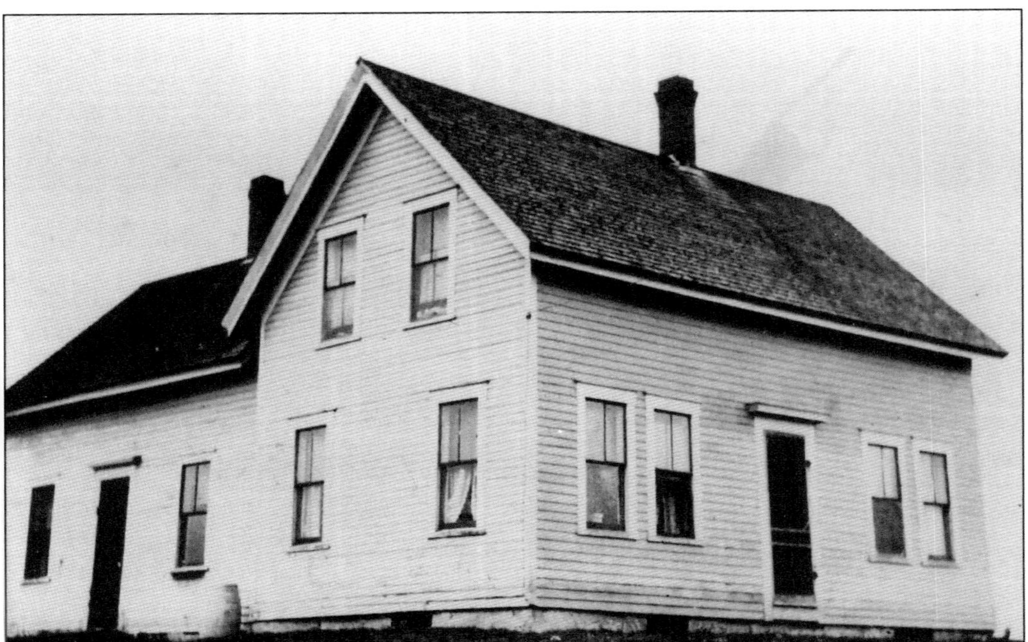

The Modest Home of Hollis Jordan. Built *c.* 1887 at Waltham, this building has granite sills. Note the rain barrel at left which collected water for house plants as well as for washing milady's hair.

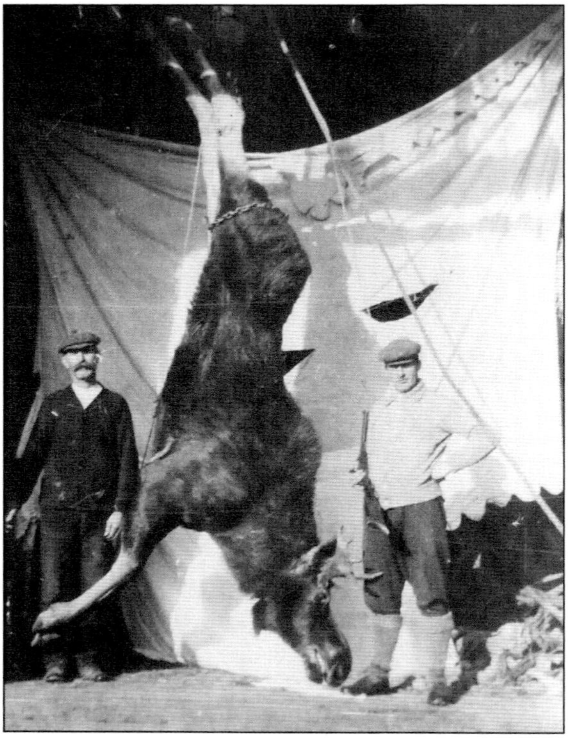

The End of a Moose Hunt, c. 1929. This moose was shot on the mile stretch by Hervey Kingman in Waltham. His brother helped hoist the huge creature up.

Moose You at Waltham? Several people got to see a moose up close as this 1940s photograph reveals. Can you see the man over the creature's back and the one on the far left?

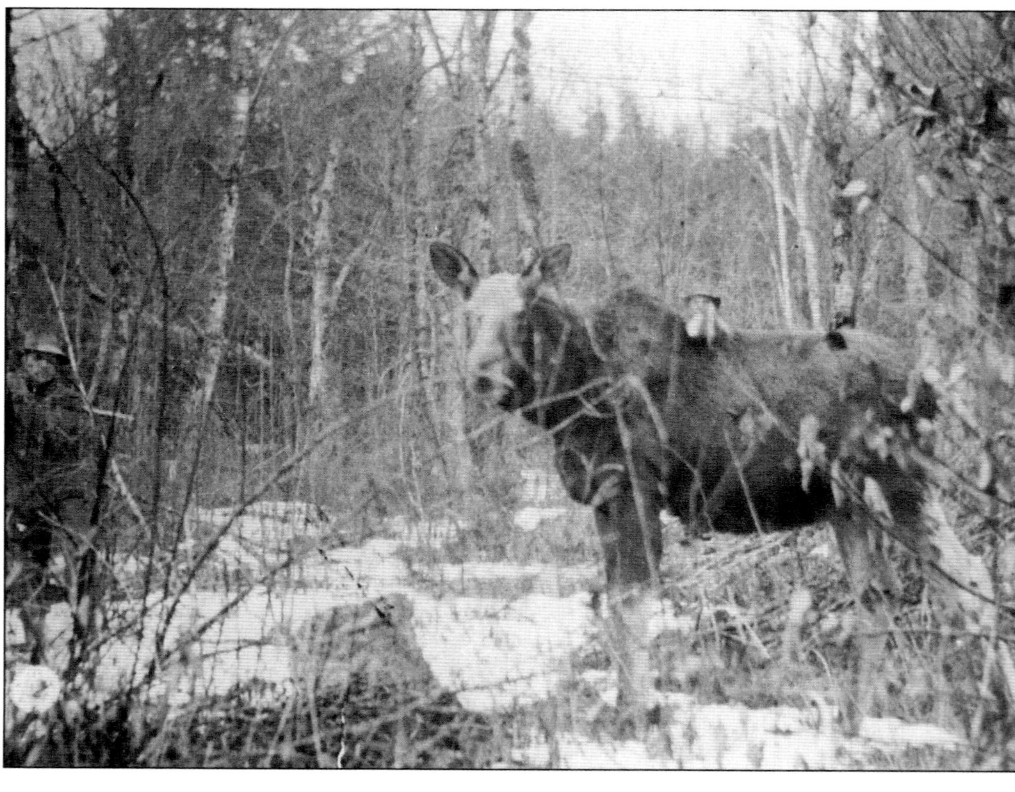

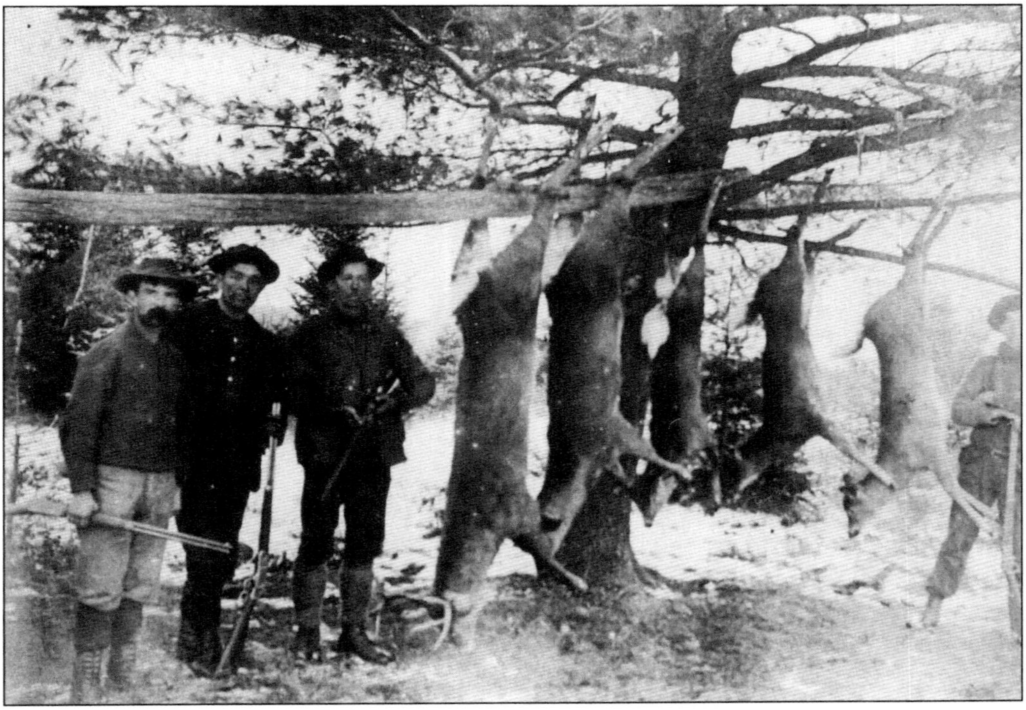

A Hunt Scene at Eastbrook. This *c.* 1890s photograph was taken when it was still legal in Maine to take two deer.

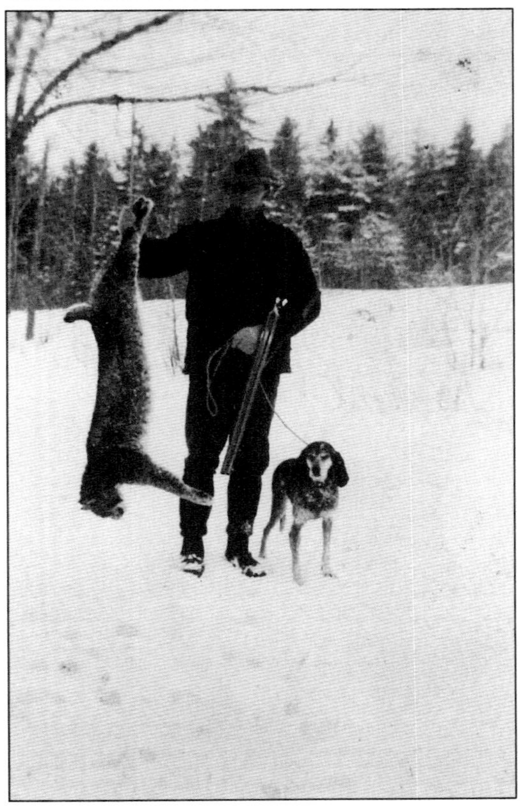

A Trapper at Waltham, *c.* mid-1900s. Francis Wilbur and his trusty hound dog had a successful bobcat hunt on this winter day.

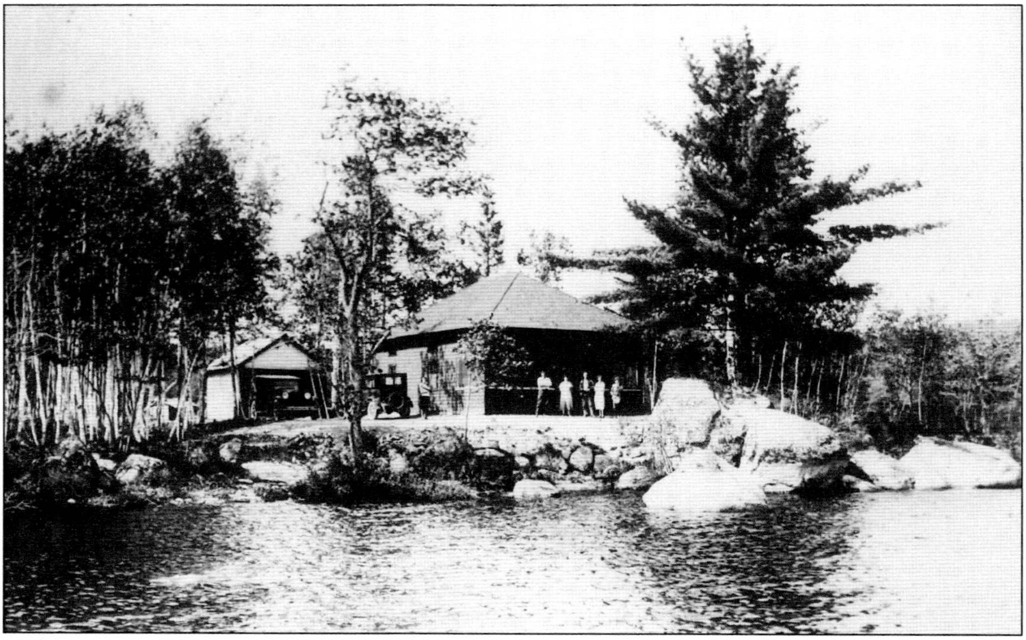

Webb Pond, *c.* 1916. Leona Wilbur's camp was located on Webb Pond in Waltham.

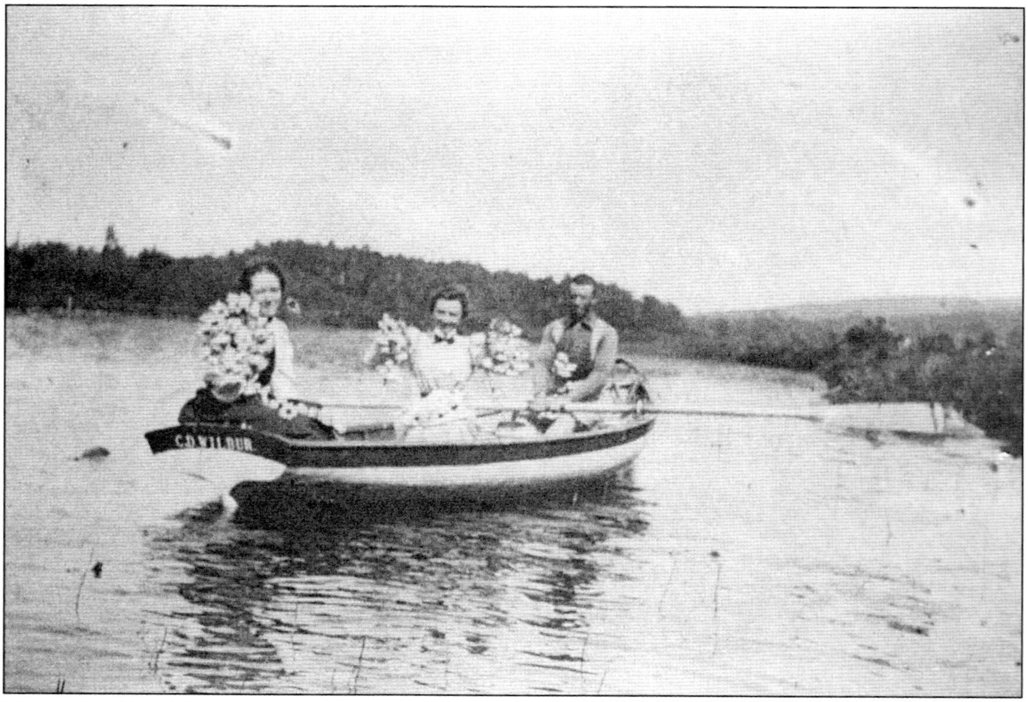

Gathering Pond Lilies. Charles D. Wilbur is seen here taking the girls out on perhaps Molasses Pond or down the Bog River to gather fragrant bouquets of pond lilies.

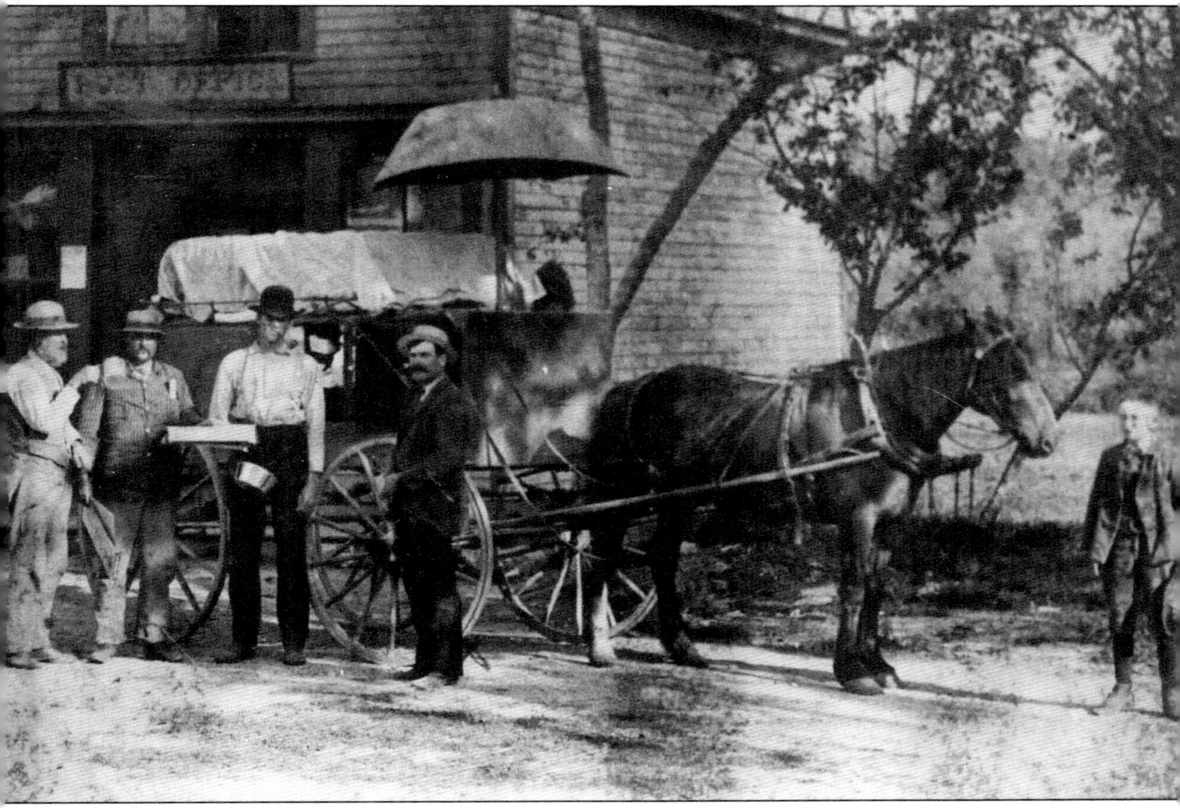

A Welcome Sight. Before there was a corner store in upriver towns, myriads of articles were bought from traveling salesmen. Needles, dishes, clothes, and luxury items were all carried in wondrous wagons. This picture is of Justin Cole and his wagon at what may be the post office in Franklin.

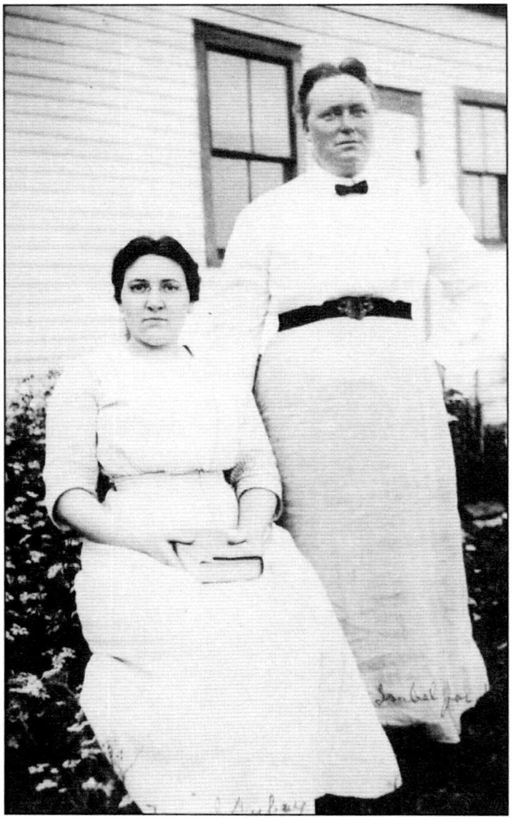

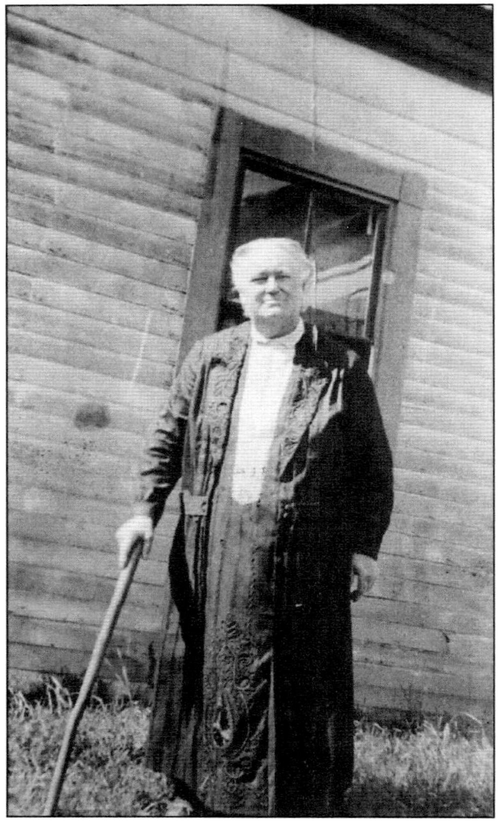

Jill of All Trades. Isabelle Jordan, who was referred to out of her hearing as "Big Belle," was a well-remembered school teacher in the Waltham-Eastbrook area. A large, husky woman, she was said to have handled a team of horses as well as any man and even shod her own team when necessary. Her specialty in the field of teaching was in mathematics. In the upper left are Isabelle and her fellow teacher Maud Dubay; in the lower right is Big Belle in her declining years.

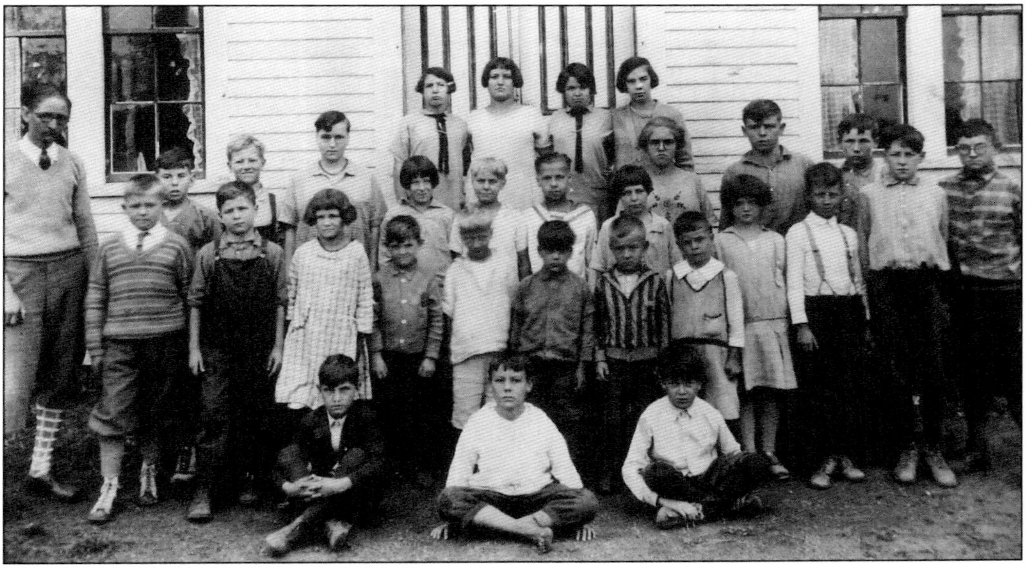

Mill School, c. 1929. The teacher, Mr. King, is on the far left. The students are, from left to right, as follows: (front row) Meltiah Bragdon, Eddie Gordon, and Raymond Piper; (second row) Vernon Haslam Jr., Warren Clark, Marguerite Bragdon, Raymond Bragdon, Ellis Wilbur, Donald Piper, Gerald Wilbur, Ernest Butler Sr., Sheila Kingman, Holmes Wilbur, and Donald Merchant; (third row) Bessie DeMeyer, Louise Gordon, Eleanor Piper, and Barbara Merchant; (fourth row) Richard Ashe, Andrew Clark, Mary Giles, Frances Butler, Carl Rankin, and Victor Wilbur; (back row) Marion Butler, Etta Gordon, Geneva Butler, and Audrey French.

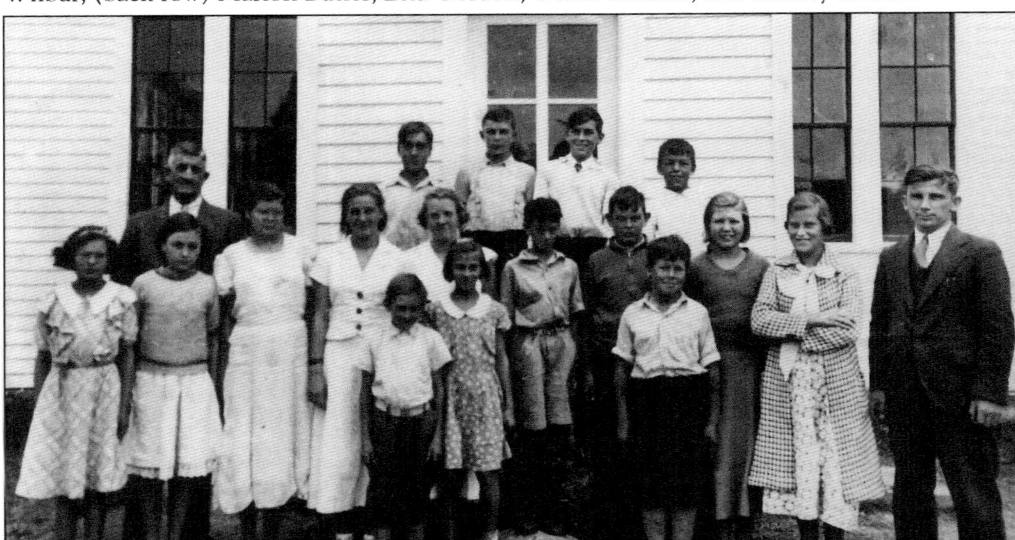

Mill School, Eastbrook, c. 1937. Mr. Wardwell's class is being visited by superintendent Sherman Scammons (left). The children are, from left to right, as follows: (front row) Henry Bunker, Shirley Bunker, William French, Marion Gordon, and Beverly Burrill; (middle row) Catherine Ashe, Virginia French, Phyllis Butler, Madeleine Giles, Pauline Kingman, Robert Ashe, and Carl Butler; (back row) Ervin Googins, Ernest Butler Sr., George Bragdon, and Gerard Wilbur.

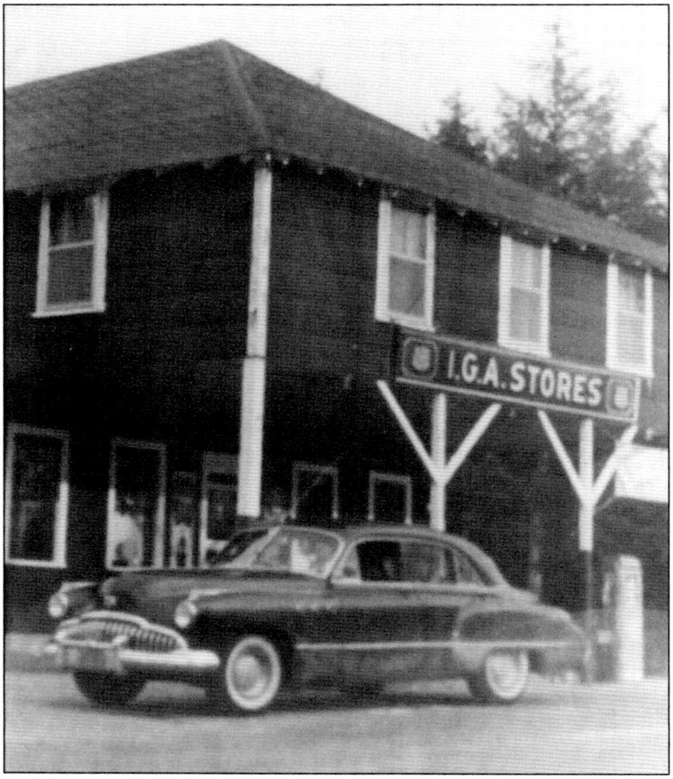

Wilbur's Store, *c.* 1949. This was the second store built on this site in Waltham by Roland Wilbur Sr.

The Waltham Town Hall, *c.* 1930.

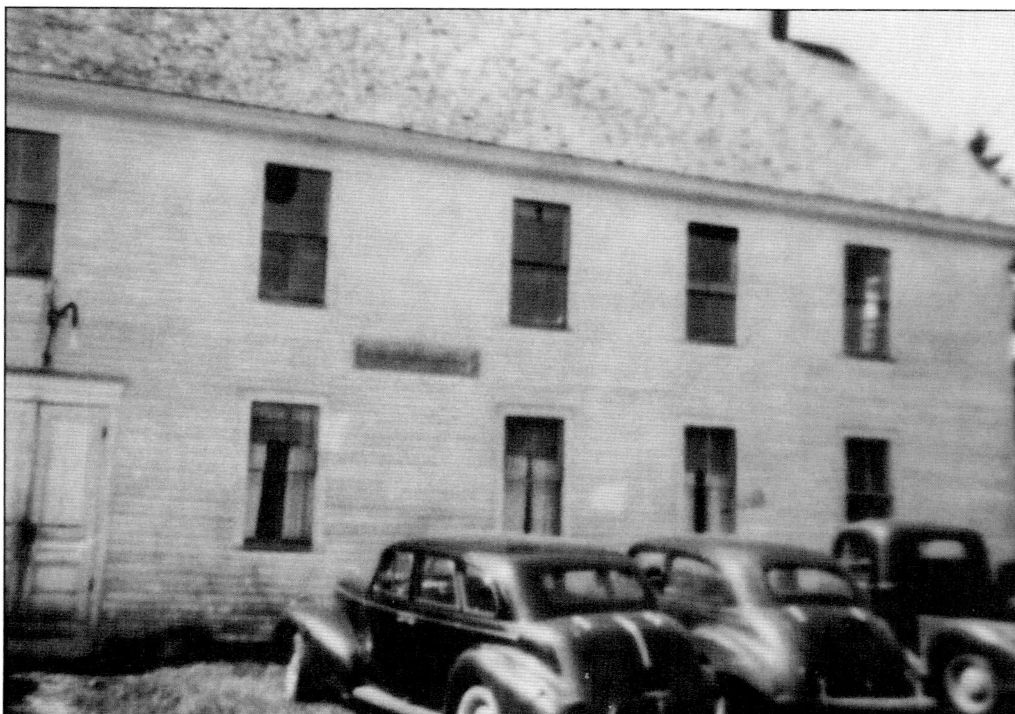

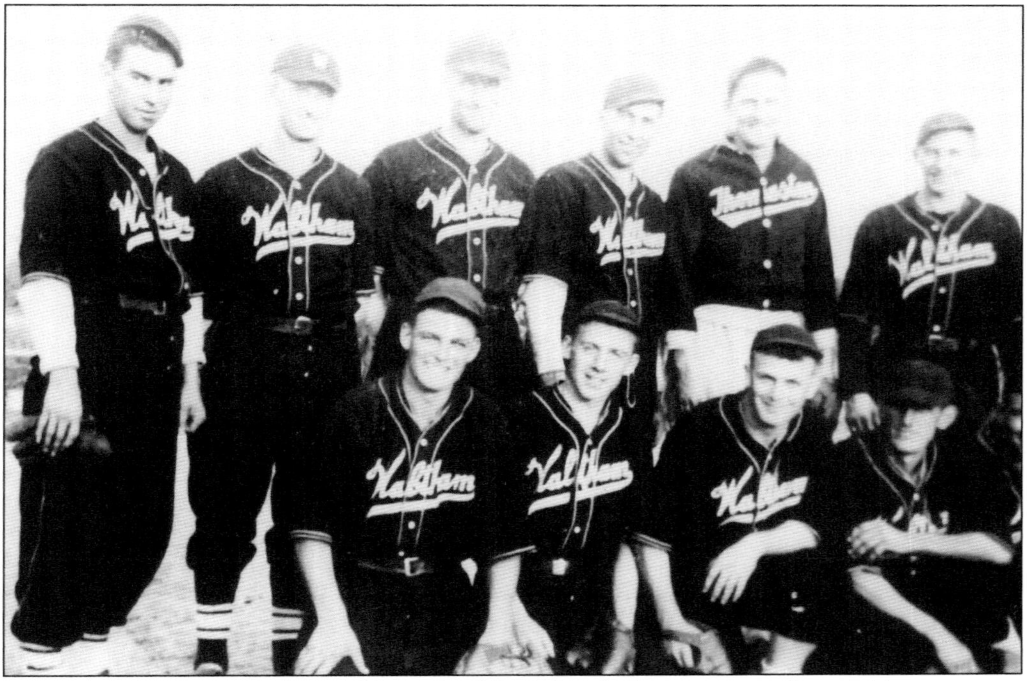

Any Local Boys Here? The Waltham Double A baseball team was a formidable opponent. This photograph was taken c. 1938–1940. Baseball competitions were a welcomed form of entertainment and remain so today in some of the river towns.

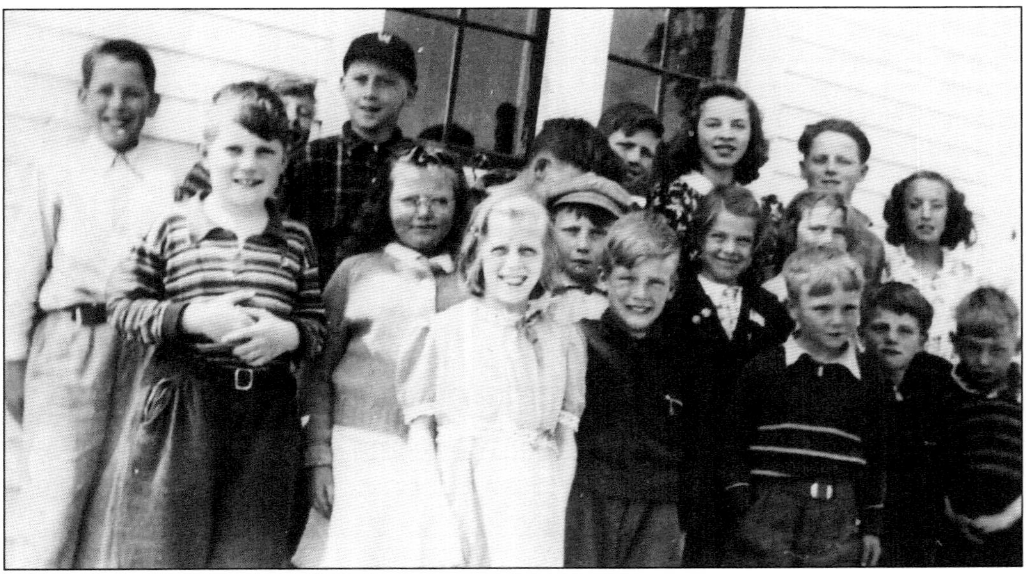
Longfellow School at Waltham. The students, from left to right, are as follows: (front row) Ernestine (Jordan) Flynn, Thomas Jordan Sr., and Roland A. Wilbur Sr.; (middle row) Robert Jordan, Marguerite (Jordan) Lynk, Reginald Jordan, Ellain (Jordan) Frost, Leota (Hardison) Higgins, Philip Jordan, and Floyd Hardison; (back row) Ralph Jordan Jr., Harvard Rankin, Robert Hardison, Merrill Hardison, Harvey Jordan, Lavina (Rankin) Stapes, Mandel Kemp Jr., and Gertrude Jordan.

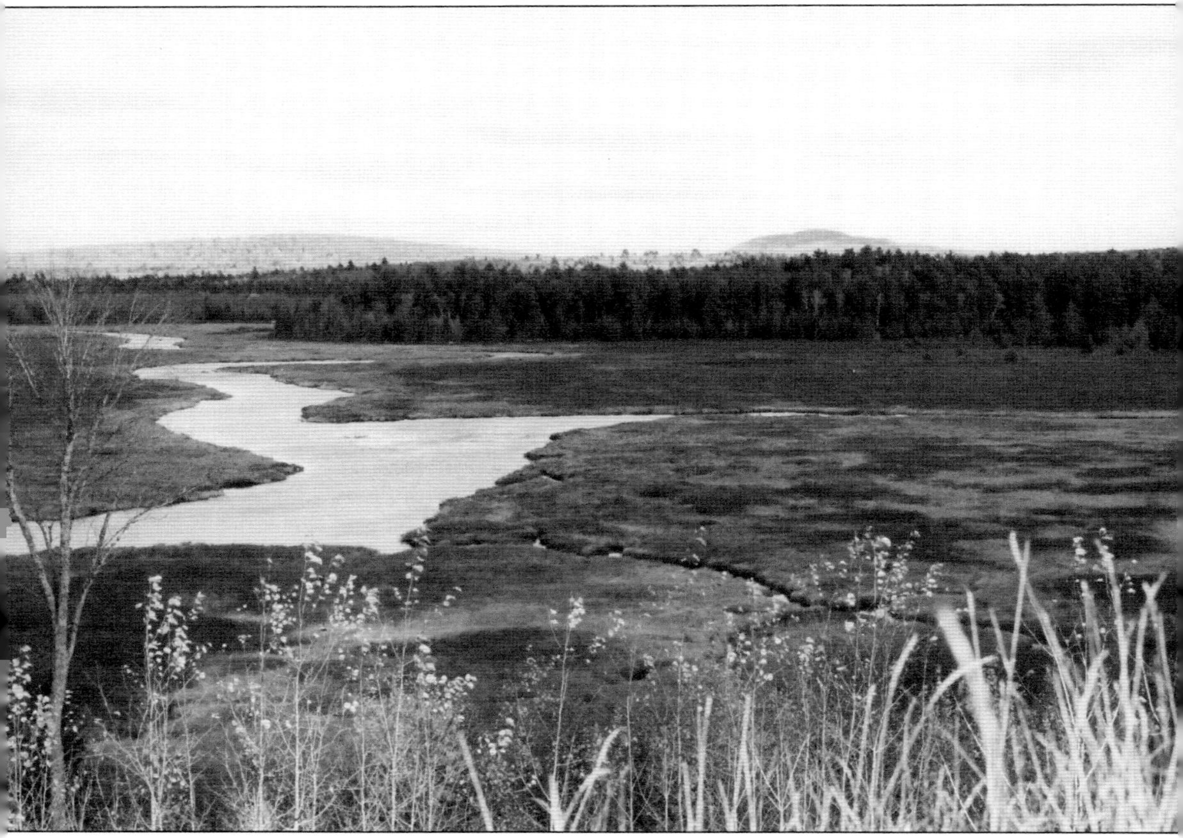

The Meanderings of the East Branch. Union River is shown here from the Whale's Back. The mountain in the background is Eagle.

Just a Boy and His Dog. Taken about 1915 on the Union River, this photograph shows a young man proudly displaying the string of trout caught by him and his Dad. Note the knapsack and old-fashioned creel in foreground.

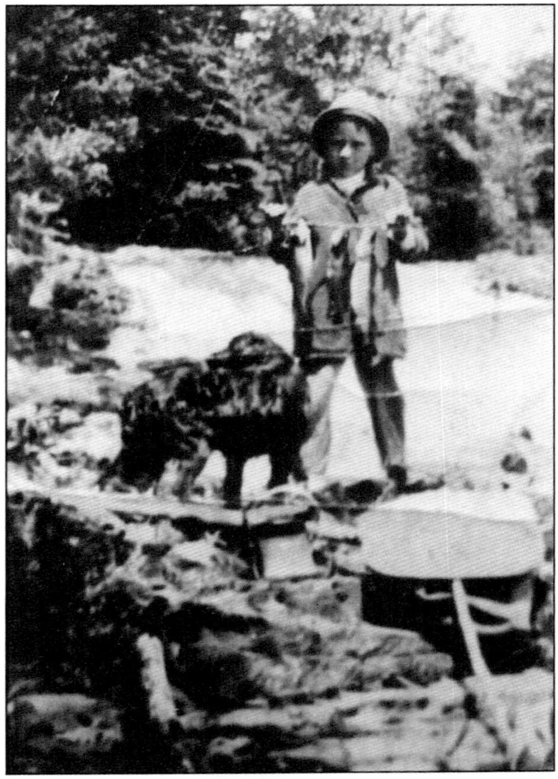

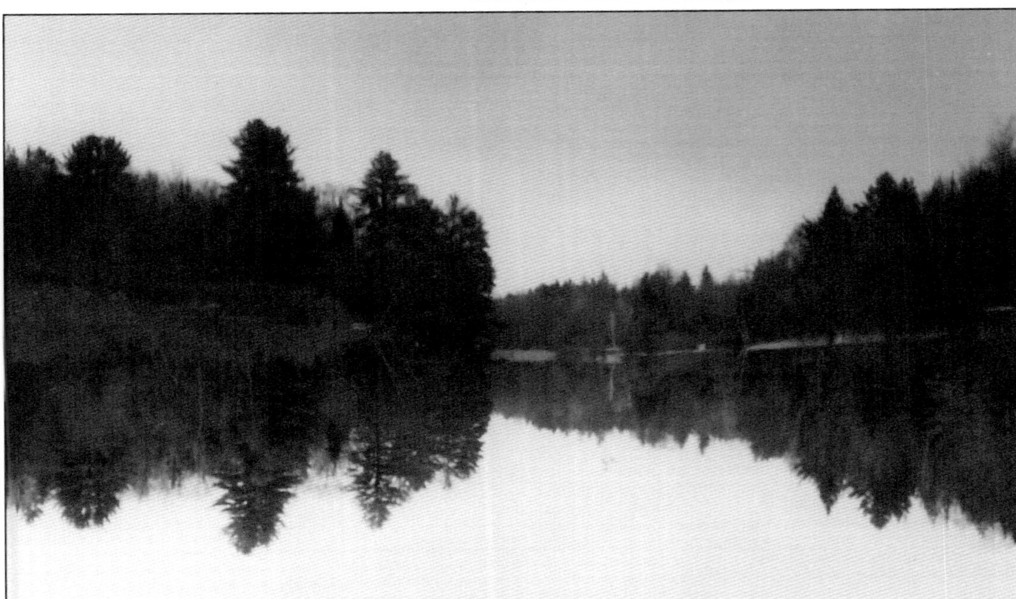

An Ancient Landmark. First mapped by the French in 1686, the Union River was called the "River of Mount Desert." It was used as a waterway of the early American Indians, and burial grounds of the Red Paint people have been discovered along its banks. This serene photograph was made on a stretch controlled by the hydroelectric dam at the foot of Graham Lake.

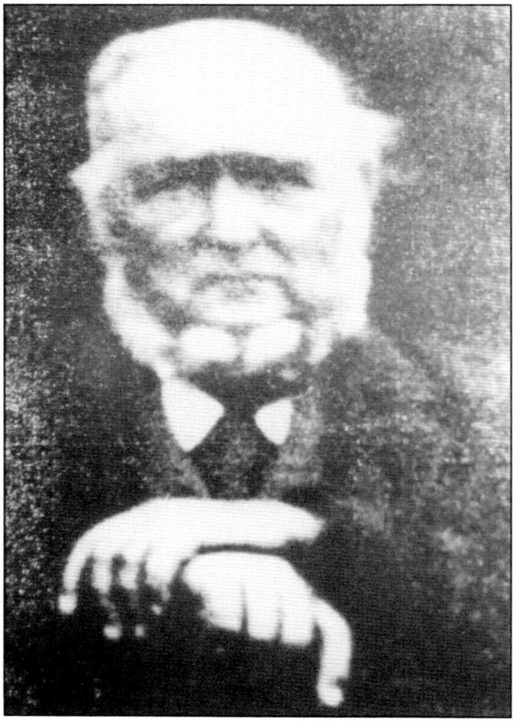

Deacon Samuel Giles. Samuel Giles, born in 1810, was the first person born in Aurora, and he reached the age of ninety-nine years before he passed away. Upon his death on August 20, 1910, he was referred to in *The Ellsworth American* as "one of the remarkable old men of Hancock County, rugged and active." He was the son of Daniel, one of nineteen children.

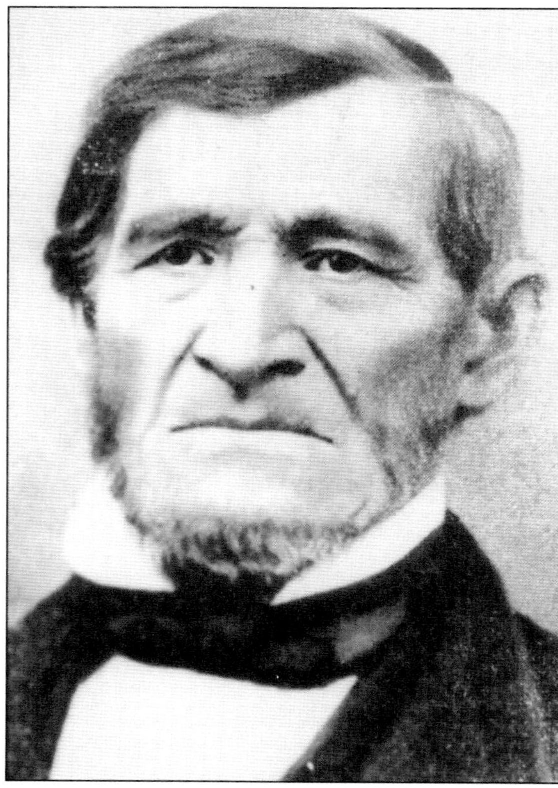

Samuel Silsby Jr. In 1805 Samuel became the first settler in Aurora. A miller by trade, he had traveled from Acworth, New Hampshire, to work with his brother, Goodell Silsby, who had settled in the nearby town of Amherst by 1803. Samuel contracted for the first two lots on General David Cobb's road just over the Amherst line in Aurora. He was soon followed by three younger brothers, Benjamin, David, and Roswell. Roswell ran a cooper's shop and Benjamin and David had a stage line to Bangor, using what is now known as the Airline Road, or Route 9. David was issued an innkeeper's license in 1825 for his establishment, called "The Mansion House." When he sold the place in 1860 it was described as "the finest stand of buildings in the county." Its worth was estimated at $10,000.

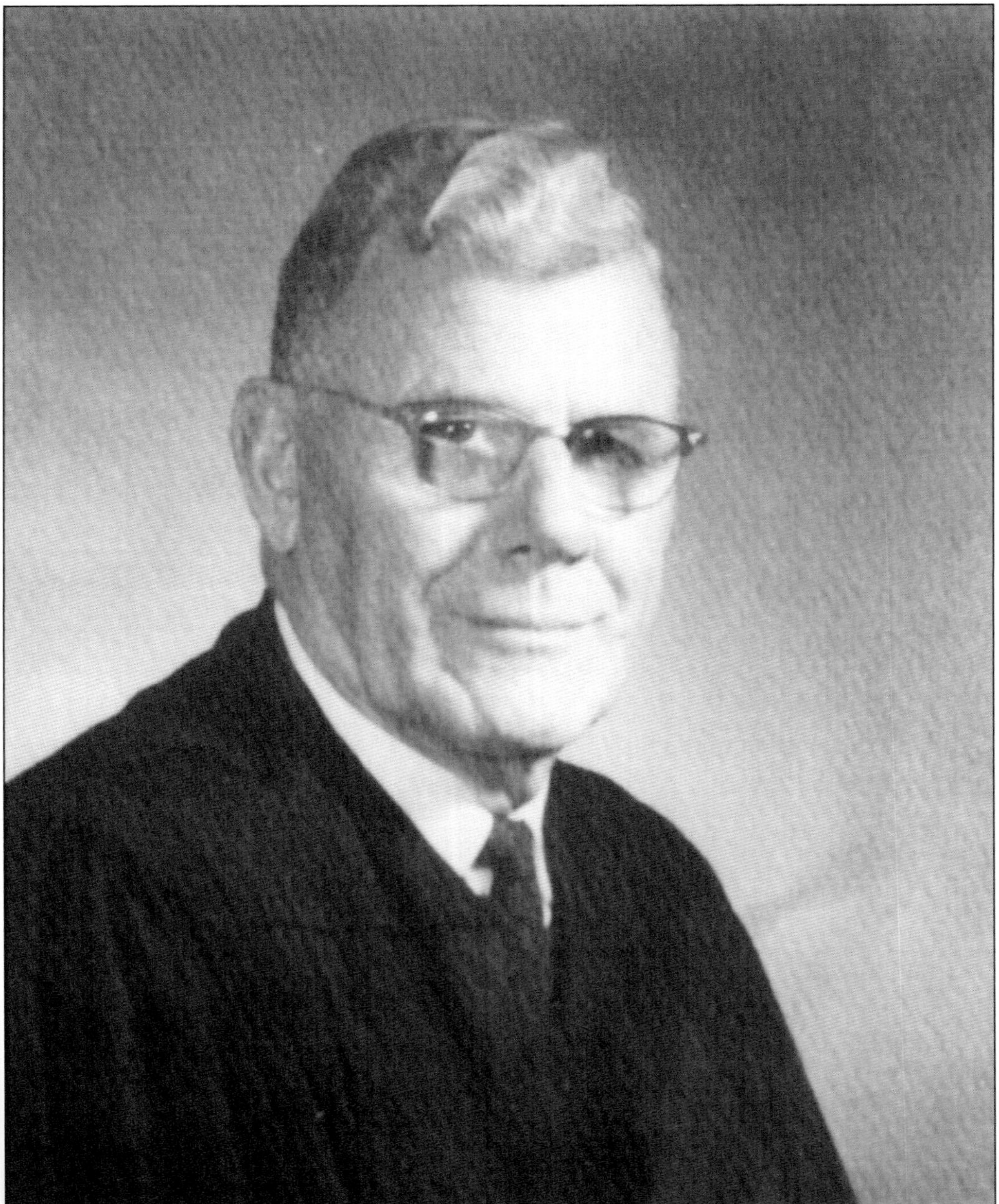

William Schoppee Silsby. Born in Aurora to Herbert and Margaret (Shoppee) in May 1902, William spent the next eighty-five years serving his town, county, and state. A graduate of the Suffolk University Law School, he founded the law firm of Silsby and Silsby in Ellsworth, was appointed superior court justice in 1961, was president of the Union River Electric Corporation, and owner of the Union River Telephone Company. In addition, he served as speaker of the Maine house, as a Maine senator for four years, was on the Governor's Council, and was instrumental in founding the Maine Ferry Service (subsequently, a boat was named for him). He led a varied life and worked as driver, cook, or crew boss on all three of Union River branches.

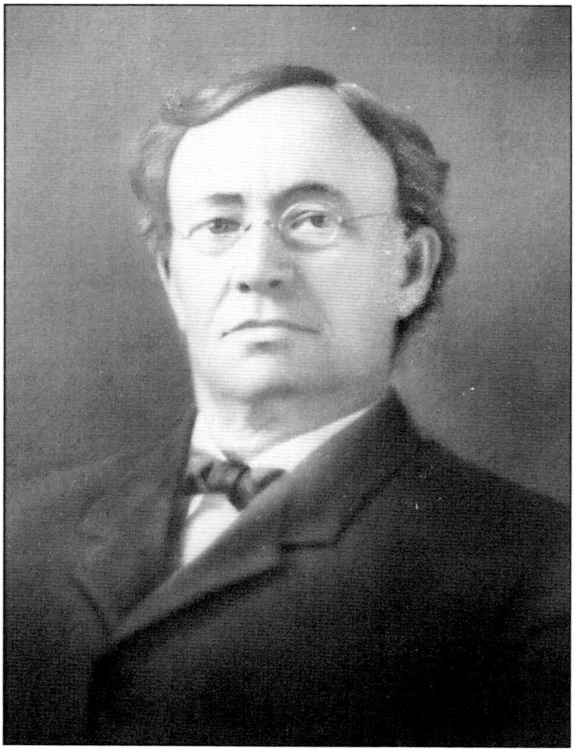

The Second Owner of Mace's Store. Albert Mace (1855–1915) was the second in line to own the family business, taking over from his father, Ansel, who founded the store in 1851. It is the oldest continuously operating general store in Hancock County. Today it is owned by Melody Mace Knadler, the daughter of Asa "Bud" Mace and his wife Jacqueline—and a member of the fifth generation removed from Ansel.

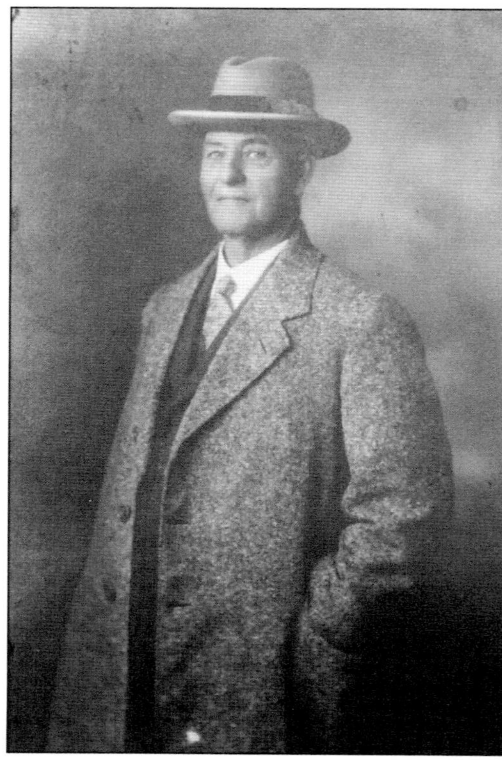

The First Maine Forest Commissioner, Appointed in 1915. Frank E. Mace, brother to Asa, was the first commissioner of forestry in the state of Maine. He also had the reputation as the last Democratic Senator in Maine from Aurora.

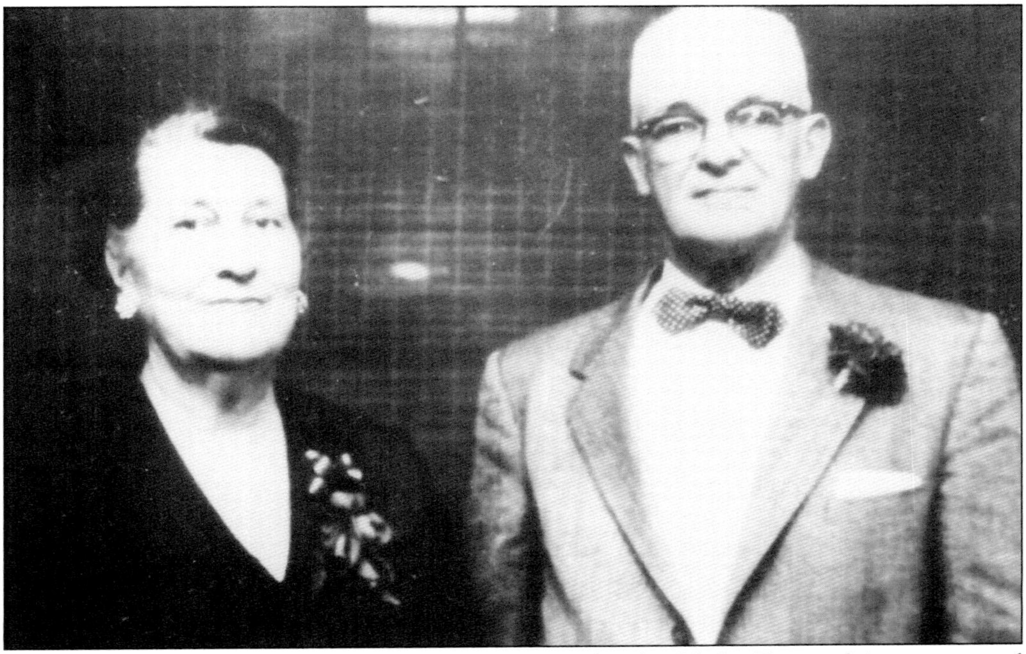

A 50th Wedding Anniversary. Asa Russell Mace and wife, Gladys Tracy of Aurora, owned and operated the Mace General Store on Route 9 until they retired. Asa, who graduated from the University of Maine with a degree in Civil Engineering, was the third generation to carry on the family business. He was representative to the state legislature in 1934, and was the first selectman in Aurora, a position he kept for forty-five years. Both were descendants of early families to Union River.

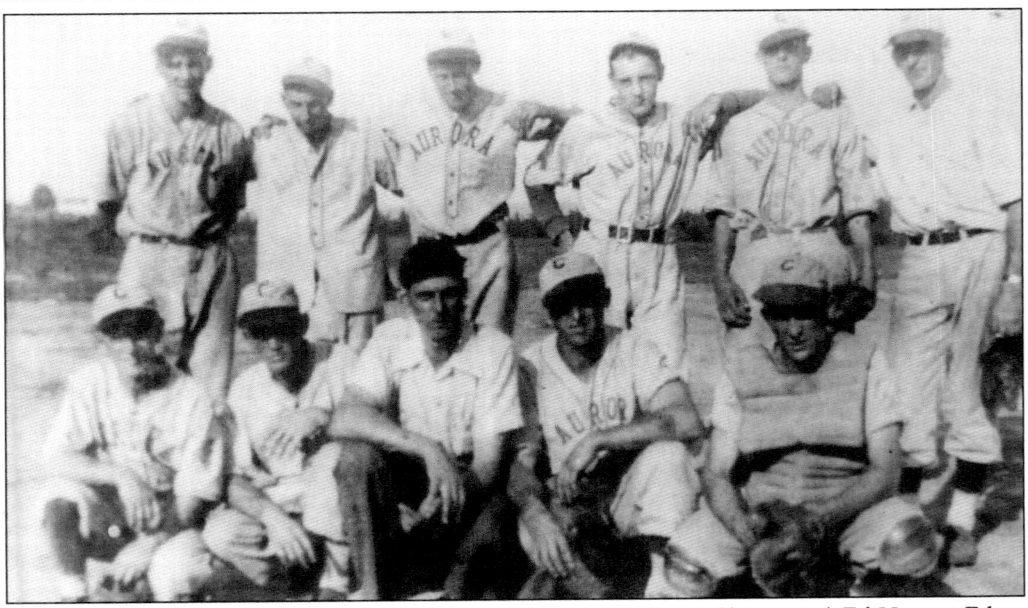

An Aurora Ball Team, *c.* 1930s. From left to right are as follows: (front row) Ed Honey, Edgar McInnich, Ronny Bradbury, Ethel Rowe, and Doug Mace; (back row) Robinson, Dick Ashe, unknown, Philmore Willey Jr., Asa "Bud" Mace, and Don Willey.

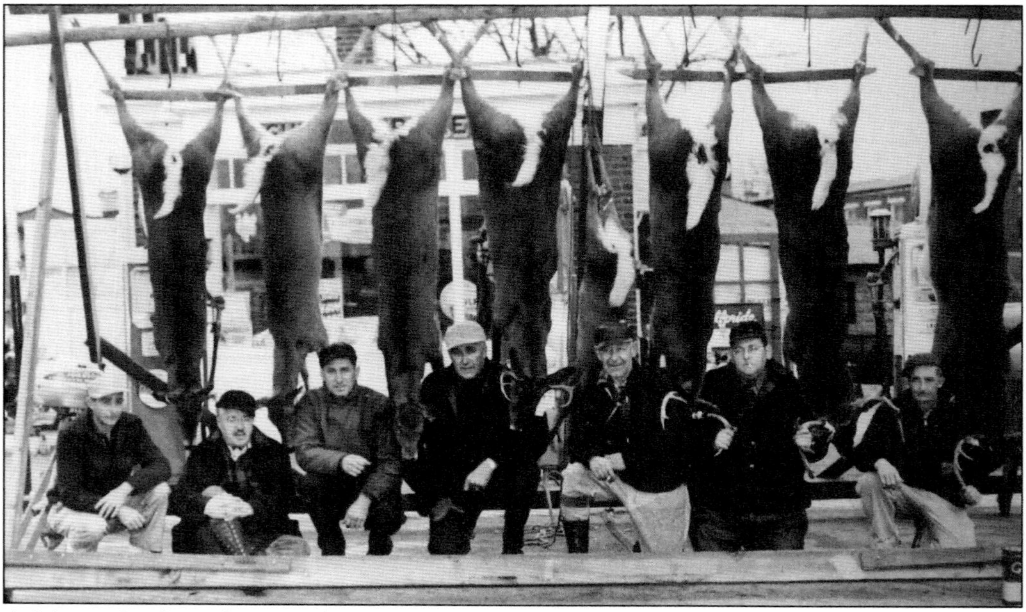

A Maine Guide Makes Good His Promise. A great number of upcountry woodsmen became certified Maine guides, and each fall they earned extra cash by taking New Jersey hunters on deer hunts. Here some of the boys, *c.* 1950, show how good Ed Honey's reputation was. Ed guided for many years at the Musson Camps in Great Pond.

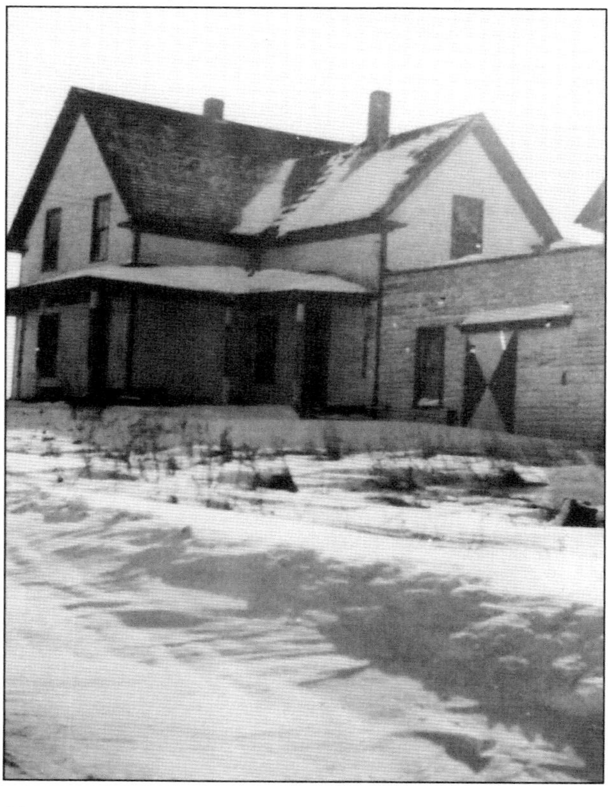

The Home of Ernest Richardson in Aurora. Built *c.* 1870, this house still stands, and is now owned by Mary (Mace) Simeon. The original Richardson came to Aurora from New Sweden, Maine. Jonathan Roberts married Polly Richardson and they moved to "the easternmost part of the state." In 1813 Jonathan Roberts was living at Edinburgh in Penobscot County but by 1832 a J. Roberts was living on Great Pond Road in Hancock County. He was a public-spirited man and was appointed school agent at Aurora soon after his move to that town. His son John was born in 1833 at Aurora and died at age twenty-five while trying to break up a log jam on the Roll Dam in 1859. His body was pulled ashore by Roswell Silsby.

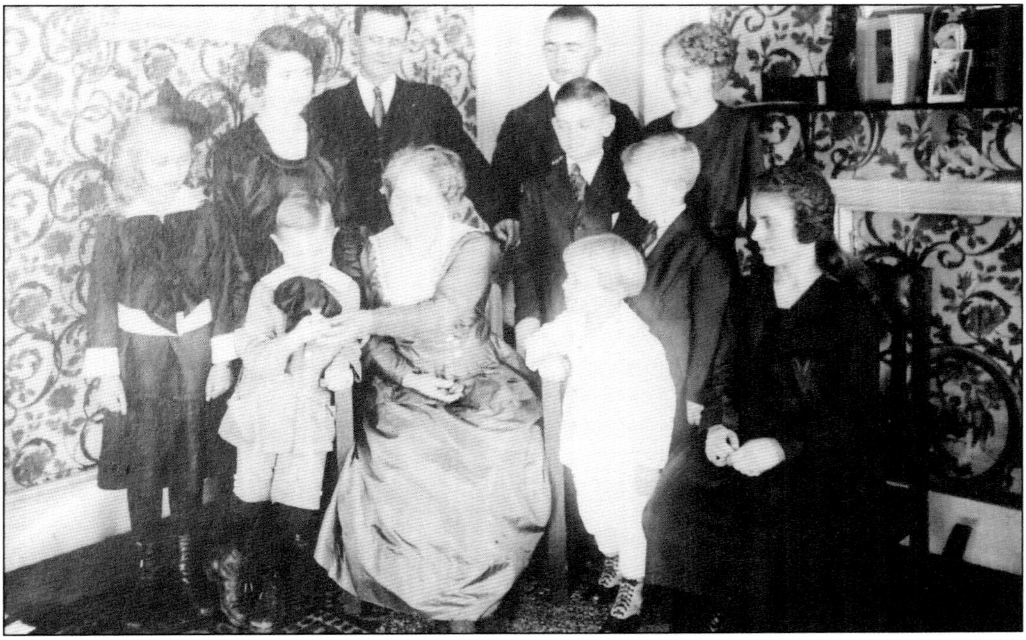

A Bangor Christmas, *c.* 1918. Ann (Murphy) Honey, with husband Harry in the background, has the family portrait taken. From left to right are as follows: (front) Frank, George, and Mary; (back) Mildred, Marion, Earl, Edward, Harry, and Margaret.

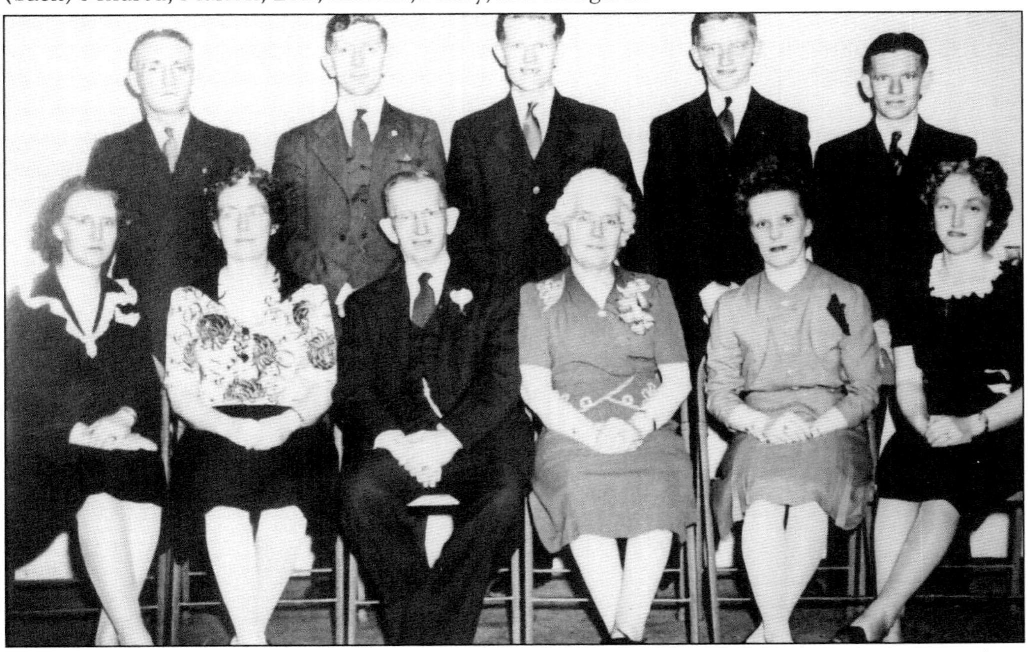

The Honey's, *c.* 1941. From left to right are as follows: (front row) Margaret, Marion, their father Harry, their mother Ann (Murphy), Mary, and Mildred Honey; (back row) Earl, George, Harry, Edward, and Frank Honey. Harry Honey was born in Lowell, Maine, and worked on the Maine Central Railroad all his life. Edward, at ninety years, and his sister Margaret are the only ones alive today. Ed will be ninety-one on his next birthday and still drives his own car.

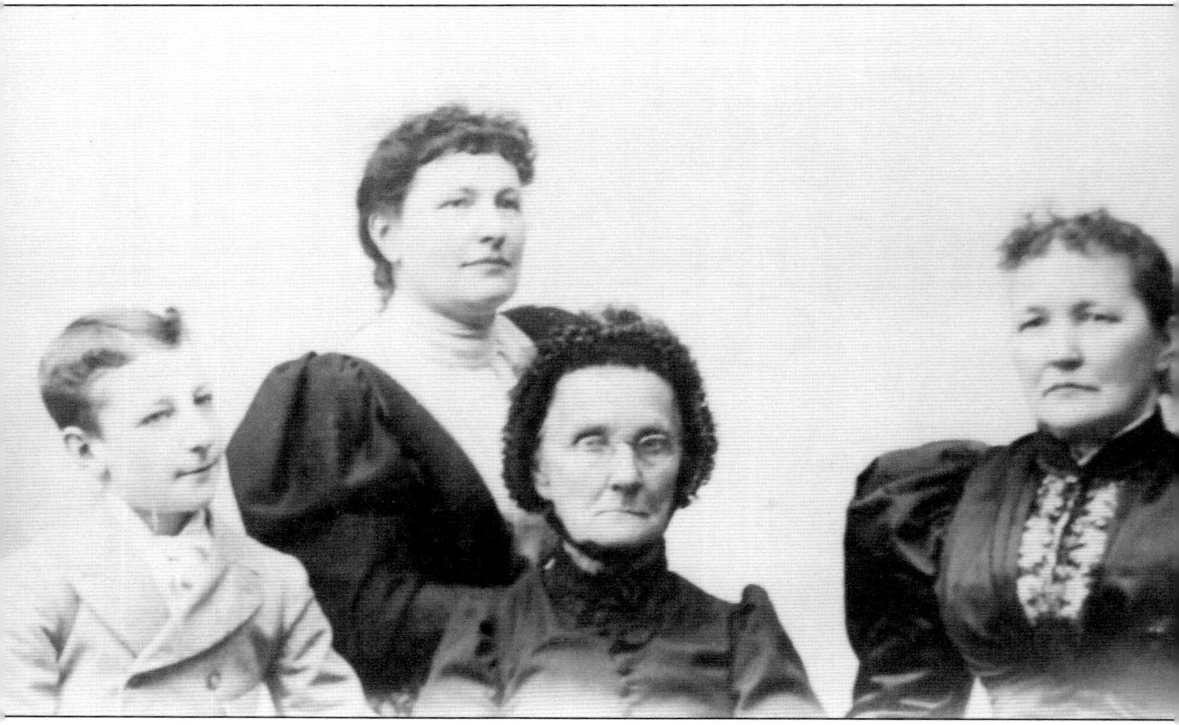

Descendants of the Eastbrook and Dedham Families. Taken *c.* 1891, this photograph shows four generations of Wilburs, three generations of Johnsons, and two generations of Jellisons. From left to right are as follows: Fred Conrad Jellison, born on September 29, 1881, to Fred Jellison and Clara (Johnson); his mother Clara, standing behind him, born on August 29, 1857, to Francis Johnson and Hannah (Wilbur); and Hannah, born in 1838 to Lyman Wilbur and Emily (Hopkins). Emily, born in 1812, is seated front center. Francis Johnson died in 1864 at age twenty-eight, and his widow Hannah remarried to Elliot Jordan in 1872.

Four

East of Union River:
Eastbrook

First called Plantation #15, Eastbrook was incorporated as a town in 1837 and was named for its location, on the East Brook branches of the Union River. The first settlers, who arrived in 1800, were Robert Dyer, Samuel Bragdon, and John E. Smith; the first settler to build a frame house was Joseph Parsons.

Settlers to this area were predominately from Massachusetts and came through early Maine towns such as Portland, Cape Elizabeth, and Kittery. Some had purchased their lands via the land lotteries held by Massachusetts while others received acres for service during the American Revolution. Each family's story makes for interesting reading; they took their Lord's charge to "Be fruitful and multiply" seriously, and descendants of these early pioneers are still on the lands today.

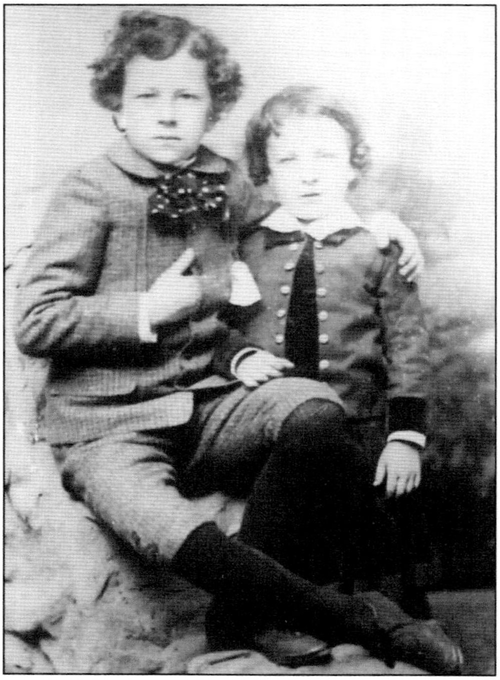

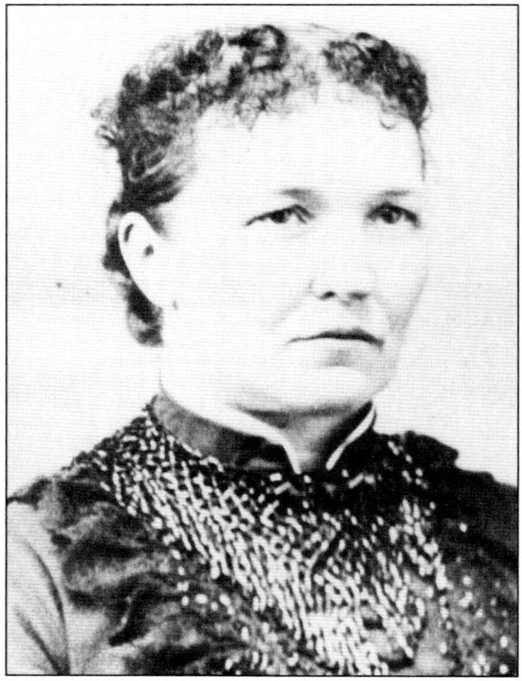

Boys of the Victorian Age and their grandmother. Fountain Rodick Jellison (left) and his brother, Fred Conrad Jellison, were born at Waltham but dressed quite well despite being raised in the country. They were the sons of Fred and Clara (Johnson) of Waltham and later Bar Harbor. Hannah Wilbur Johnson was the boys' grandmother and was married to Francis Melvin Johnson (below).

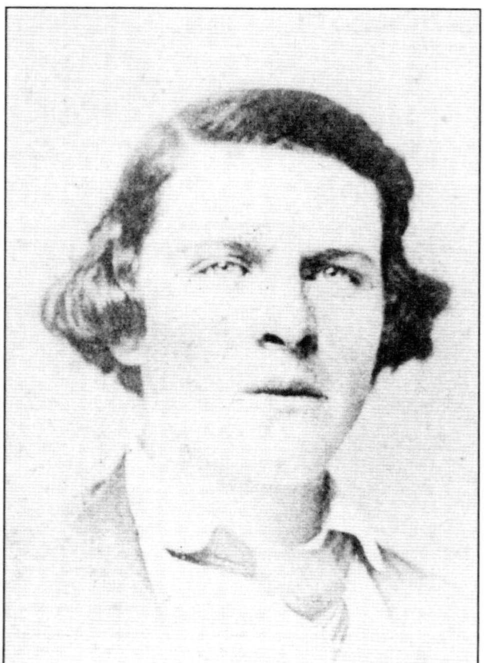

Waltham-Dedham Descendants. Francis Melvin Johnson and Hannah Brown Wilbur were married at Dedham in 1856 and had Clara and Lyman before Francis died suddenly in 1863. Hannah went to work at The American House in Ellsworth. The two children were brought up by their grandparents, Lyman and Betsy (Ford) Wilbur in Eastbrook.

Eastbrook, *c.* 1880. Orwell and Eliza (Winchester) Googins pose with their daughter Minnie, who seems to distrust the whole event.

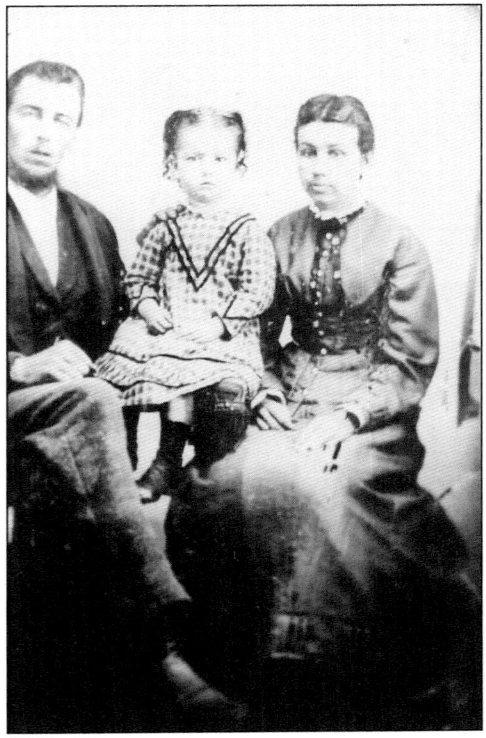

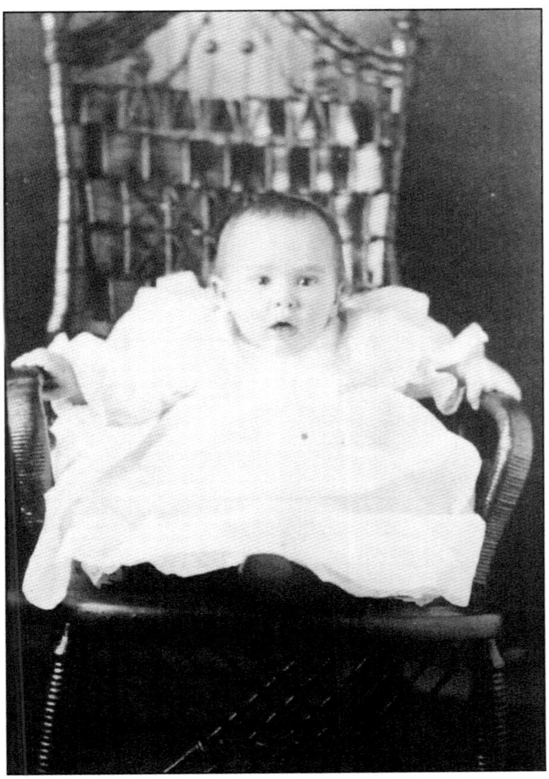

Big Chair, Little Tot, *c.* 1888. Eva Springer of east Franklin went on to become a graduate of the Maine Central Institute in Pittsfield in 1906.

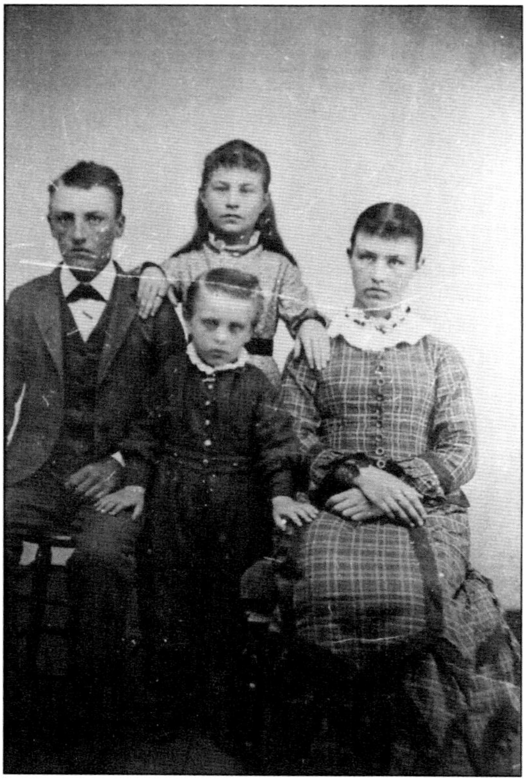

A Tintype Portrait, *c*. 1870. This unidentified group poses solemnly for a family picture.

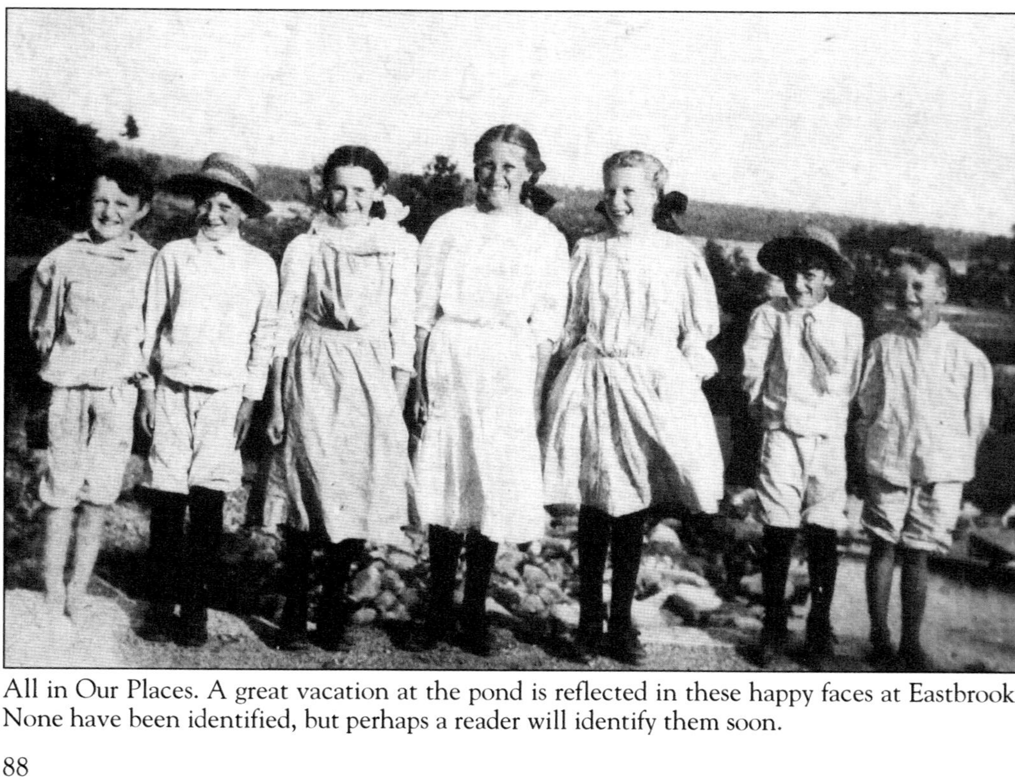

All in Our Places. A great vacation at the pond is reflected in these happy faces at Eastbrook. None have been identified, but perhaps a reader will identify them soon.

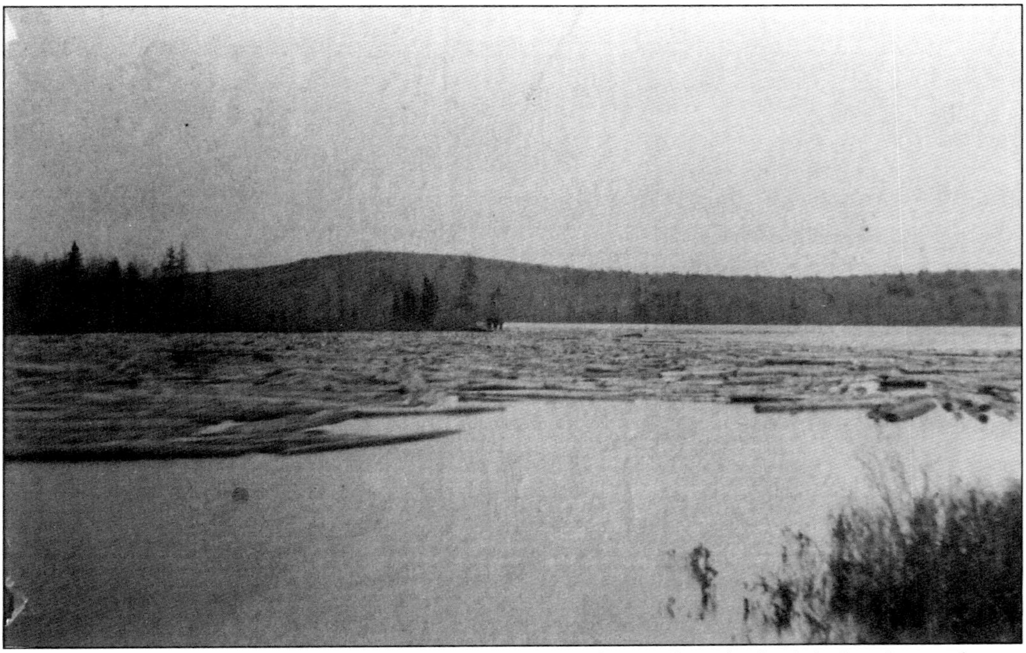

Logs on the East Brook. Logs were left in the East Brook to soften the bark before being driven down the Middle Branch of the Union River on the way to mills in Ellsworth Falls.

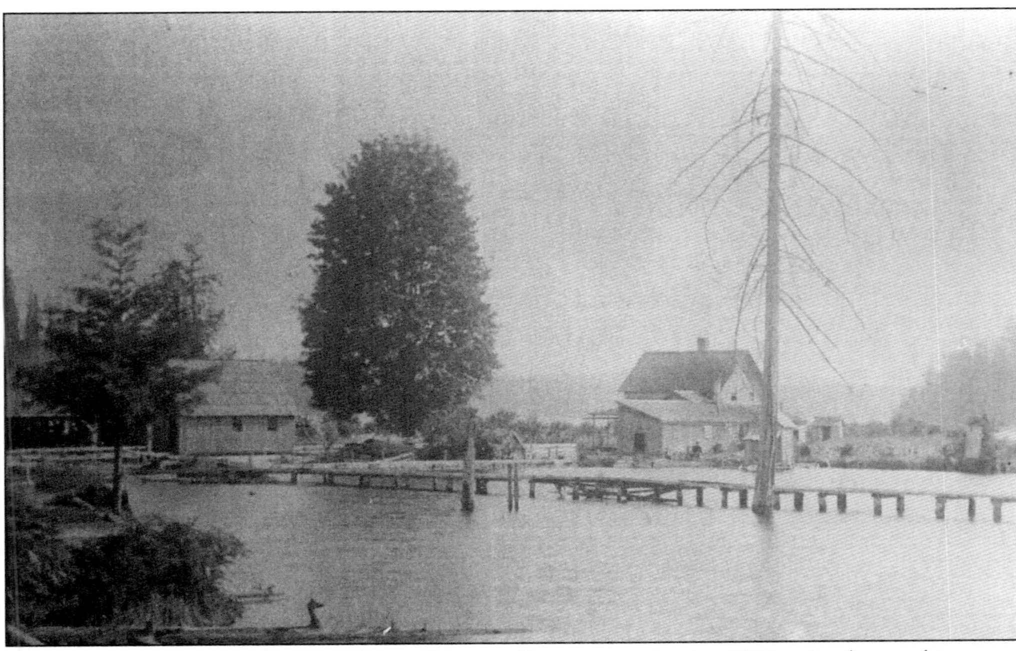

Scammon's Mill at Eastbrook. This mill was still operating in the 1900s. As the working men were too busy to take pictures with the new-fangled contraption, the camera, these scenes were prizes in any town's collection.

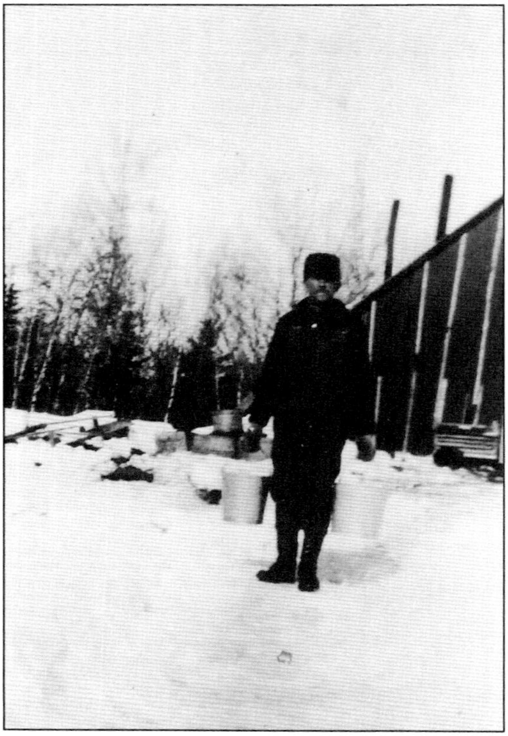

Unknown at Eastbrook. Shown is a cookee, a very necessary component of a woods camp. He carried water, kept the wood box filled, and was one of the original "go-fers."

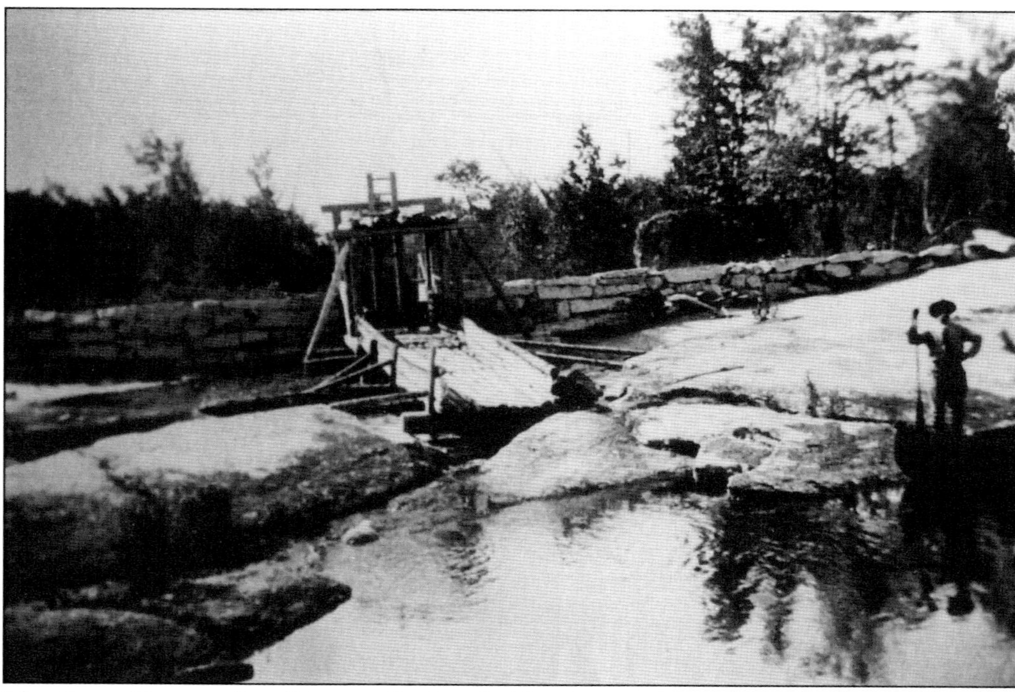

The Stone Dam on Bog River at Eastbrook. This logger, standing on the large ledges that border the river, is ready to put in and free any logs that have become lodged at this narrow place in the stream.

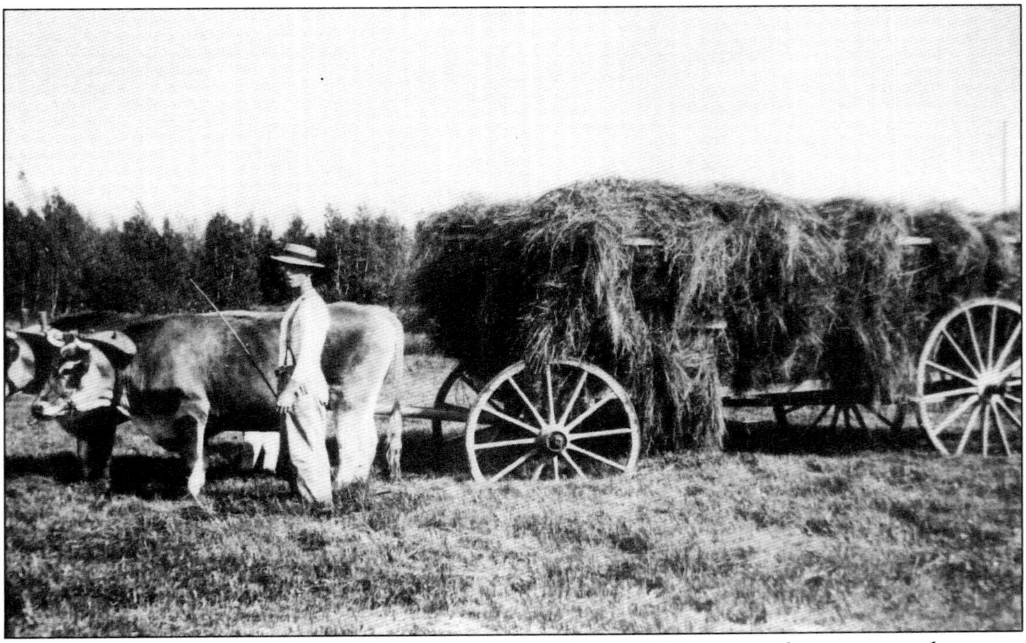

An Early Harvest in Eastbrook. Howard "Doc" Wilbur with his team of oxen pause for a rest before hauling this rick of marsh hay to the barn.

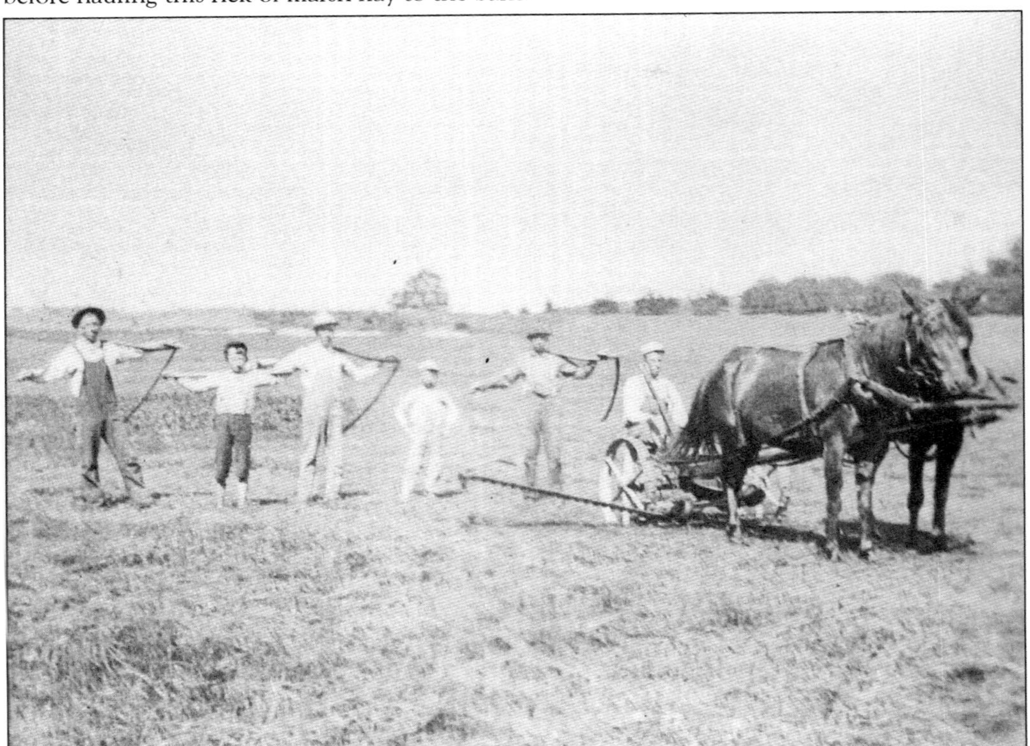

Haying in Eastbrook, c. 1899. Leona Wilbur's team and mowing machine were a big advance, but with a never ending crop of rocks, hand scythes were still needed.

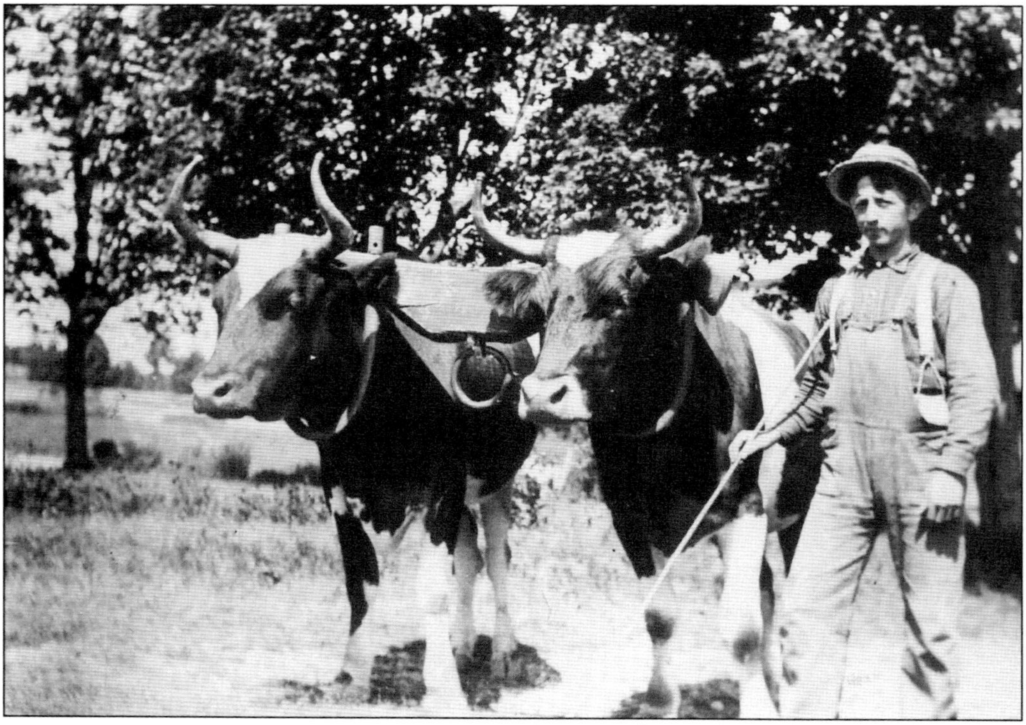

Jasper Wilbur and a Yoke of Oxen in Eastbrook.

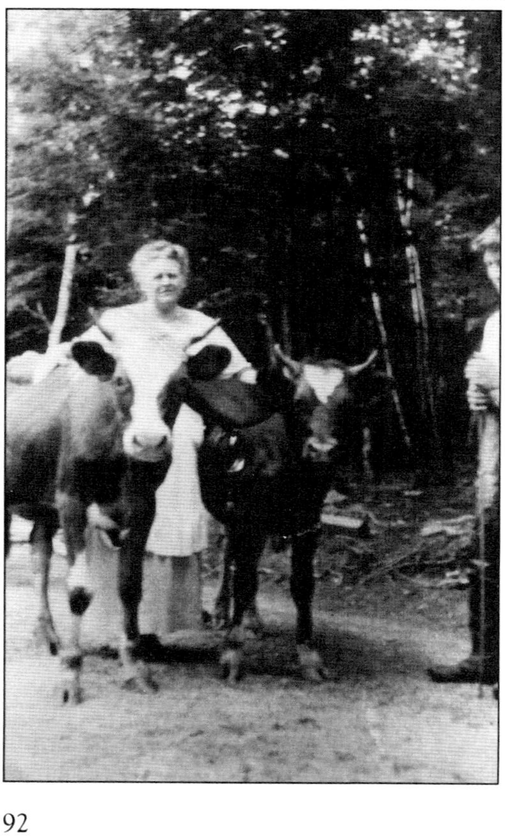

Gentle Beasts of Burden. Great care was taken of the family team of oxen for they were, literally, worth their weight in gold. Mrs. Susan Thayer is shown here petting Walter Googins' oxen at the Thayer camp on Webbs Pond. Walter is on the far right with his guiding wand.

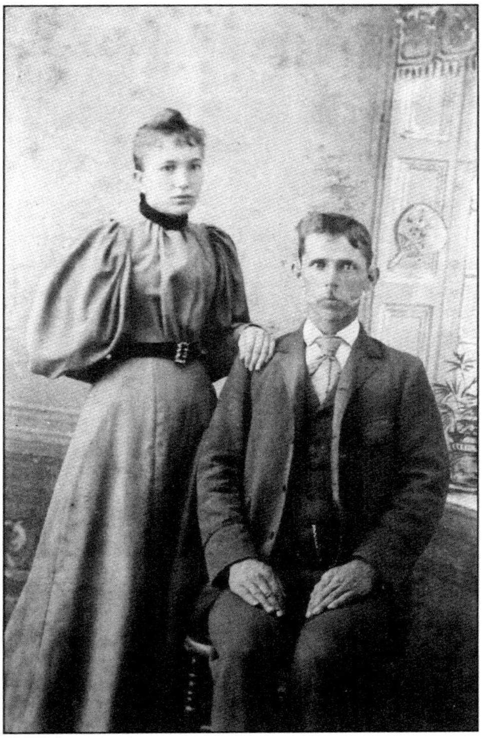

An Eastbrook Couple, *c*. 1880s. Adelbert Merchant and his new bride, Jennie French, are shown here on what may be their honeymoon. This image is from a tinted tintype.

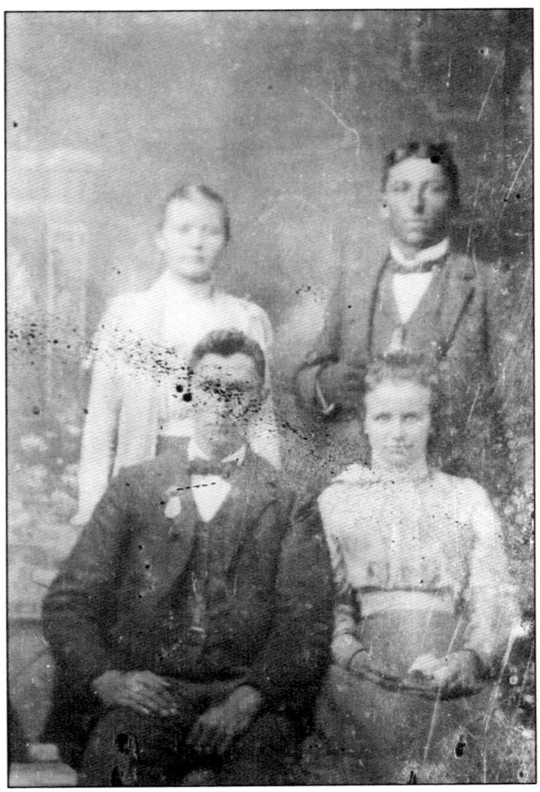

Tintypes Age Quickly. In this early 1890s tintype, which has been scratched and worn over the years, the faces of Mahlon and Maud (Wilbur) Wilbur, in front, and Ellery and Marcia (Dinsmore) Wilbur still shine brightly.

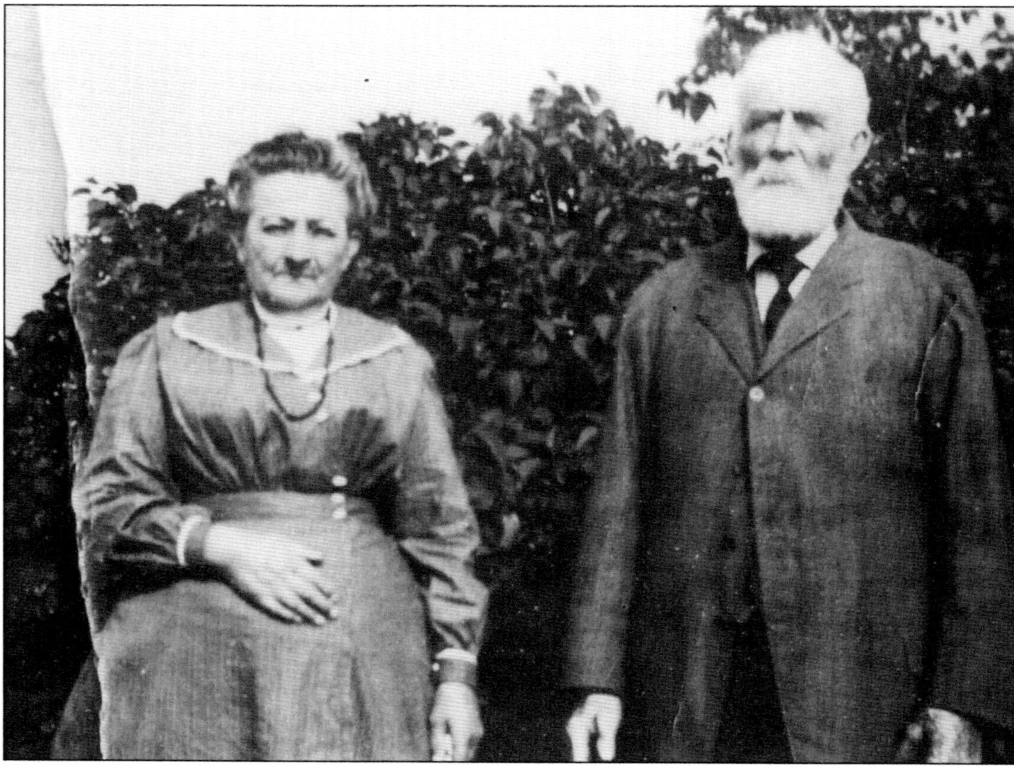

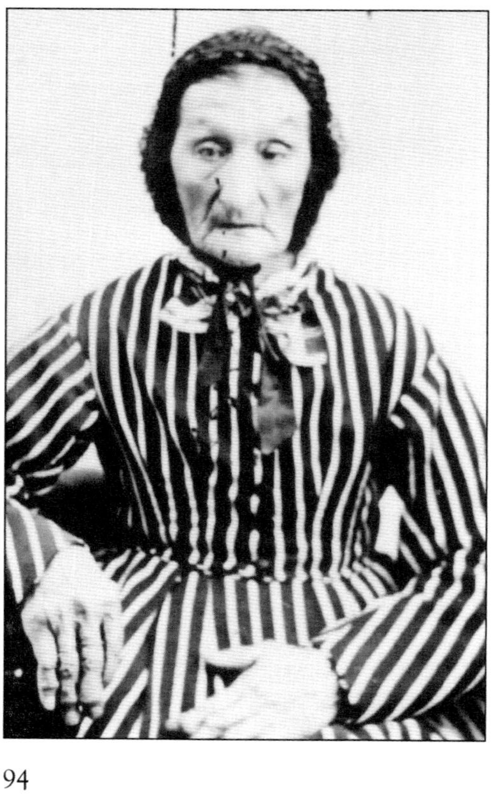

A Photograph Was Serious Business. Taken *c.* 1900, this photograph shows George and Mary Wilbur, who lived in one of the oldest homes in Eastbrook, the John Ford Wilbur house.

The Matriarch of Eastbrook. Sarah (Snyder) Hooper was the daughter of Frederick Snyder, who came straight from Germany to America. She died in 1892 at the age of ninety.

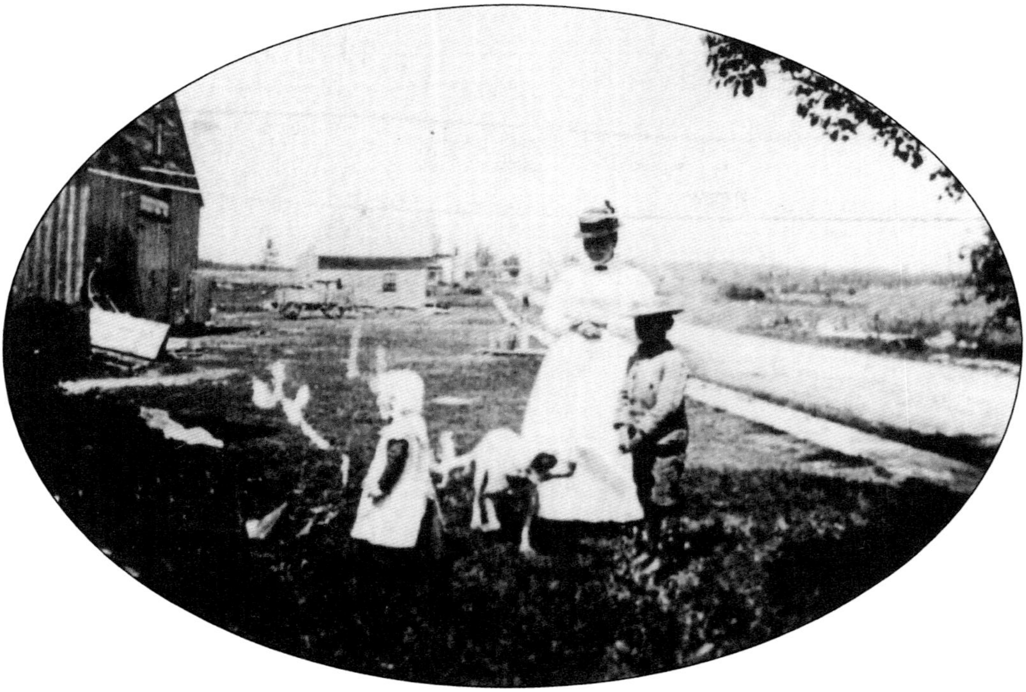

A Pastoral Scene on Waltham Ridge. Cecelia (Hastings) Giles, the granddaughter of first settler Lebbeus Kingman, is shown here with two children at the turn of the century.

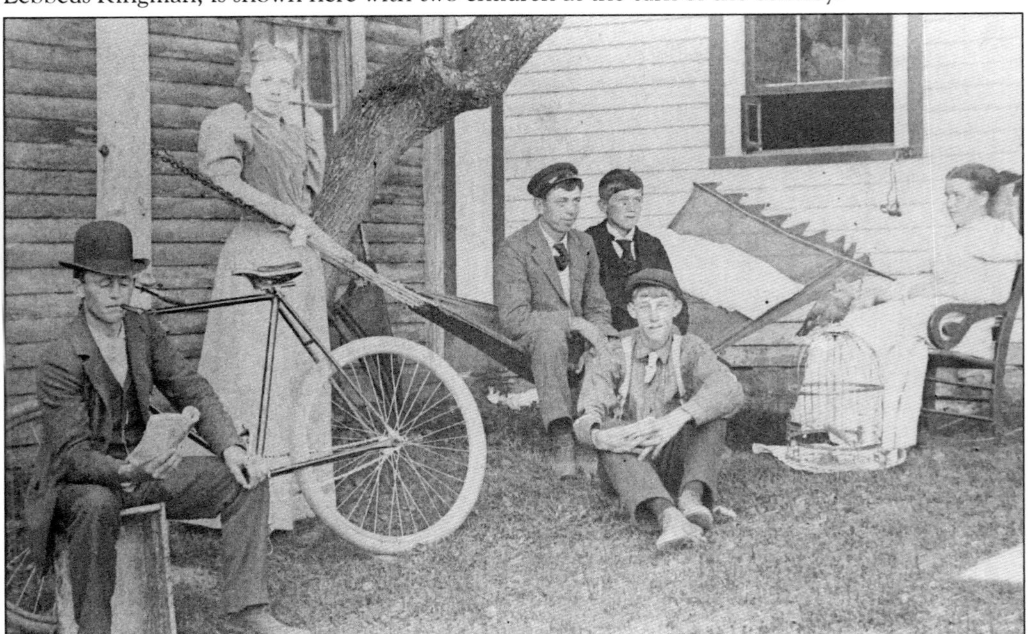

A Spoof at Eastbrook. An inventive photographer posed this family one summer's day in the 1880s. David Wilbur (left) smokes a cigar and reads, while an unidentified lass carries oars to a canoe; Harold Kingman and a friend swing on a hammock; Amon Googins sits on the grass; and Helen Lowrie pets her parrot.

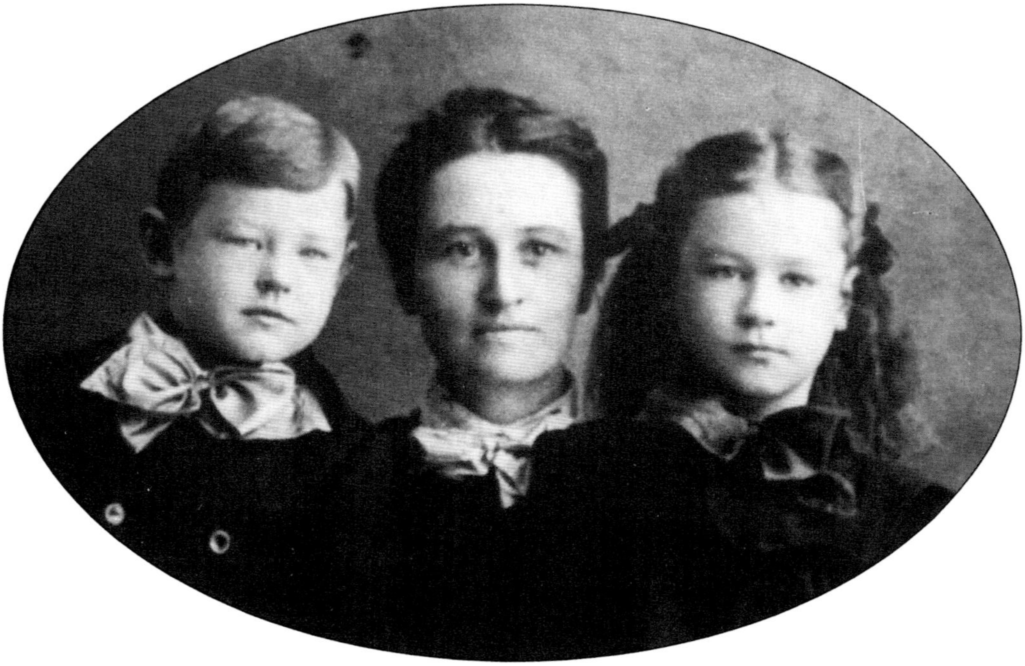

Mother, Dear Mother. The love Marian Letitia (Hooper) Fullerton felt for her children, Curtis Hooper Fullerton and Frances Emmeline Fullerton, can be seen in this oval.

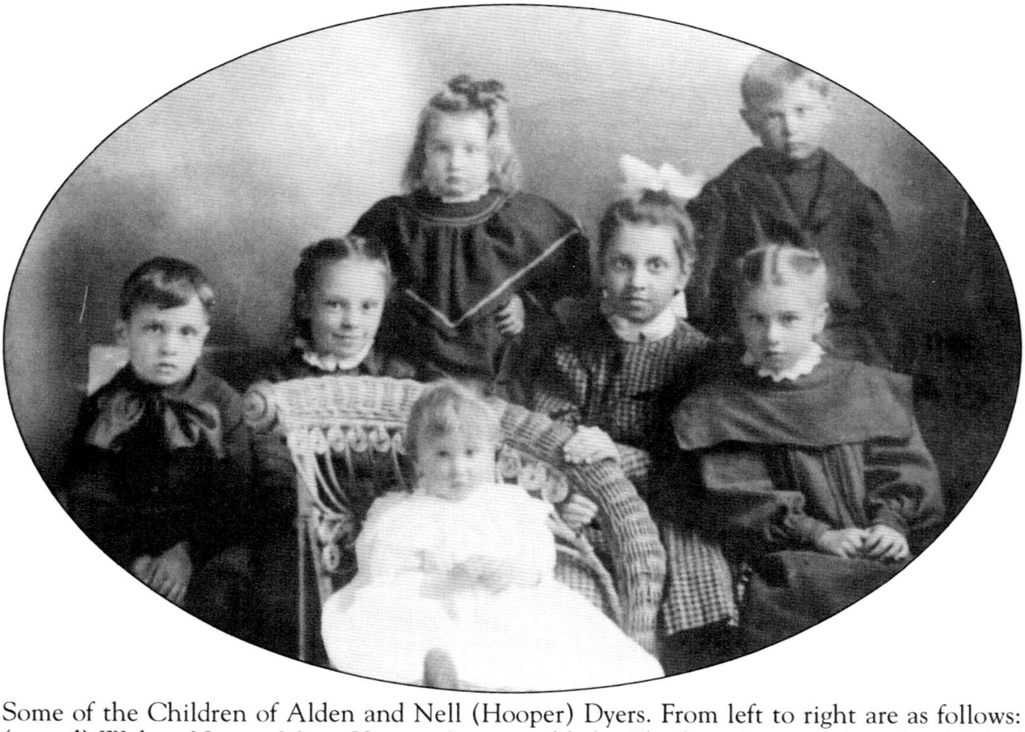

Some of the Children of Alden and Nell (Hooper) Dyers. From left to right are as follows: (seated) Walter, Nancy, Mary, Harriet Anne, and baby Charlotte Lavinia; (standing) Ethel and Mitchell.

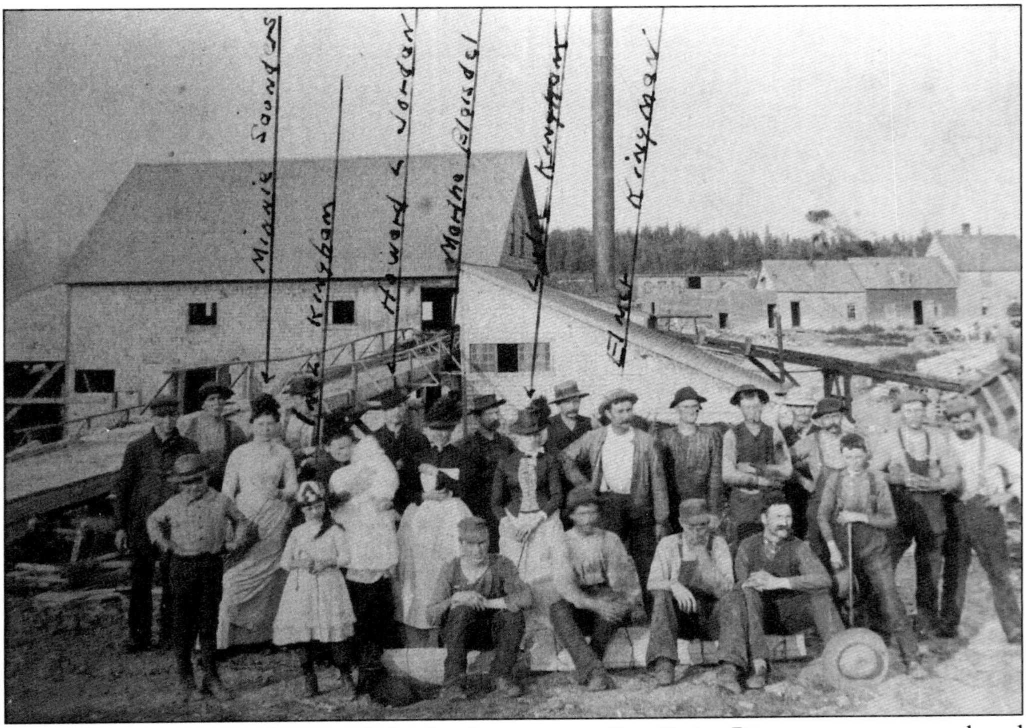

Kilkenny Stream in Franklin, *c.* 1880. Men from surrounding Union River towns were employed at this lumber mill, which later become a tannery. Some of the people shown here have been identified: Minni Saunders is third from the left, Inez Kingham stands next to her, and Howard L. Jordan, Martha Blaisdal, Lura Kingman, and Elmer Kingman are pointed out.

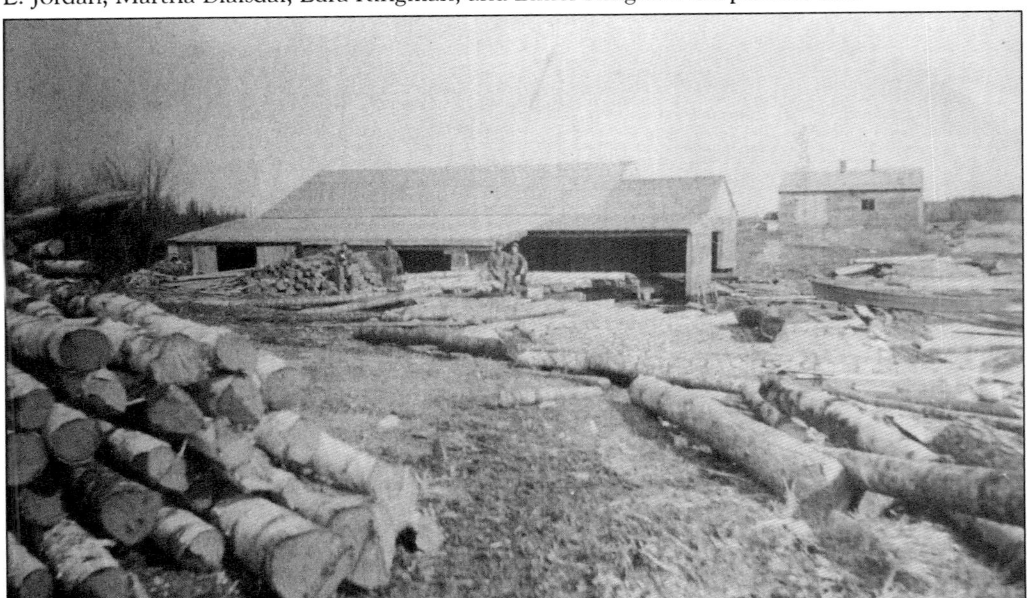

The Clark and Russell Mill of Webb Brook. The date of this photograph remains unknown. This appears to be a hardwood mill; note the birch pile on the left.

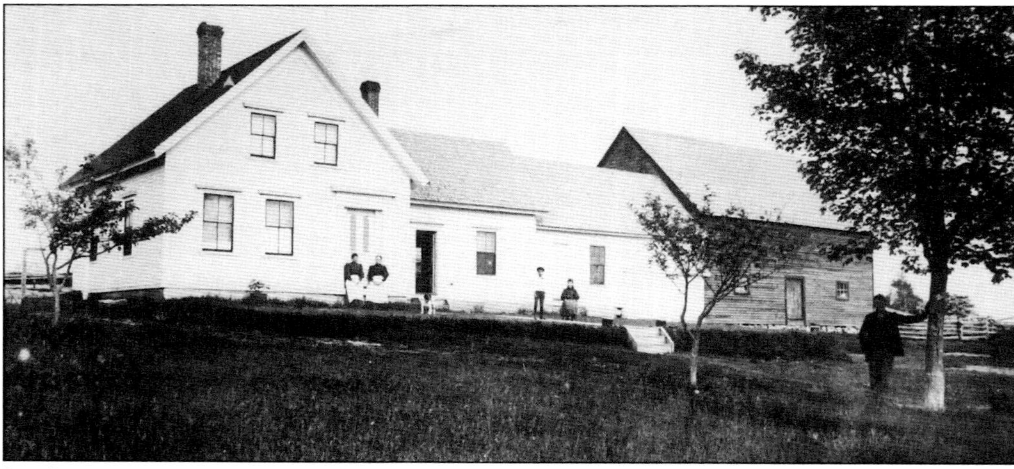

Ira Scammon's House in Eastbrook. Severe thunder and lightning storms were legendary along the Union River. Many a story is told of a "ball of blue" coming into the kitchen and rolling around the iron cook stove before exiting through a hole it would burn in the wall. Ira Scammon's house in Eastbrook wasn't as lucky, for it burned to the ground in 1908 after it was struck.

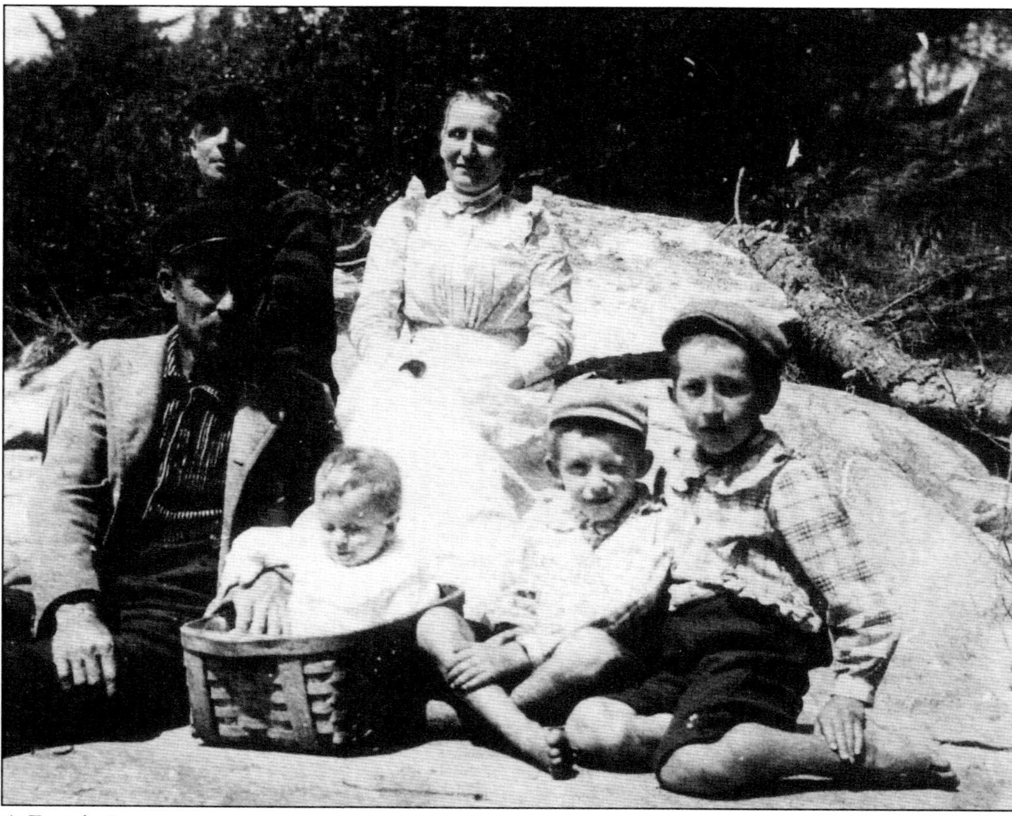

A Family Picnic at Eastbrook. Albert Manley Giles and his wife Ella (Whittier) are shown here with their children. Manley, who was born in 1906, is in the picnic basket; the two young boys are Wesley and Harold.

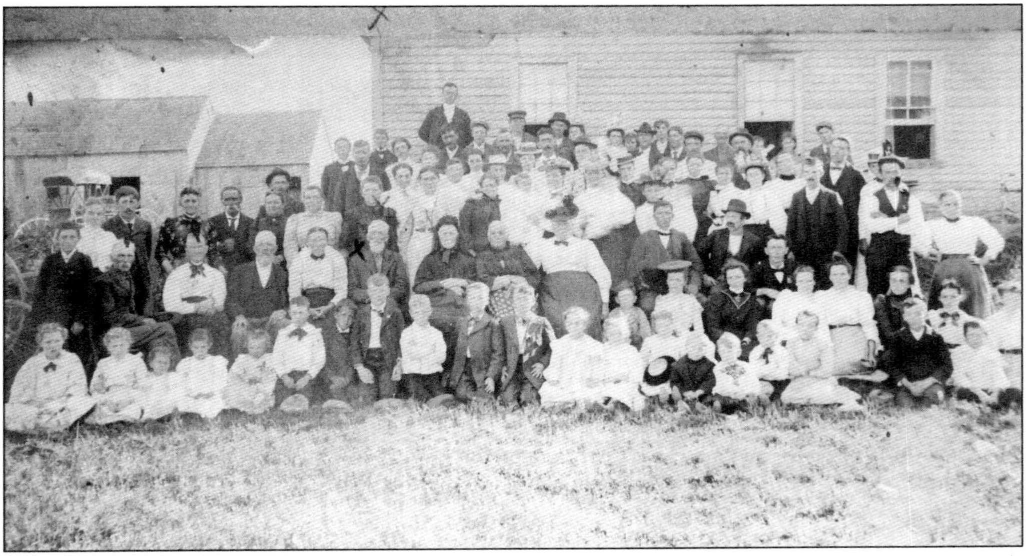

Descendants of Ebenezer and Betsey (Ford) Wilbur. This gathering occurred at the Joseph Wilbur Home in Eastbrook, *c.* 1903. The "x" marks Jasper Wilbur's photograph.

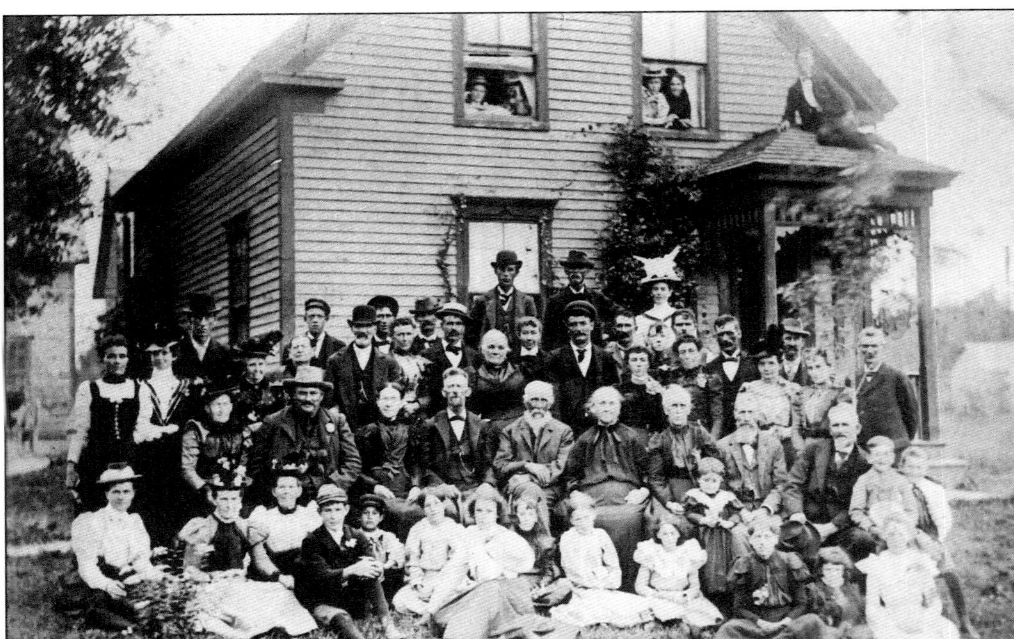

A Smith Reunion at Eastbrook. These people are descendants of James Smith of Biddeford, who came to the Union River by 1764. The Smiths are likened to being as many as "the grains of sand on an ocean beach."

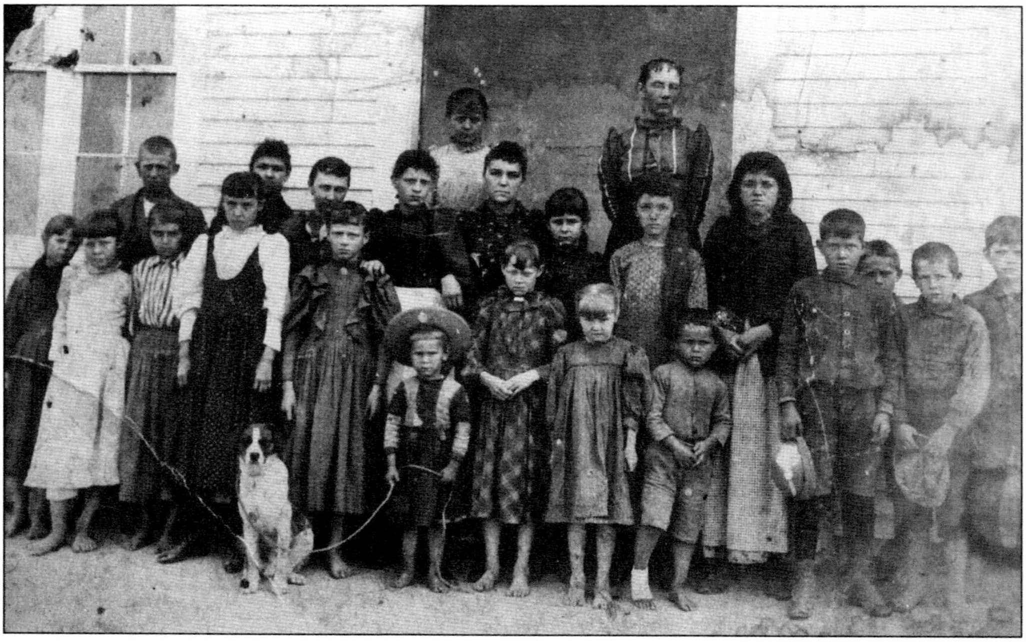

A Rare Old Photograph of Ridge School. This school stood in Eastbrook, *c*. 1894, and the teacher this year was Miss Effie Morrill. In the back with her is Marcia Dinsmore. The others, from left to right, are as follows: (front row) Blanche Bragdon, Grace Dinsmore, Delia Wilbur, Rosalie Crimmins, Marcia Hardison, Melvin Bragdon (with dog), Mary Hardison, Mattie Jellison, Leslie Wilbur, (with bandaged foot), Henry Lawrie, Fred DeMeyer, and Cleveland Bunker; (back row) Nahum "Kepps" Bragdon, Mabel Curtis, Lettie Dyer, Stella Butler, Sadie Wilbur, Lige Bragdon, Vin Lawrie, Lucy Bunker, and Lyman Wilbur.

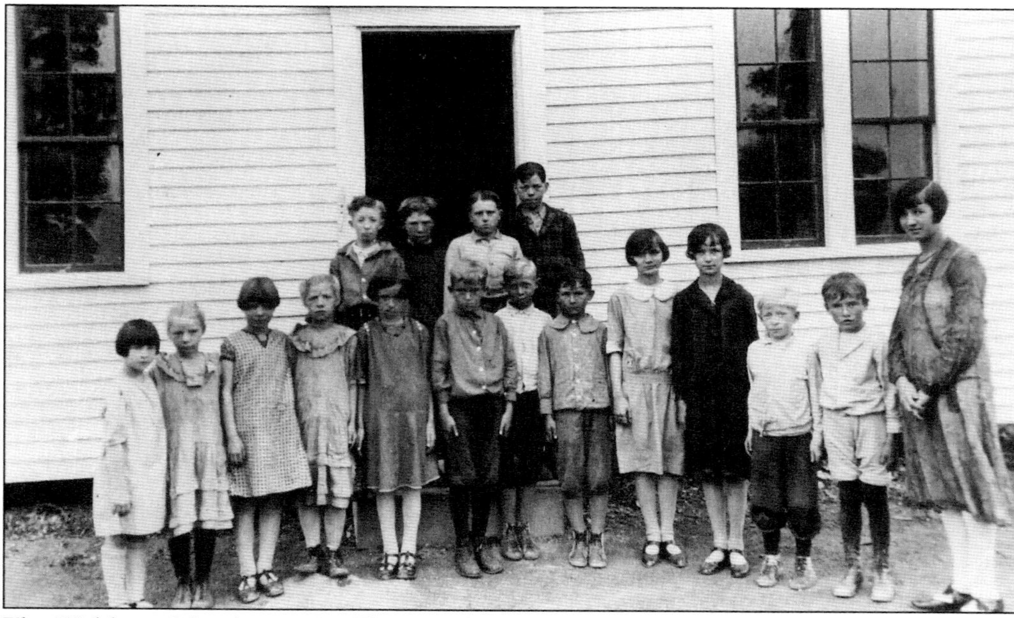

The Waltham School, *c*. 1924. This is a class of Martha Jordan, but none of the students are named. The school was torn down some years ago.

Five

West of Union River:
Dedham, Clifton, Eddington

Nathan Phillips of Massachusetts was the first settler who prospected around Phillips Lake in 1801. He built a log cabin near where the present Lucerne Inn is located. Once a part of Township #8, Dedham was incorporated in 1837. It is known for its great beauty and has been dubbed the "little Switzerland of America." The original stage stop was called the "Half-Way House"; today it has become the Lucerne Inn. Other early settlers were the Burrills, Dodges, Davises, Fitts, Greggs, Haynes, Manns, Osgoods, and Johnsons. Dedham is home to the first permanent hatchery for the preservation of the Atlantic salmon in the United States, which celebrated its 100th birthday in 1989.

Clifton was first called Jarvis Gore, named after the original land grantee, Leonard Jarvis. The name was then changed to Hillsboro in honor of first settler John B. Hill, but Clifton was eventually settled on due to the distinctive cliffs overshadowing the town. Clifton has lost part of its border to Dedham and Eddington. Two first settlers were Benjamin and Israel Barnes, followed by Chicks, Penneys, Orcutts, Parkes, Crosbys, DeBecks, and Days.

Eddington was named for Colonel Jonathan Eddy, who was given 9,000 acres in Penobscot Valley in payment for his service in the War of the Revolution. He served as the first registrar of probate in Penobscot County, the first postmaster, and the first justice to the Court of Common Pleas. Other early settlers were Comins, Hapworths, Buzzells, Mahoneys, and Grants.

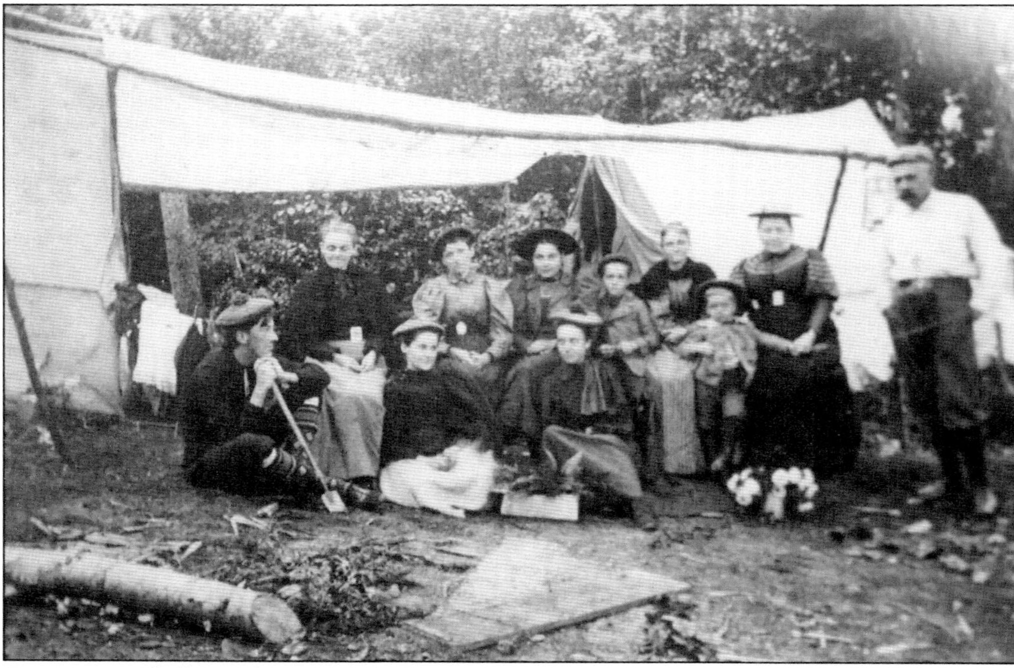

Camping at Phillips Lake 1891. This is where it all started, with tents and lean-tos eventually becoming cabins and small cottages ready to accommodate city-weary people. From left to right are Frank Rowe, Clara Wood, Charlotte Cates, Ida Wood Gouch, Bob Files, Charlotte Hanson, Carl Gouch, Annie Gartes, Ralph Gouch, Sarah Files, and Mullen Cates. The Files built their own cottage in 1904.

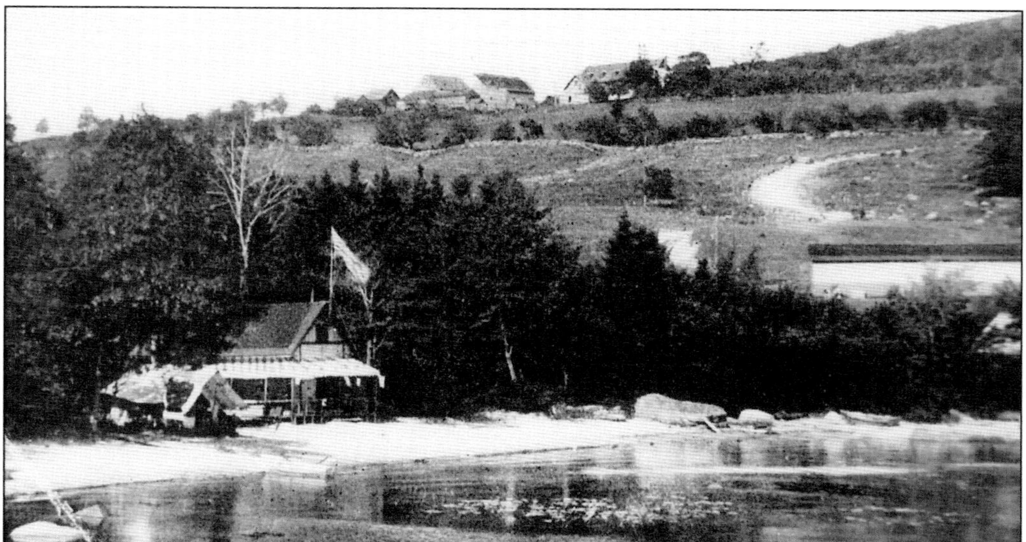

Early Camping on Phillips Lake, c. 1890. Looming on the horizon is the well-known Lake House, often called the Half-Way House, and now known as the Lucerne-in-Maine. The large set of outbuildings housed horses and feed for them, as this was a regular stop on the stagecoach line. Both mail and passengers were delivered to this hotel half way between Ellsworth and Bangor.

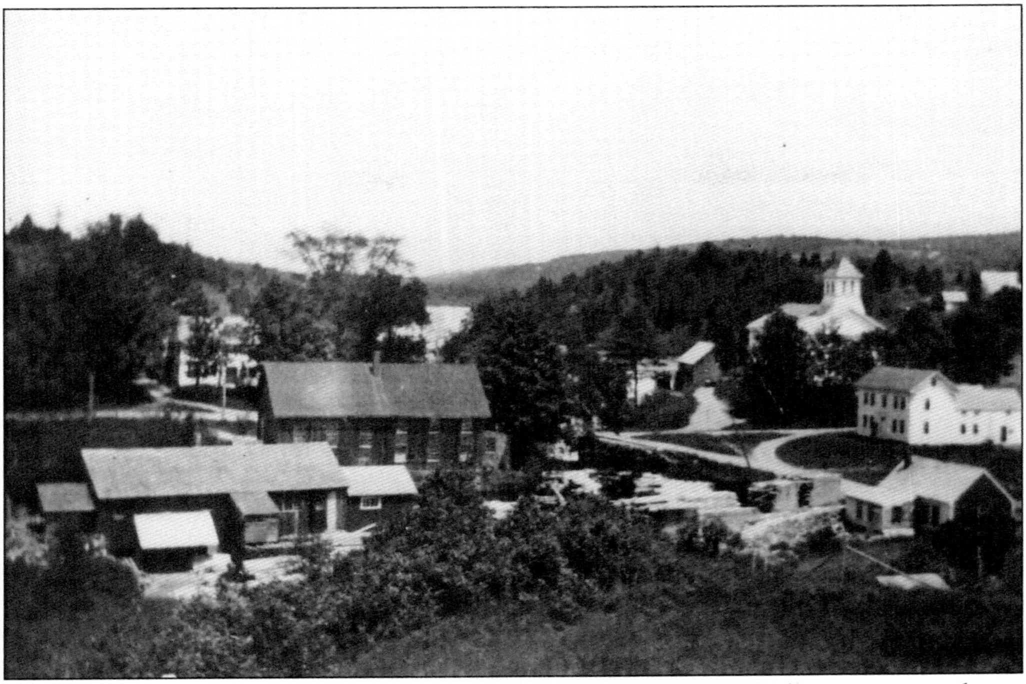

Dedham Village, *c*. 1900. All the components of an early New England village square are shown here—the Congregational church on the hill, the smaller homes as well as those where the mill hands boarded, and the lumber mill which kept the townspeople employed.

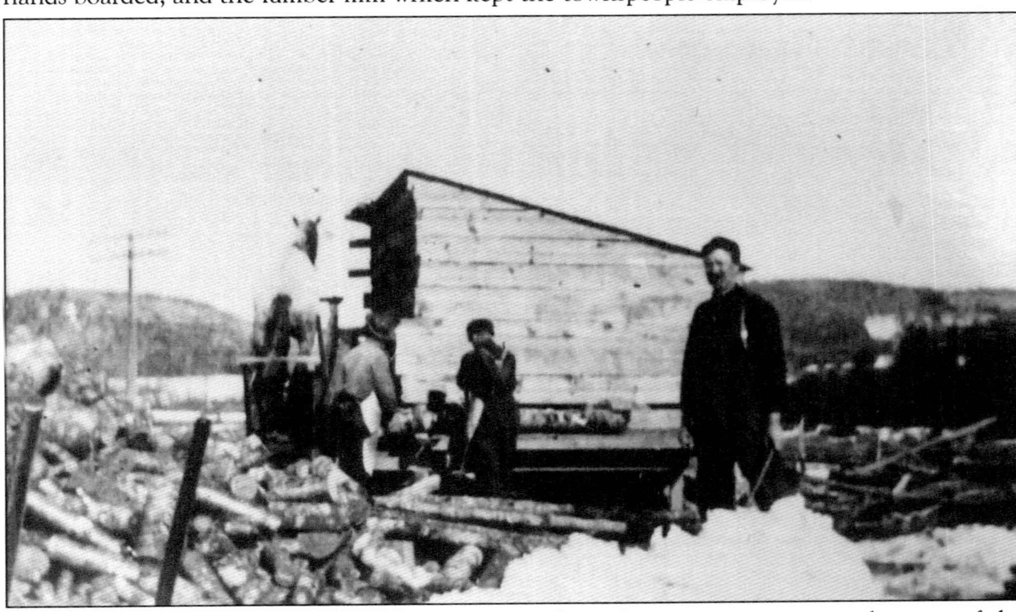

Cutting Pulp on Fitt's Pond. Wood operations such as this were necessary at the turn of the century, when everyone burned wood for warmth. Early snows and ice made the ground around the ponds firm enough to work on. The horse on the treadmill to the left provided an easy source of power for the saw. The men in the background wear heavy aprons for protection around the wood pile and saw. Fitt's Mountain is in the background.

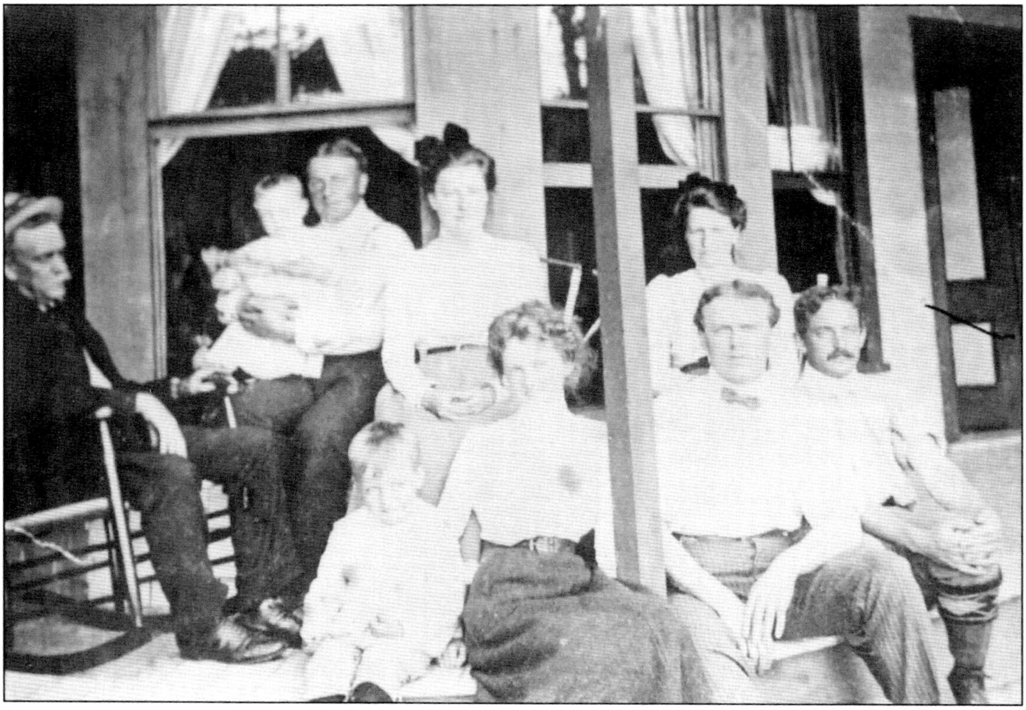

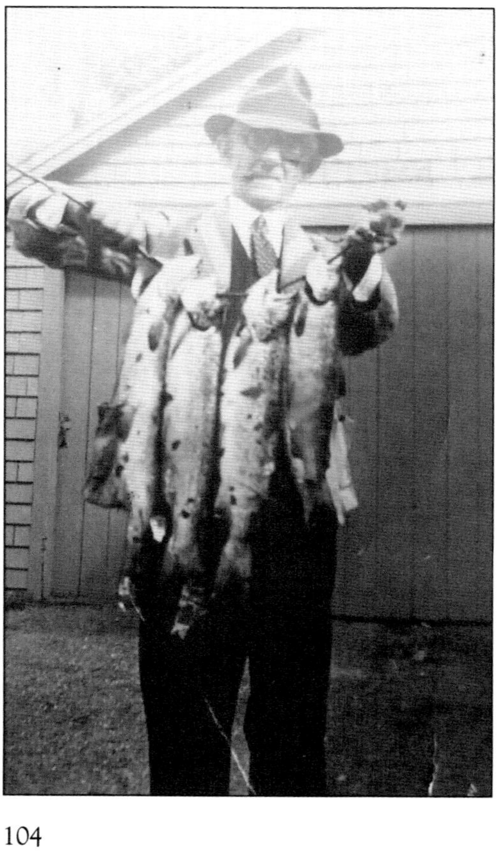

Parker Cottage, *c.* 1900. Spending an afternoon on the porch at Lucerne was a ritual in the hot days of summer at the turn of the century. From left to right are as follows: (front row) John P. Ramsay, Daisy Hodge, Harold Hodge, and Percival Hubbard; (back row) George W. Parker, Katherine Stewart, John L. Parker, Fannie Wing, and Marion P. Hubbard.

A Great Catch, *c.* 1902. Mark Crowley proudly shows off his four salmon caught at Green Lake.

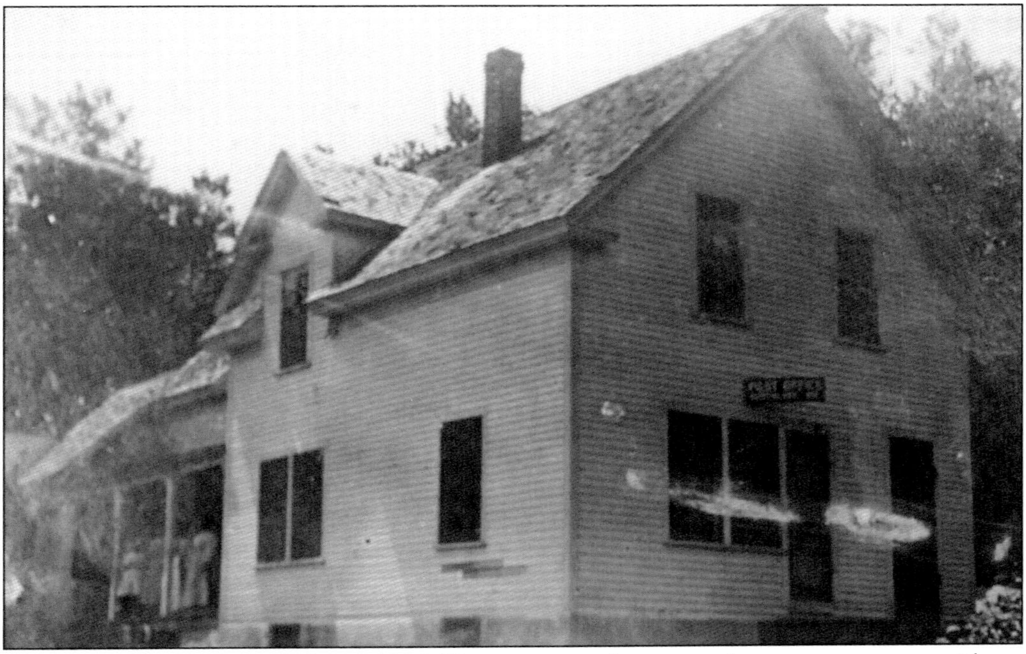

The Post Office at Green Lake, *c.* 1920. This was once the scene of many permanent residents as well as those who summered here for their health.

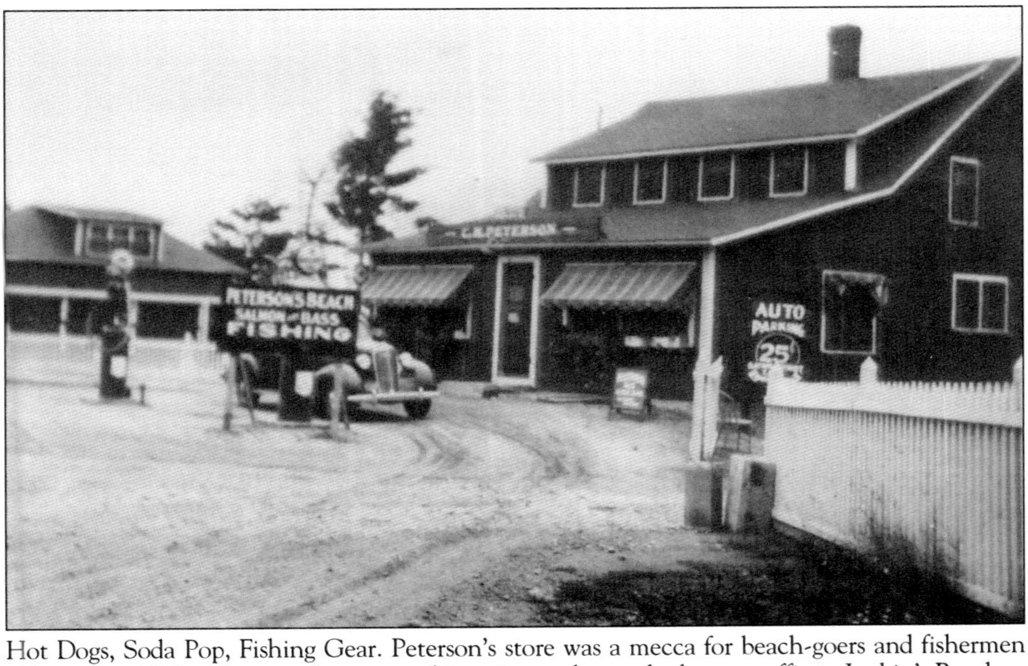

Hot Dogs, Soda Pop, Fishing Gear. Peterson's store was a mecca for beach-goers and fishermen alike in the 1930s. Charging for auto parking gives a clue to the heavy traffic to Jenkin's Beach.

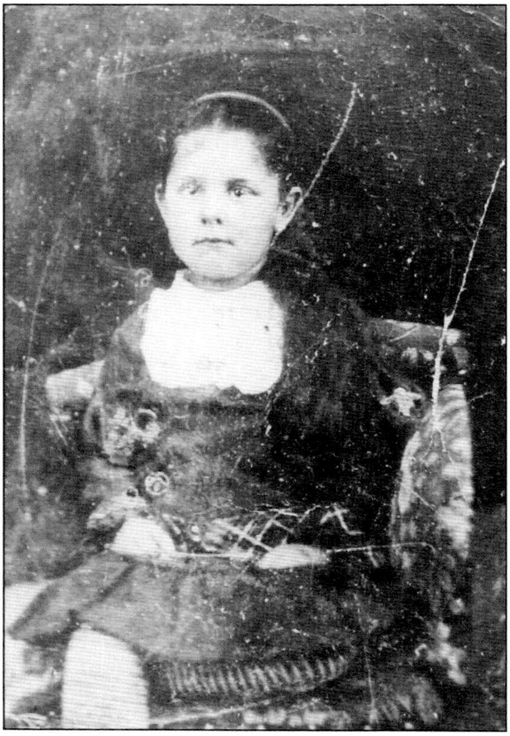

Ethel Maud Spencer, *c.* 1870s. Born in Clifton to Marietta Clark and Rockwell Spencer, Ethel married Charles Paul Bennoch, a descendant of John Bennoch, who founded Edinburgh and Orono. Ethel and Charles had the first filling station in Dedham, where they brought up a large family. Another family business was Goose Pond Beans.

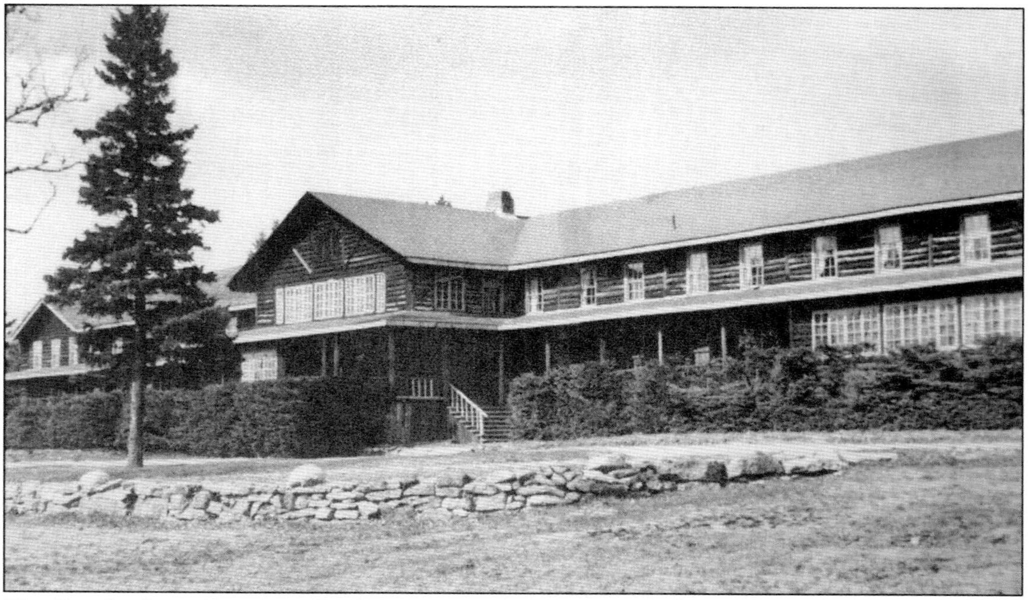

The Log Lodge at Lucerne. Built in 1927–28 at the cost of $200,000, it contained seventy-five rooms and was billed as "the largest log building in the country." Passengers from Boston, Philadelphia, and other points could leave the train at the Lucerne-in-Maine railroad station after an overnight trip. Special features included a summer camp for children and other guest houses for a "wonderland" adventure. It enjoyed a brief heyday before burning under mysterious circumstances in the 1960s.

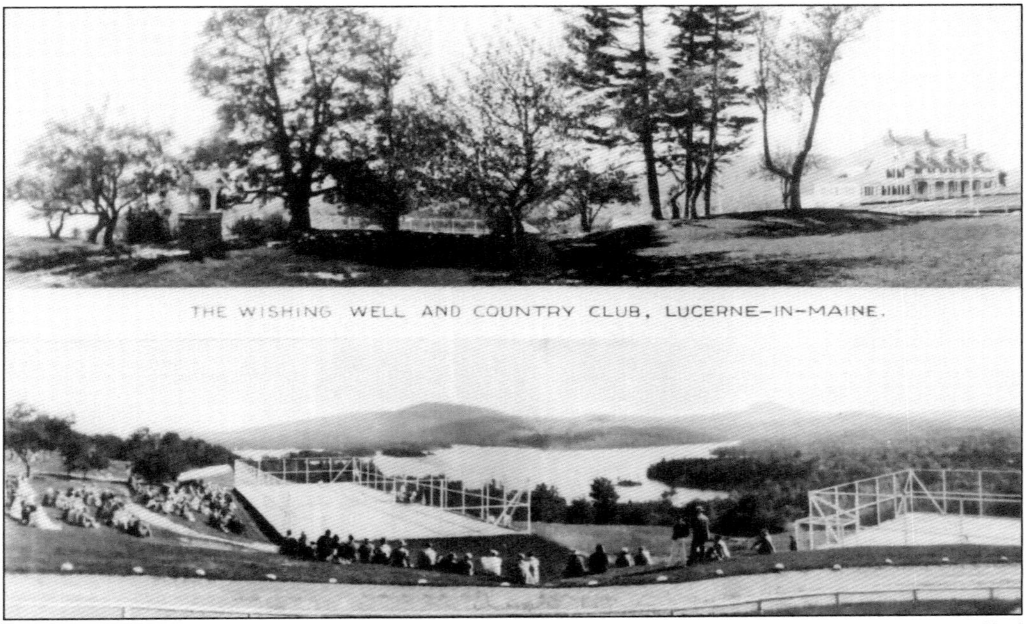

A Panoramic View of Phillips Lake in Dedham. This famous stage stop at Dedham, now called Lucerne, still stands as regally as when this photograph was taken.

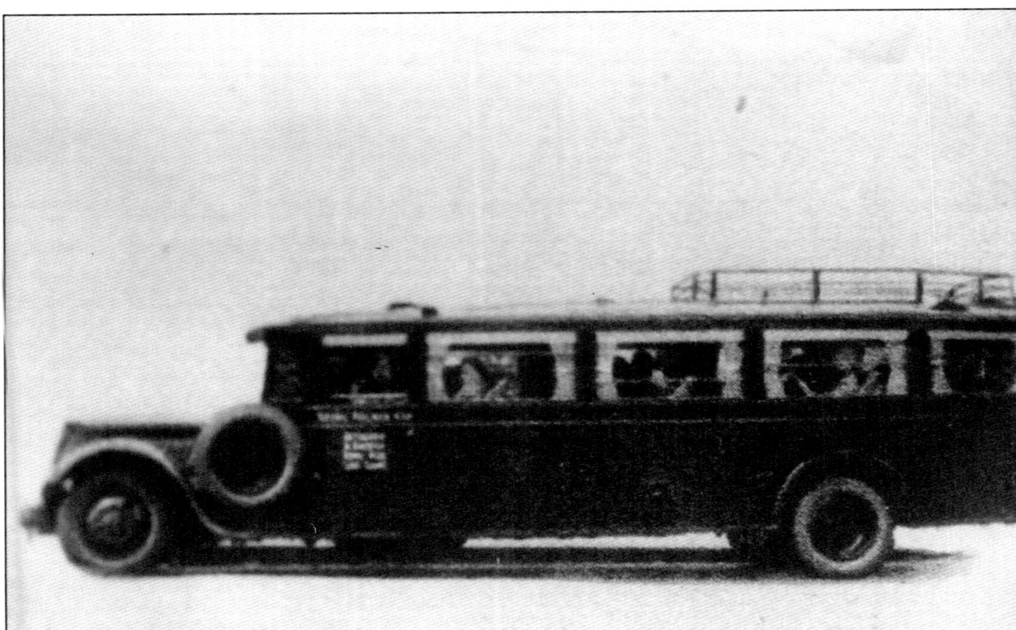

All Aboard for Maine, c. 1920s. As a vacation spot close to the big cities on the East Coast, hundreds came to take advantage of the healthy surroundings. Here the Royal Blue Line Tour Company arrives after an overnight ride from Boston.

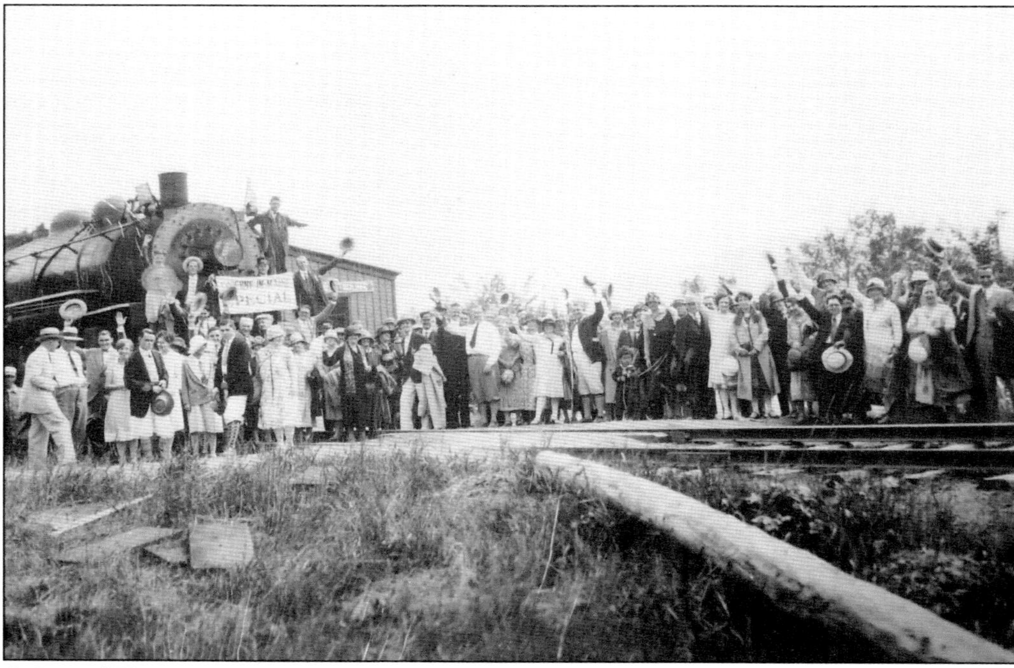

A Special Train at Lucerne, 1928 or 1930. The Maine Shore Line Railroad made a special stop at Lucerne-in-Maine. Built in the late 1880s, there were official stops in the town of Dedham.

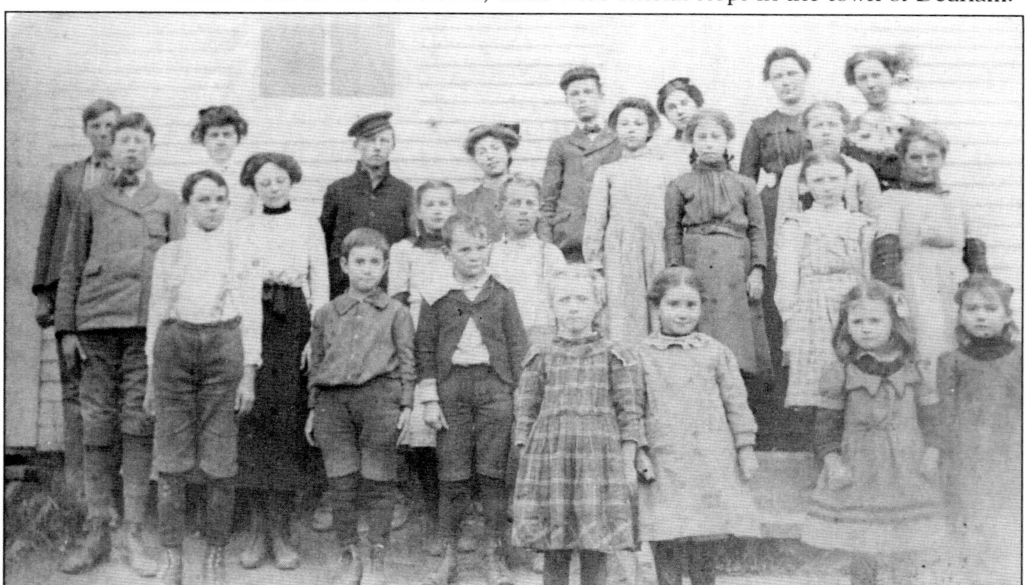

The Fall Term at Dedham, 1902. This school was in the village next to the home of Arthur and Mary Dresser. Louisa M. McIntyre, the teacher, is second from the left in the back row. The following children are identified, but not in order: Walter Fogg, Clifford Burrill, Ethal McLaughlin, Lester Waining, Aimee Miller, Henry Sweet, Alice Betterly, Leonora Miller, Maurice Miller, Leslie Burrill, Ethel Fogg, Alice Black, Hattie Townes, Lora Kinney, Marcia Burrell, and Alta Black.

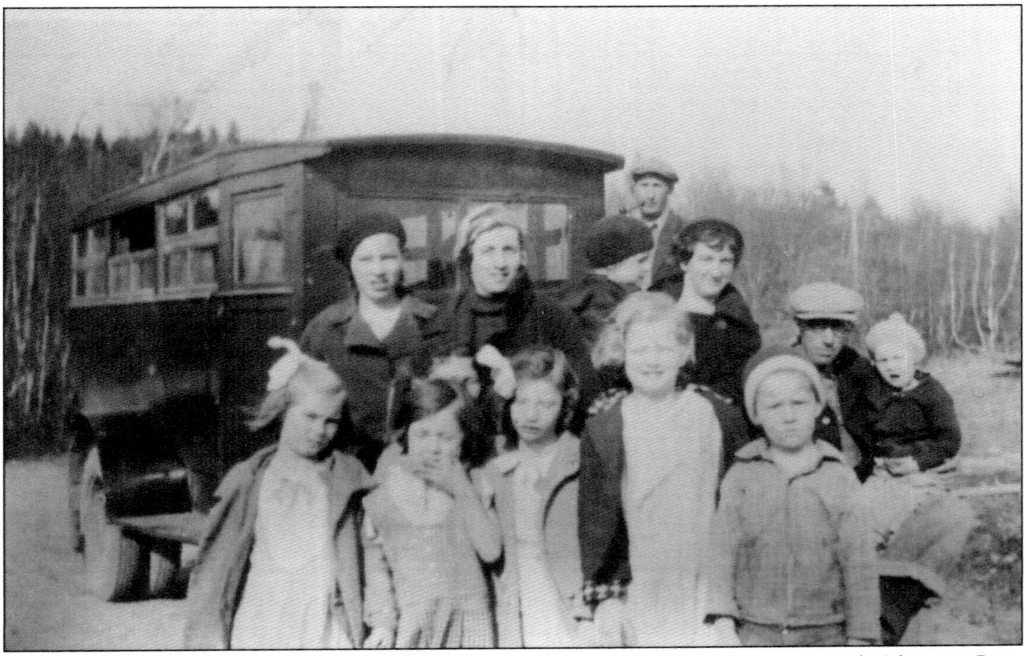

A School Bus in Dedham, *c.* 1933. From left to right are as follows: (front row) Glenice Gray Bernot, Millicent Coffin, Priscilla George, Joyce Young, and Own Young; (second row) Florence Young Yoder, Doris Coffin, Gertrude York, and Irene Gray in the arms of Gardiner Coffin. In the background is Walter Gray beside the first school bus in town.

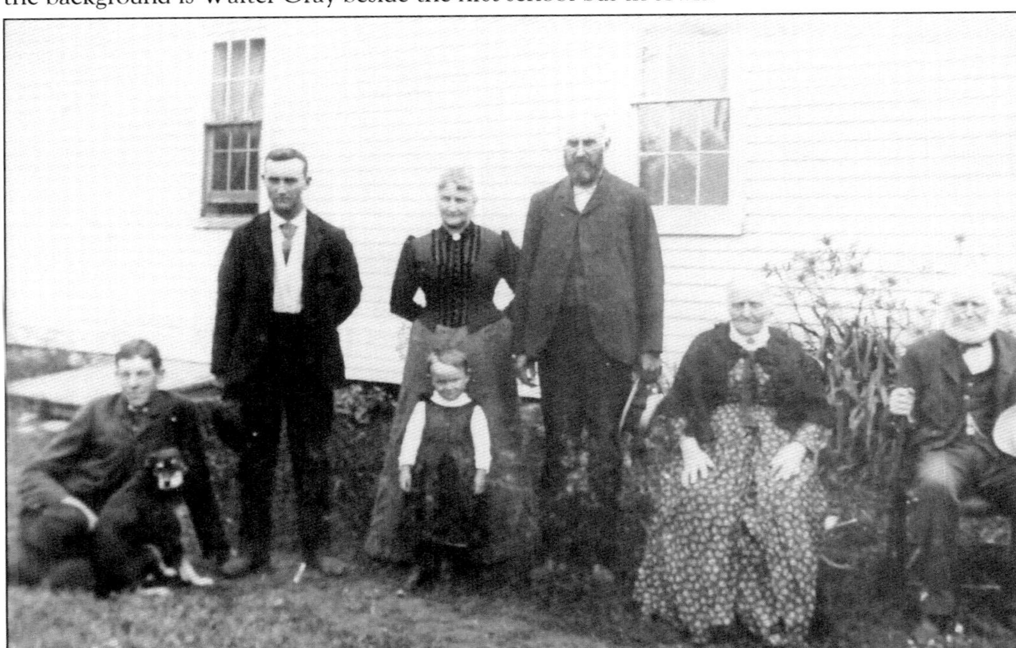

The Summer of 1892. The family patriarchs, on the right, are Elijah and Content (Sweet) Comins; in the center are Jerome Comins and Ella (David) Comins; to the left is Henry Comins standing beside a hired man and a pet dog; and in the front is Jerome Herbert Comins.

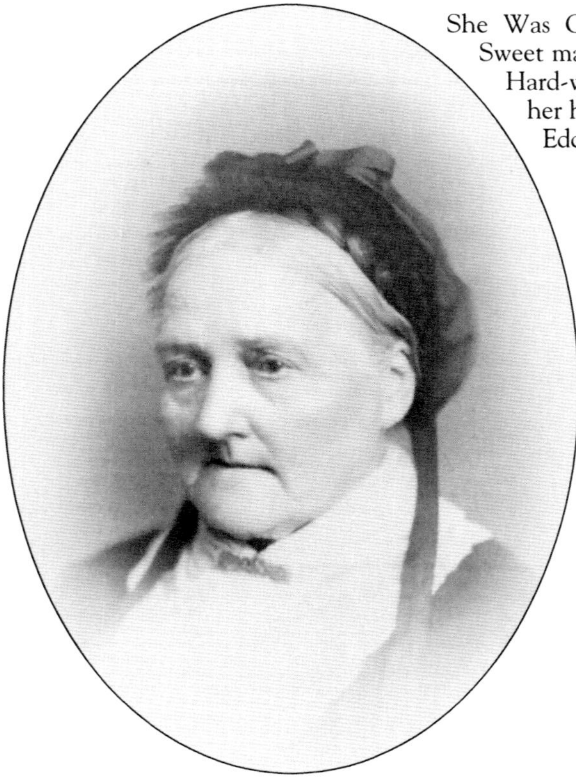

She Was Content and Sweet, *c.* 1880s. Content Sweet married Elijah Comins on March 24, 1834. Hard-working and thrifty to a fault, she helped her husband become a self-sufficient farmer at Eddington, Maine.

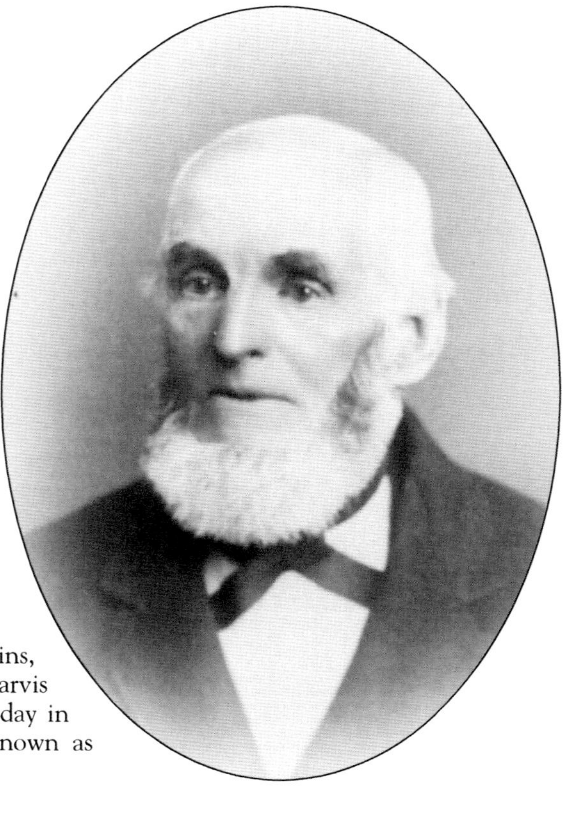

An Early Settler of Eddington. Elijah Comins, the son of Coolidge Comins, was born at Jarvis Gore. His good works are remembered today in the community, and the town hall is known as Comins Hall.

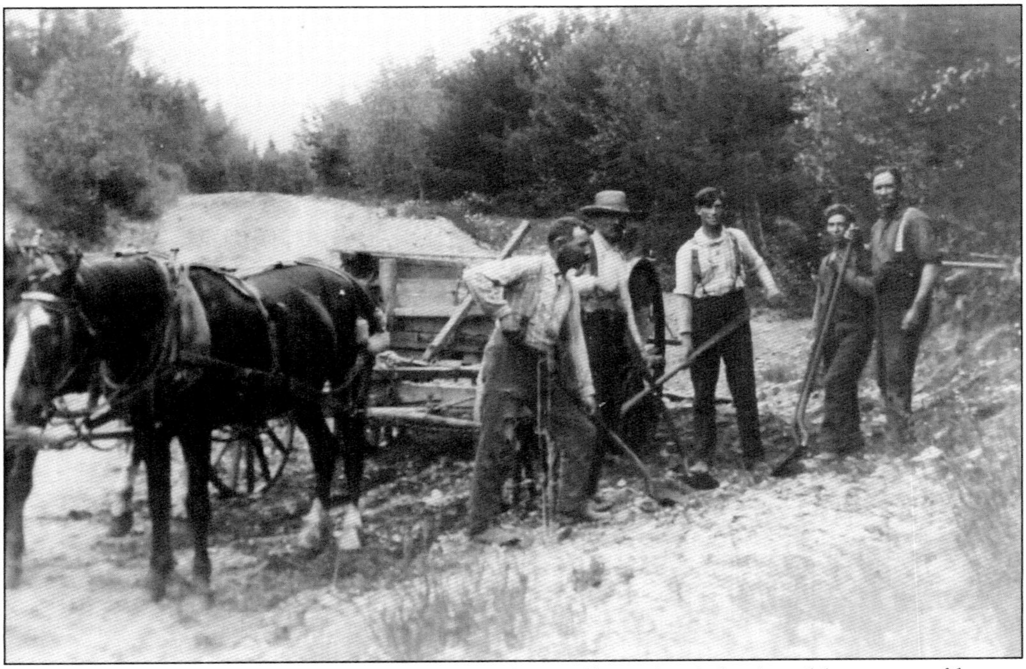

An Early Road Crew at Clifton, *c.* 1880s. Melvin Jellison (with hat) and his team of horses work with his crew widening the town road. Picks and shovels were their only tools.

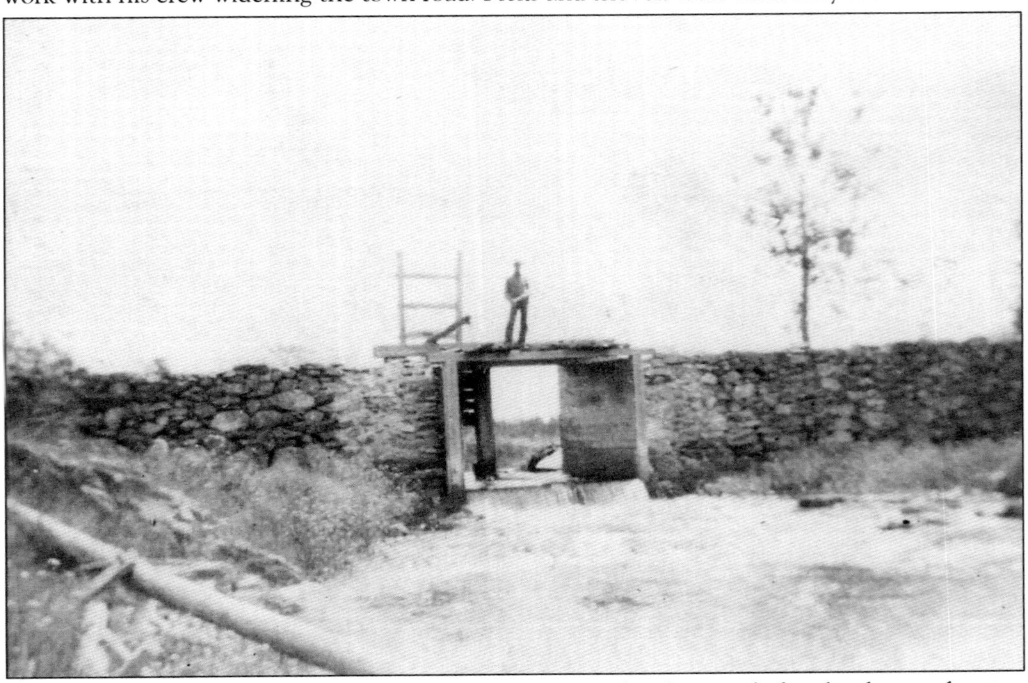

Archer's Dam in Clifton, 1870s. Waterways were second only to rich farmlands as a drawing card to settlers along the Airline Road. This dam is thought to have been on Bradbury's Brook. George lived over the line in Amherst on the ancestral land of Anselm Archer, who came from Cherryfield with his brother Robert about 1810.

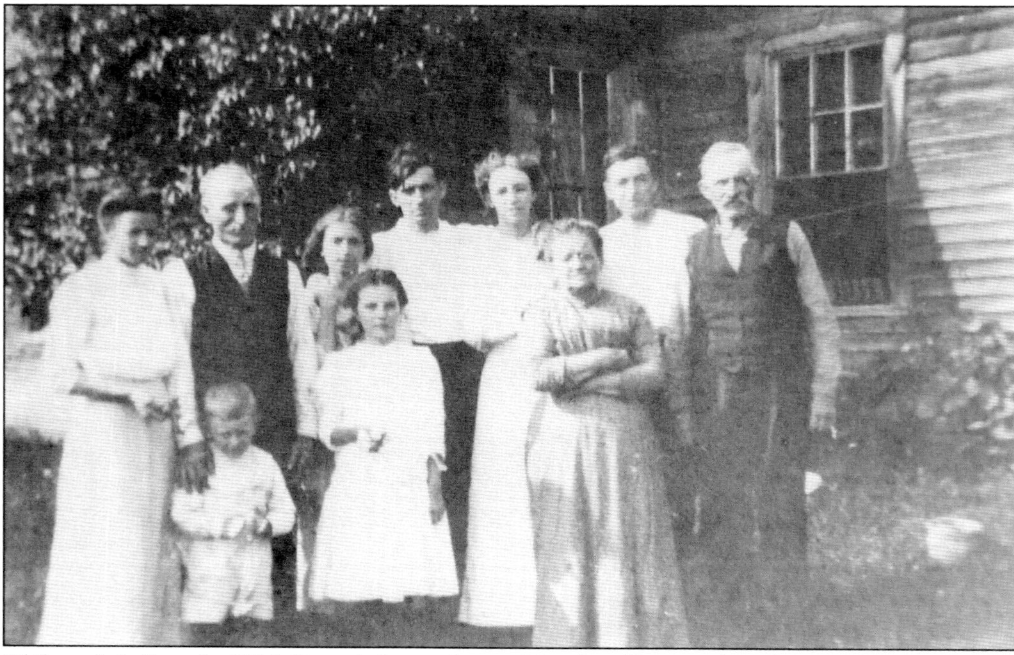

Clifton, July Fourth, 1913. From left to right are Maud and Leonard Williams, Blanche Jellison, Kilby Jellison, Mr. and Mrs. Jesse Jellison, and Melvin Jellison with his wife, Brooksey (DeBeck), standing in front of him. Leon Williams and his sister Ethel are in front on the left.

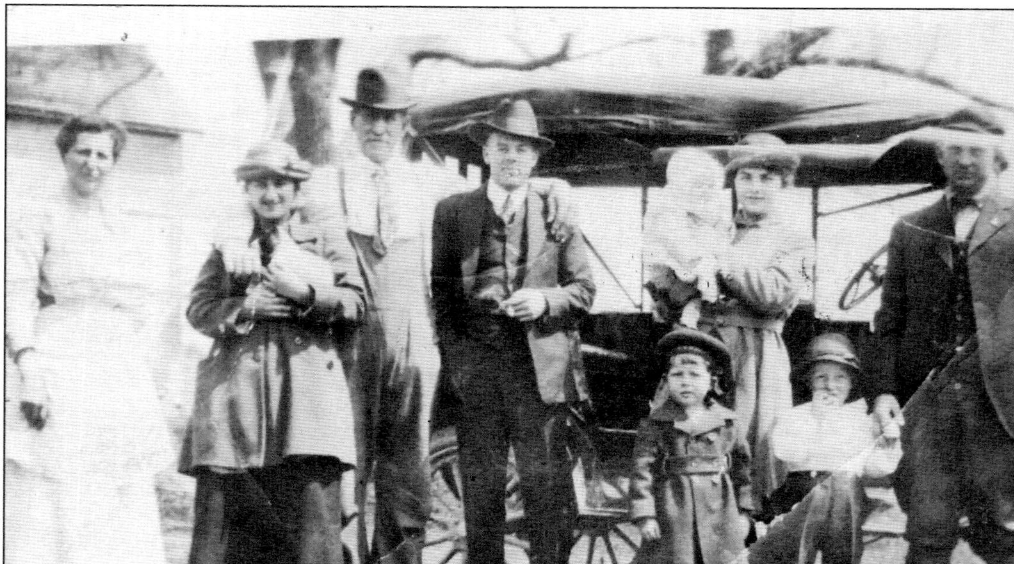

A Bragg Family Gathering, *c.* 1920. Receiving a welcome at their Uncle George Bragg's home in Clifton was the couple on each side of George—Osborn Blanchard and his new wife Ollie. Osborn was the son of Bertha and George Blanchard of Springfield. The lady on left was George's second wife, Eleanor Phinney. On Osborn's left is Ida, George's daughter, holding her son Gerald, with her son Milton standing in front of her; both were the sons of Earl Jellison. On the right is Harry Bragg, the son of George and Mary, holding his son Harry Jr.'s hand.

Alonzo Wilson Bragg. This is perhaps one of the oldest known likenesses of Alonzo Bragg Sr. Born in 1828 at Vassalboro, he married Eliza Jane Chick in 1854 at Great Pond and settled in Clifton. The family moved to Pokiak, New Brunswick, just before the Civil War draft, and recently discovered letters indicate it was to avoid service. The image is from a tintype created before his marriage.

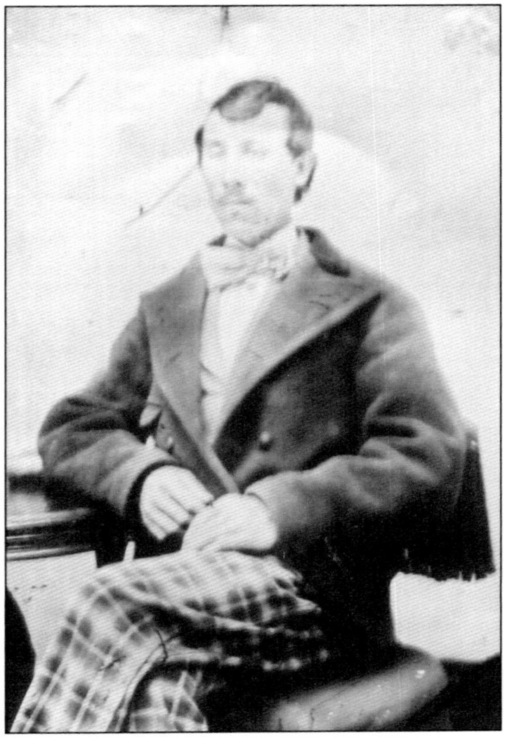

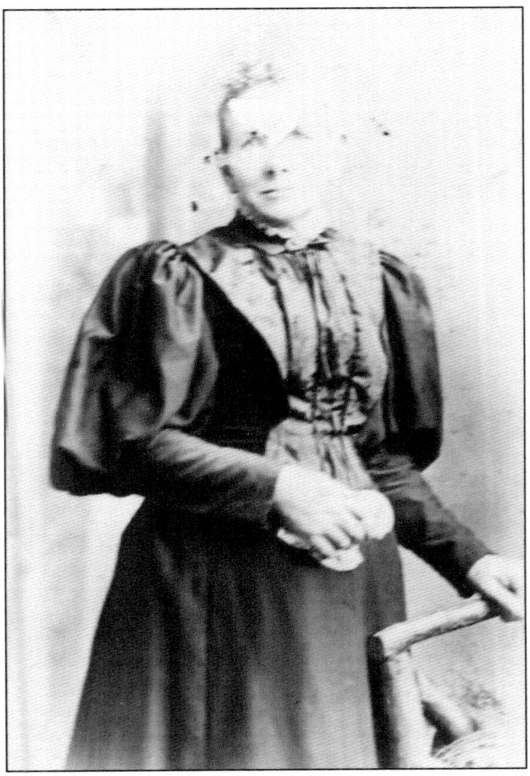

Descendants of Loyalists. Eliza Chick, the daughter of Nathaniel and Betsey (Williams) Chick, was a descendant of Nathaniel Mills, owner of the *Massachusetts Gazette and Post Boy*. He wrote inflammatory articles against the American colonists at the outbreak of the American Revolution. She married Alonzo Wilson Bragg in 1854 when she was fifteen and he was twenty-eight.

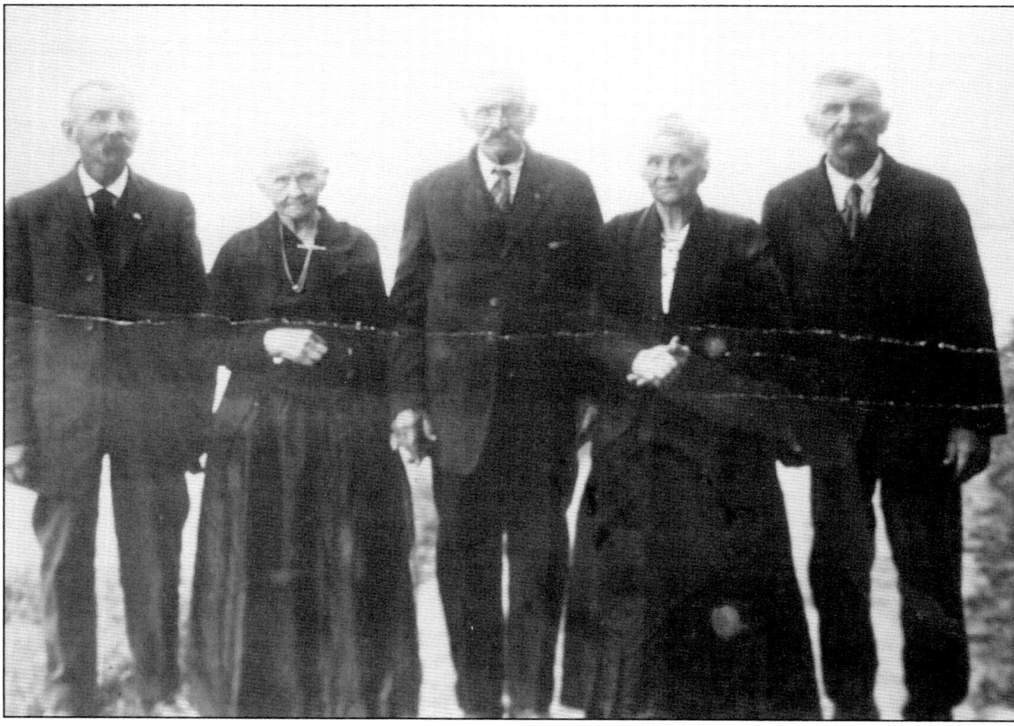

A Jellison Reunion, *c.* 1901. Shown here are five of the children of John and Elmina (Day) Jellison of Waltham, Maine. From left to right are George W. Jellison, Lucy A. Jellison, Melvin Sylvester Jellison, Loantha B. Jellison, and Charles F. Jellison.

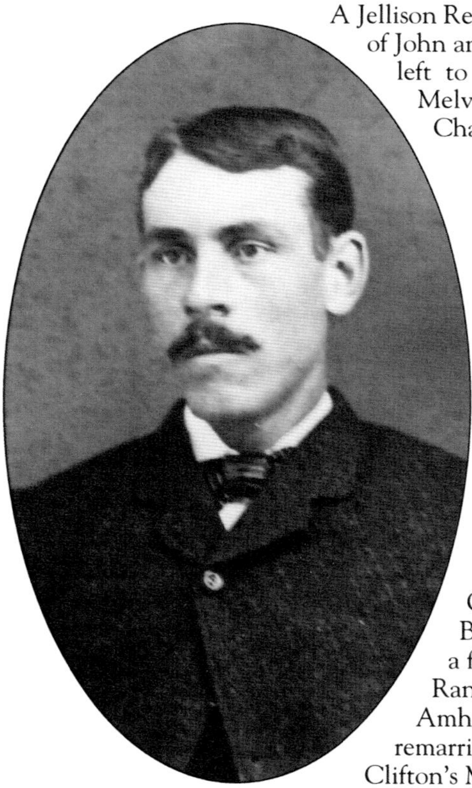

George Wilson Bragg. Born in 1866 at Pokiak, New Brunswick, the son of Alonzo and Eliza, George was a farmer. On January 19, 1895, he married Mary Jane Rankin, the daughter of William and Maria (Mosley) of Amherst. Mary Jane died in 1907, and George eventually remarried to Eleanor E. Phinney. All of them are buried in Clifton's Maplewood cemetery.

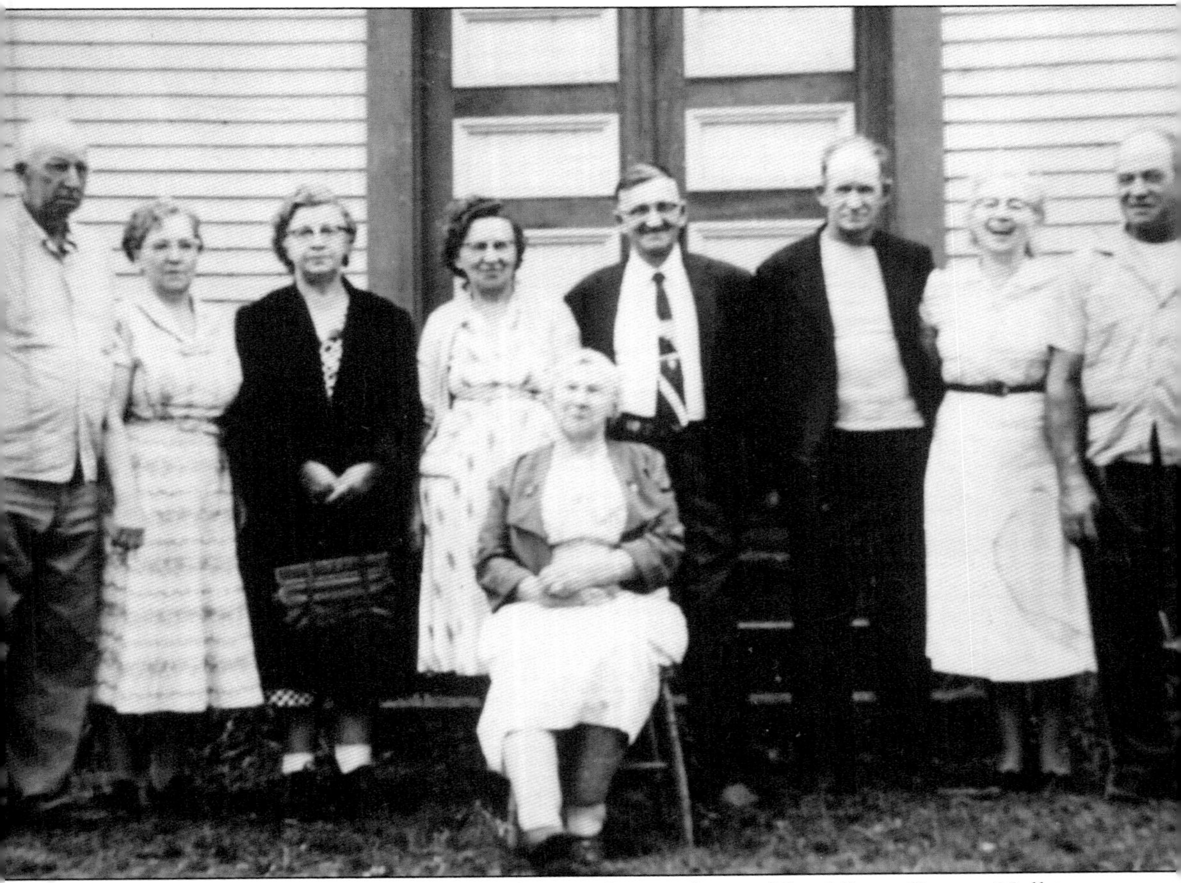

A Giles Family Reunion. This photograph was taken in front of St. Albans Grange Hall in the mid-1970s. Seated in the center is Della White Giles, the widow of Harry E. Giles, the son of Charles and Antha (Clewley). From left to right are John Giles, Relief Giles Knowles, Gertrude Giles Leavitt, Grace Giles Murray, Clarence E. Giles, George Giles, Dorothea Giles, and Floyd Giles.

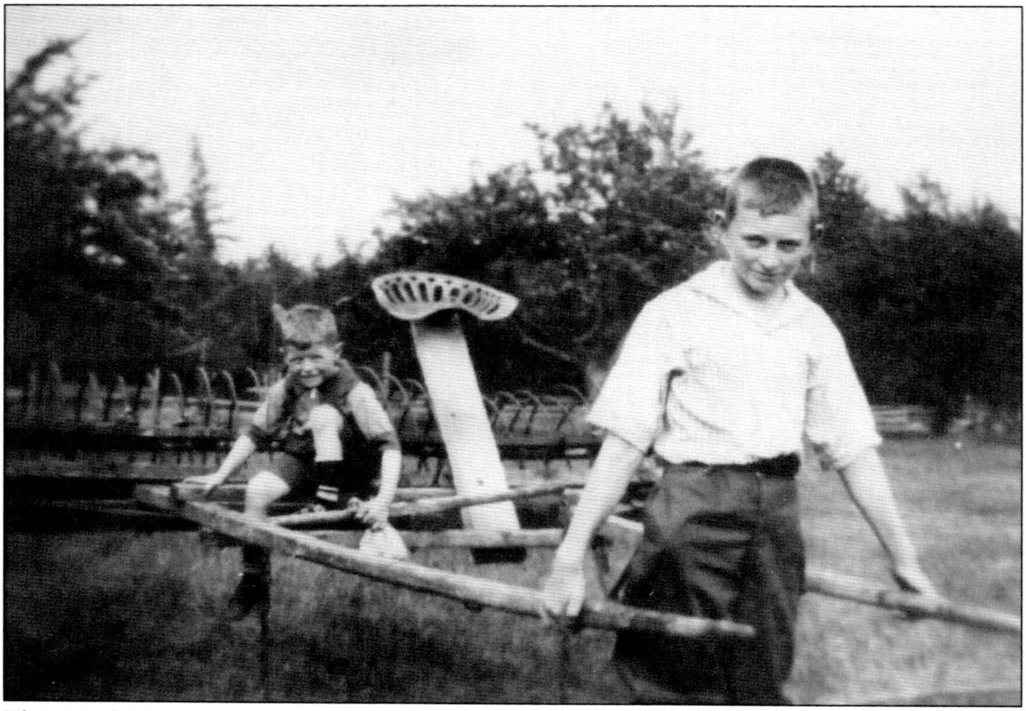

The Carefree Days of Summer, *c.* 1918. Raymond Leon Williams gives his young cousin, Fred Demers, a ride on the hay-tedder on the farm in Clifton.

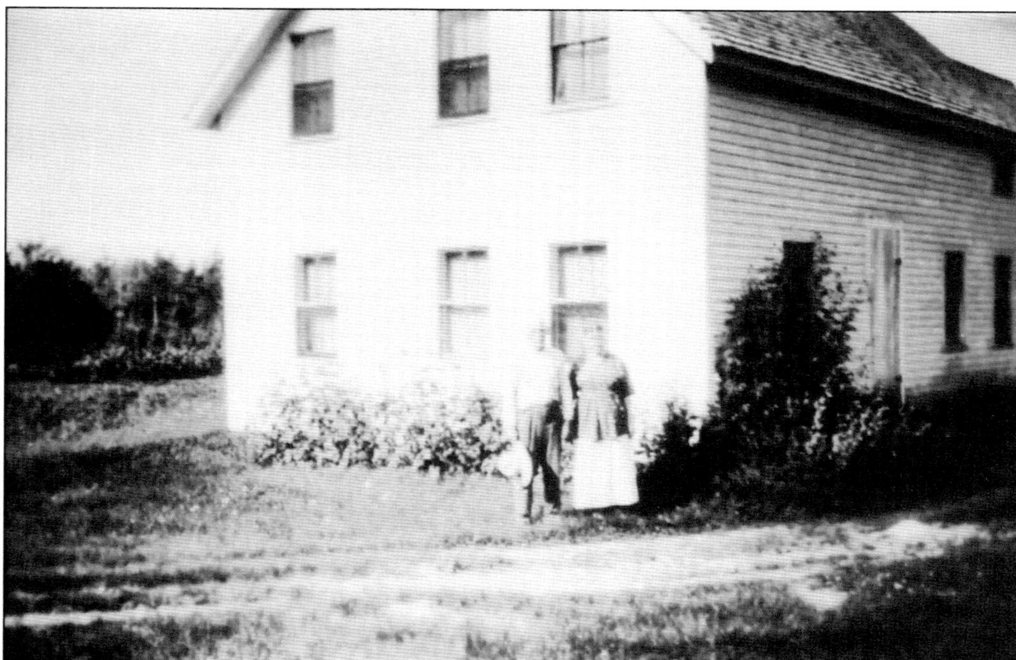

The Williams Homestead. Joshua and Martha Williams stand in front of their house in their Sunday best. This two-story home with ell burned in the 1930s and was never rebuilt.

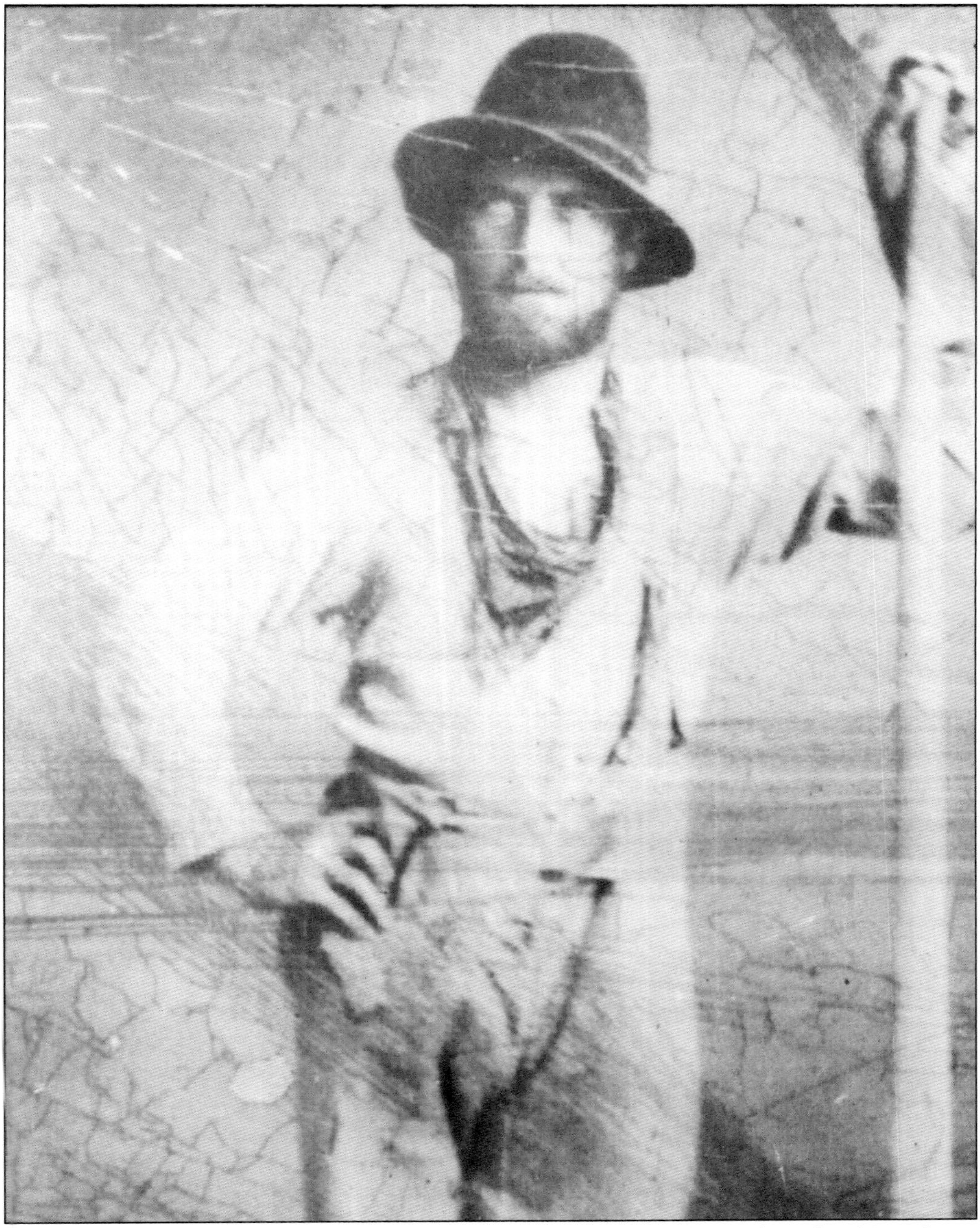

The Inventor of the Peavey. In the spring of 1857 on the stillwater branch of Penobscot River, Joseph Peavey had a brainstorm after seeing the difficulties men had picking apart a log dam. He went straight to his blacksmith shop and guided his son Daniel on how to make an improvement on the log pick. Using an iron clasp with a hook on the side, and fastening an iron point on the end of the pick, he invented what is known as the Bangor or Rafting Peavey. The Peavey Manufacturing Company has been in business for almost 140 years, and is located just 5 miles from the site of the origin of the peavey. Today, Peavey tools help in the furniture business, farms, and orchards, and are known internationally.

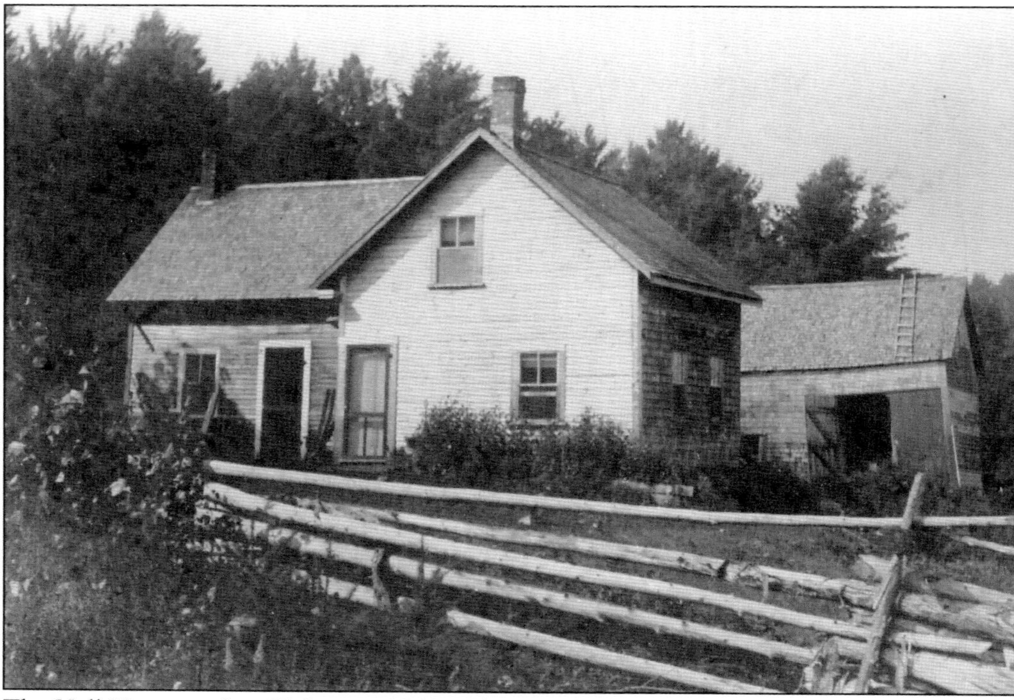

The Hall Homestead at Clifton, c. 1860s. This was the home of Samuel Hall, born in 1825 in Knox, Maine, and his wife, Lucy J. McDonald. They were married in Knox on September 24, 1845. Samuel was a farmer all his life, and settled in the rich meadows of Clifton on Route 9.

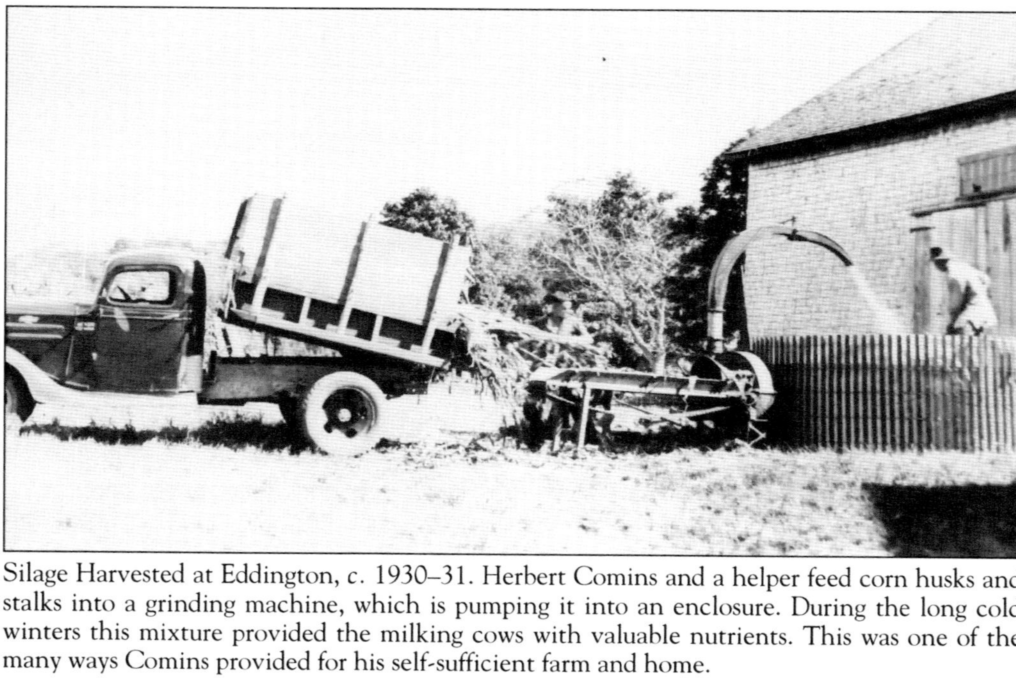

Silage Harvested at Eddington, c. 1930–31. Herbert Comins and a helper feed corn husks and stalks into a grinding machine, which is pumping it into an enclosure. During the long cold winters this mixture provided the milking cows with valuable nutrients. This was one of the many ways Comins provided for his self-sufficient farm and home.

Six

South to North Bend: Surry

First occupied by the French on Newbury Neck, the area was surveyed in March 1762 as Township #6, a first-class township, by David Marsh. Known as "The Surry Gore," it included a section that extended as far as the Falls on the Union River at Ellsworth. When Maine became a state in 1820 it became a permanent part of the city of Ellsworth. The first English settlers were Symonds, Weymouths, Flyes, and others soon followed, including Lords, Floods, and Hammonds. Clarks, Treworgys, and Youngs settled on a neck of land named for their Massachusetts home, Newbury. It was incorporated in 1803 and given the name Surry, a name suggested by John Ross in a letter to General David Cobb, then president of the Massachusetts Senate.

The Jarvis family, one of the most notable families in eastern Maine, settled early on in what is now Surry. Brothers Leonard and Philip Jarvis, Boston merchants, began buying up lands of the original grantees from the State; by 1800 they owned 98,386 acres of land in townships 3, 6, 7, and 8. Leonard Jarvis died in Surry in 1813.

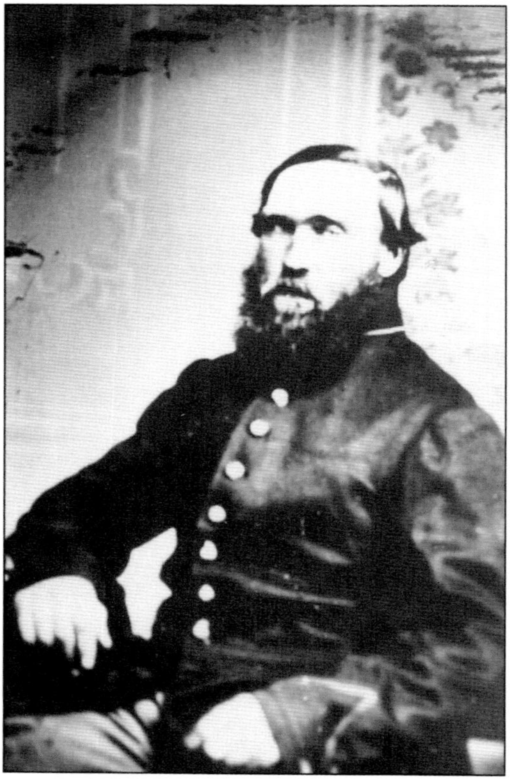

A Patriot Who Did Not Come Home Again. James Meader Gaspar was born in Surry in 1825 and died in 1864 in the Battle of Cedar Creek during the Civil War.

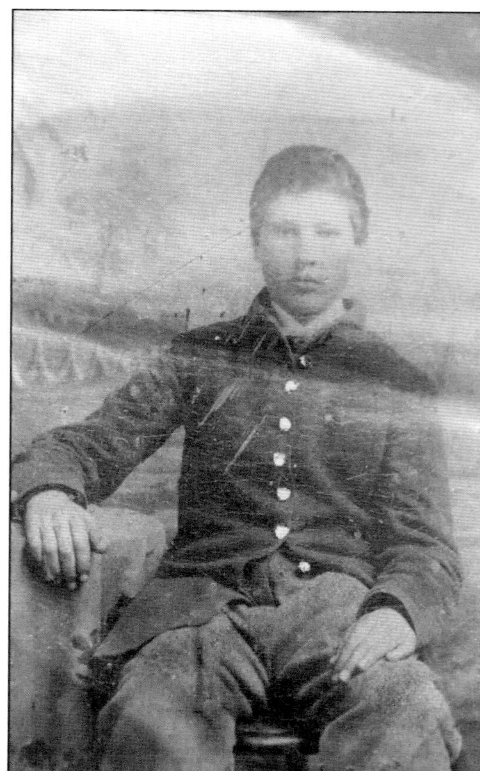

A Tintype, c. 1860. While it is not known whether Charles Conary served in the Civil War, the uniform he wears was typical of that worn by drummer boys during that conflict.

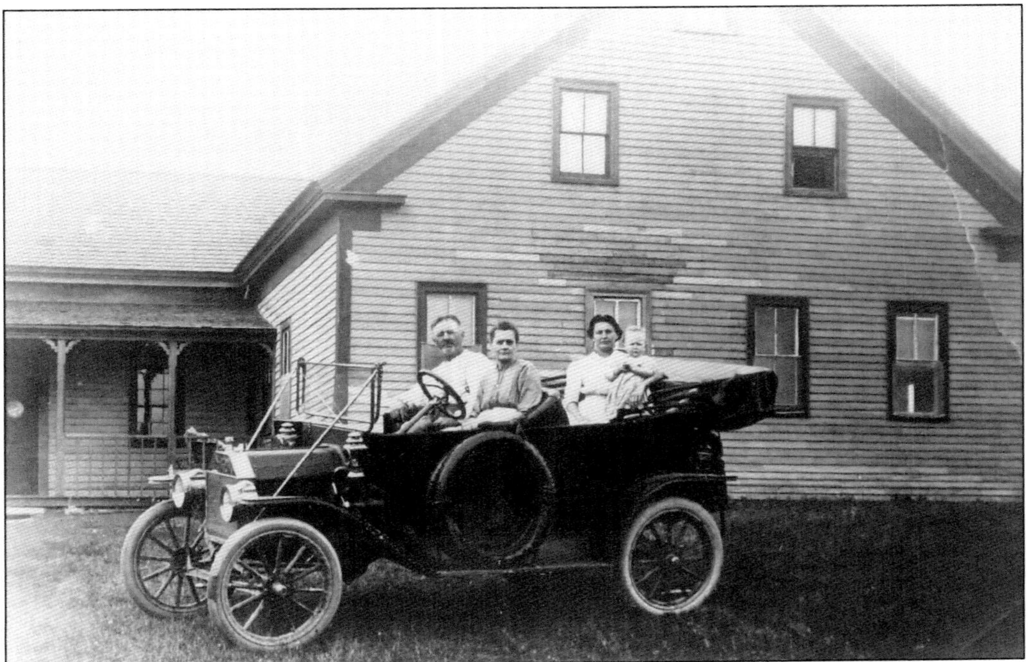

The Pine Hill Home, *c.* 1916. The front seat passenger is Manoel Almond Gaspar, whose grandfather, Francisco Manoel Gaspar, came from the Azores as a youth and jumped ship on the coast of Maine in 1816. In the touring car with him is his wife Celia; their daughter, Annie Gaspar Smith, is in the back seat with her son Franny. The home shown here is still standing.

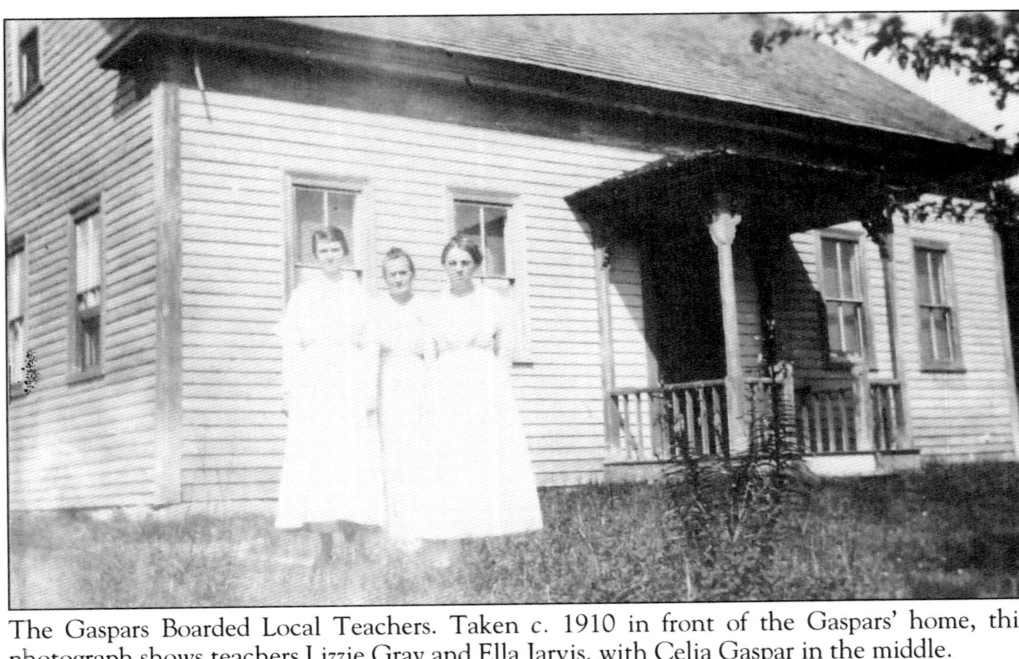

The Gaspars Boarded Local Teachers. Taken *c.* 1910 in front of the Gaspars' home, this photograph shows teachers Lizzie Gray and Ella Jarvis, with Celia Gaspar in the middle.

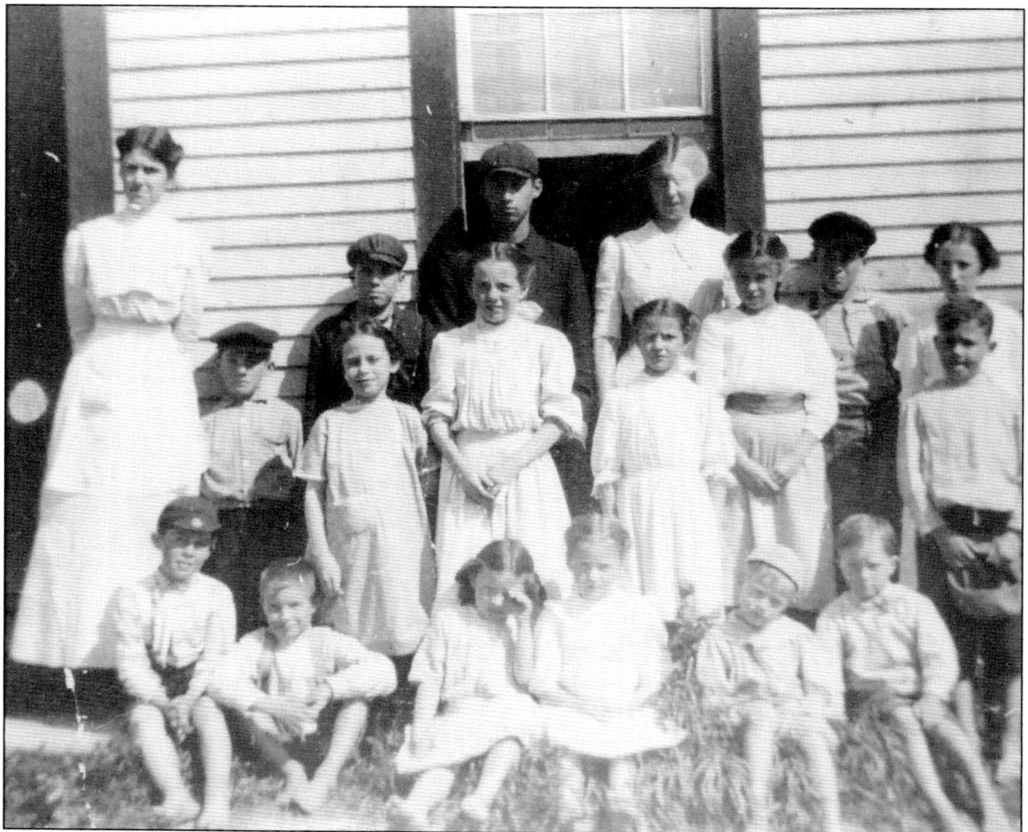

The North Bend Road School, *c.* 1915. None of the students are named, but the teacher is Lizzie Gray.

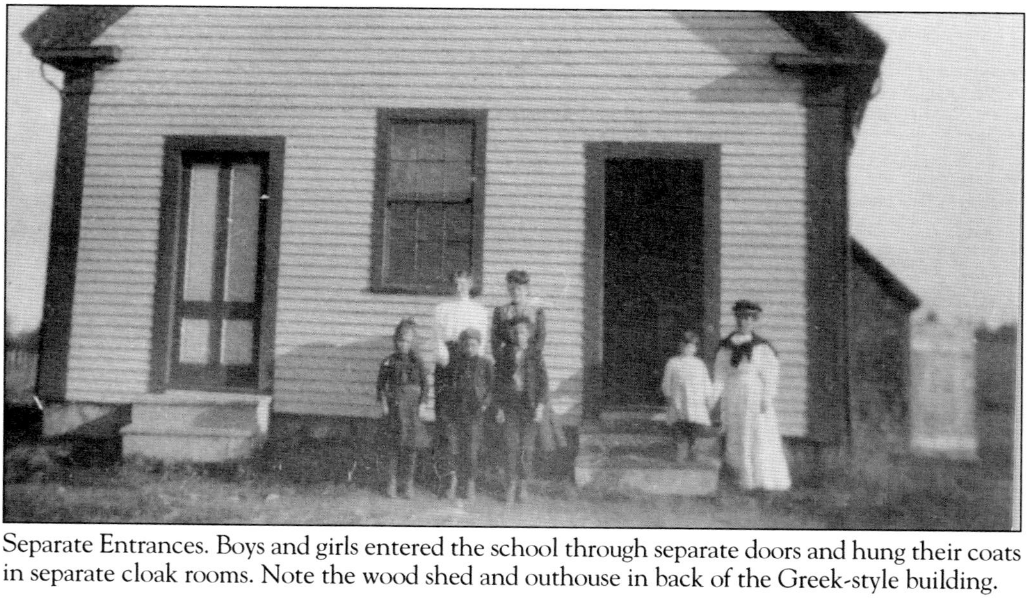

Separate Entrances. Boys and girls entered the school through separate doors and hung their coats in separate cloak rooms. Note the wood shed and outhouse in back of the Greek-style building.

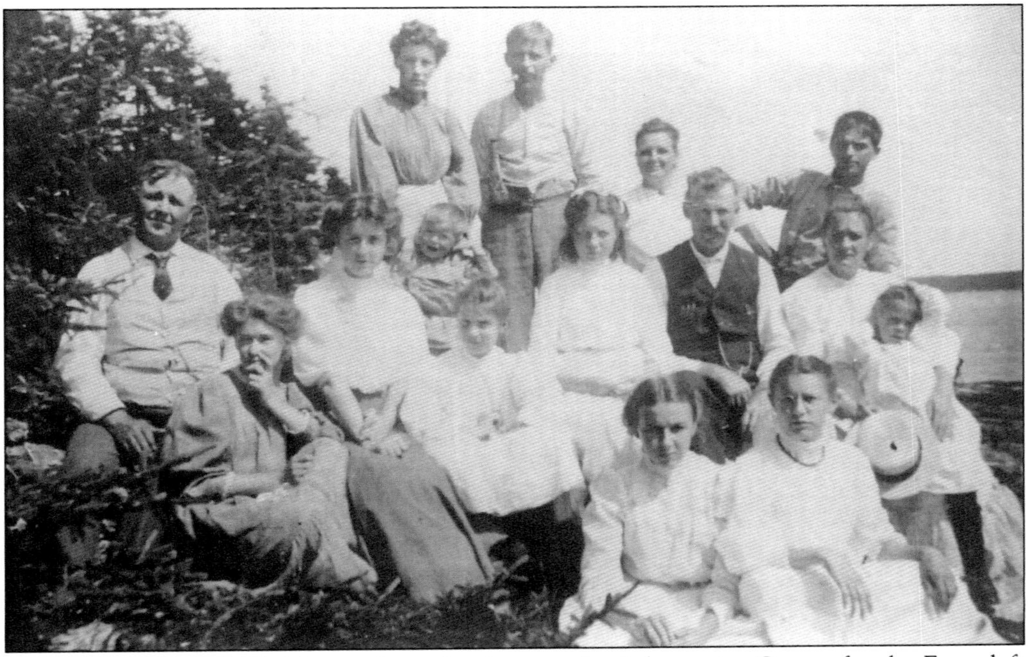

Newbury Neck, *c.* 1907. This is the only photograph of the entire Gaspar family. From left to right are as follows: (front row) Glenola (Clark) Gaspar and Annie Gaspar; (middle row) Manoel Almond Gaspar, Lillian Withee, Corinna Clark, Addie and Clara Carpenter, John Jellison, and Celia Gaspar (holding daughter Ruth); (back row) Venetia and Roscoe Gaspar with son Manny, Mrs. Jellison, and Everett Gaspar.

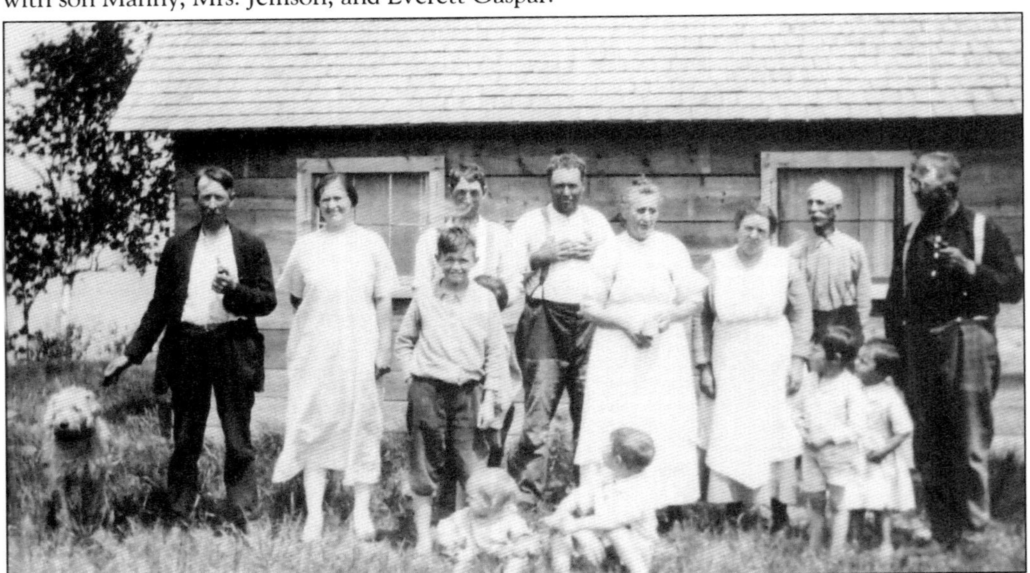

A Reunion at the Camp of the Neck. Newbury Neck was a favored picnic place for many years. Shown here are, from left to right, as follows: (front row) Henry, Ralph, and twins Larry and Florence Smith; (back row) Charles Conary, Annie Smith, and Will Thorne; (in front of Will Thorne) Franny Smith, Francis Smith, Celia Gaspar, Helen Thorne, an unknown man, and Manoel Gaspar. The Conarys' dog, "Ding-Dong," is on far left of photograph.

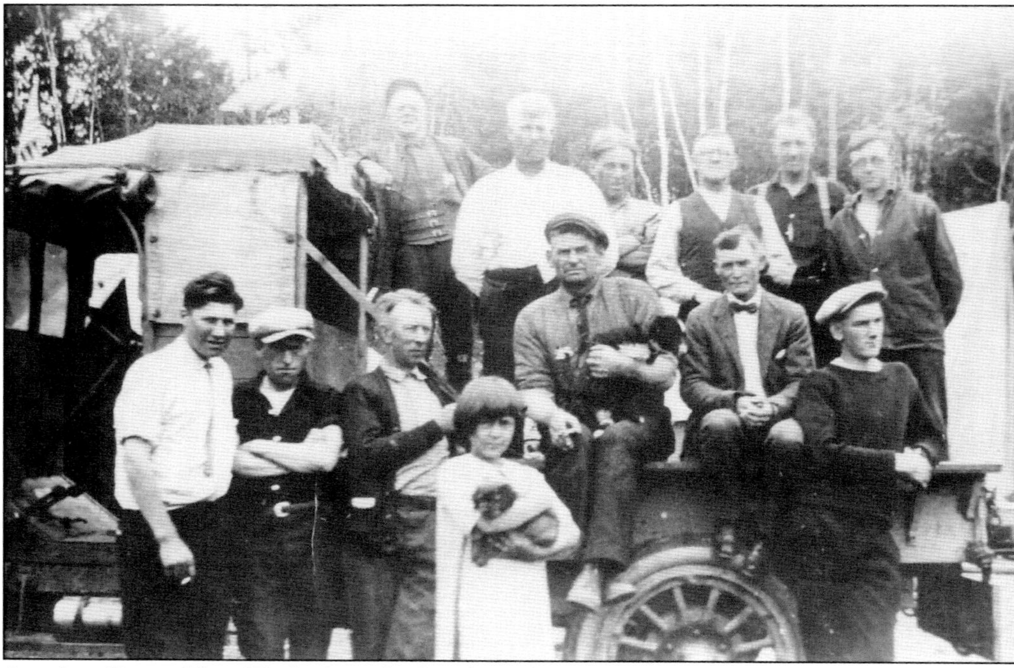

Another Group That Worked on the Road. In the 1800s and well into the 1930s, men could work off their town taxes by helping to fix up the town's roads. Cleve Conary (front row, third from left) is in charge of this group. Note the wooden spokes on the vintage truck. The name of the little girl holding puppy is unknown.

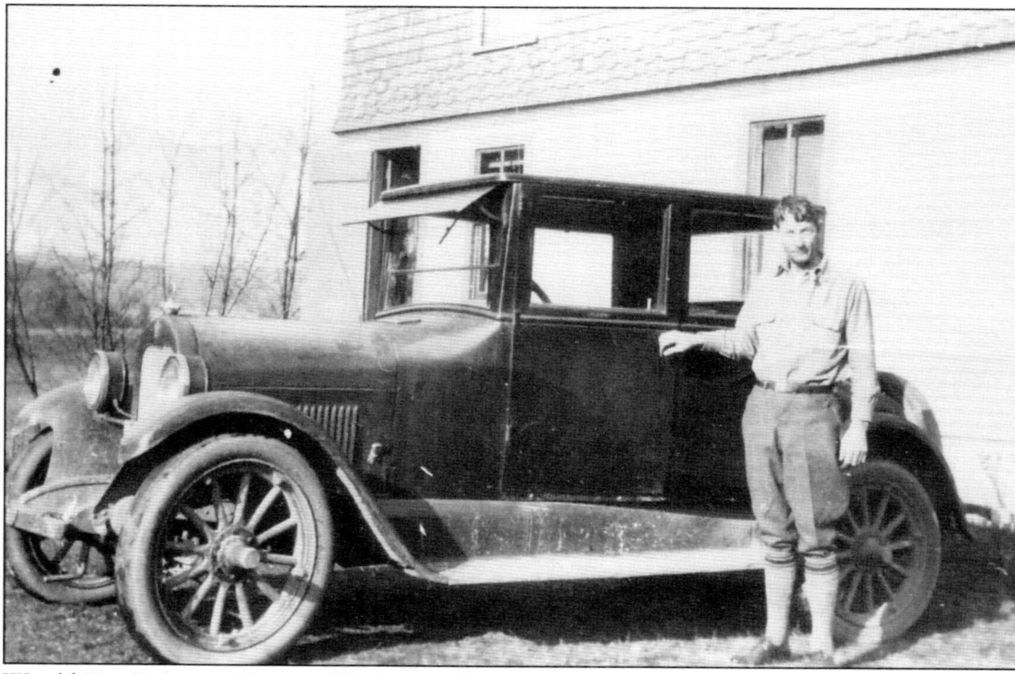

Would You Believe a Durant? With a crank in front to get her started and durable hard-rubber tires, Will Thorne's new car was the talk of Surry in 1916.

The Road Foreman and an Antique Truck. Conary sits on the wooden running board of this vintage "workhorse," dubbed a FWD. Running lights were little more than lanterns wired for electricity. Iron wheels complete the description of a rugged vehicle.

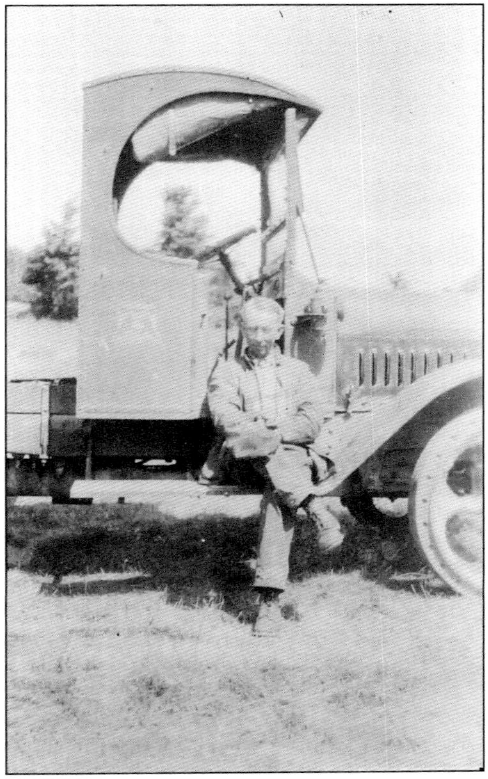

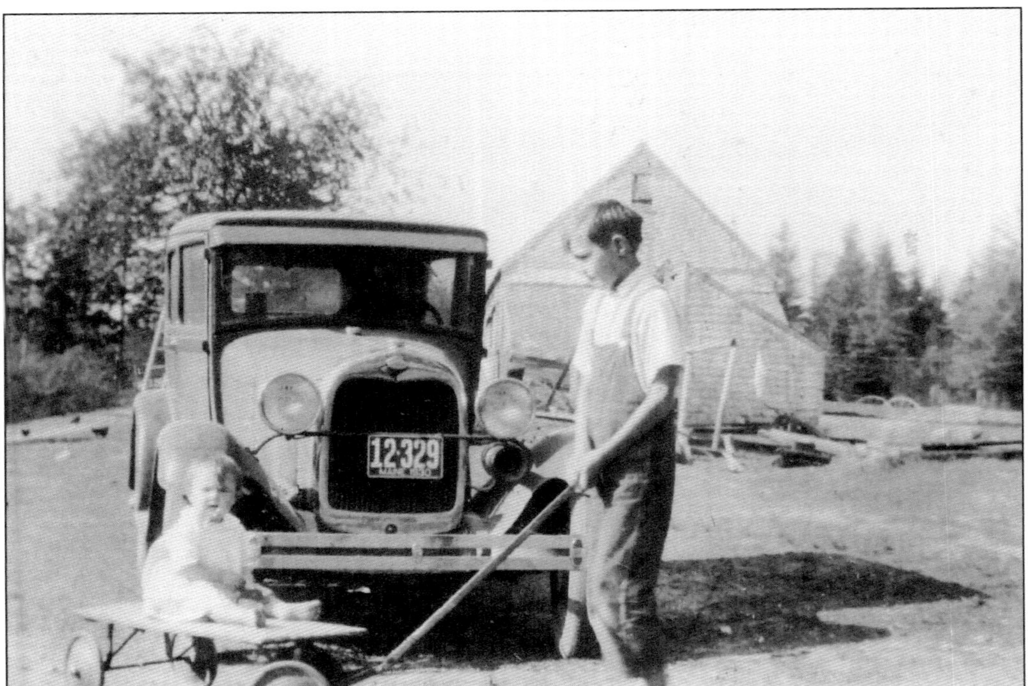

Newbury Neck in 1930. Henry Smith gives his little sister a ride in his sideless wagon.

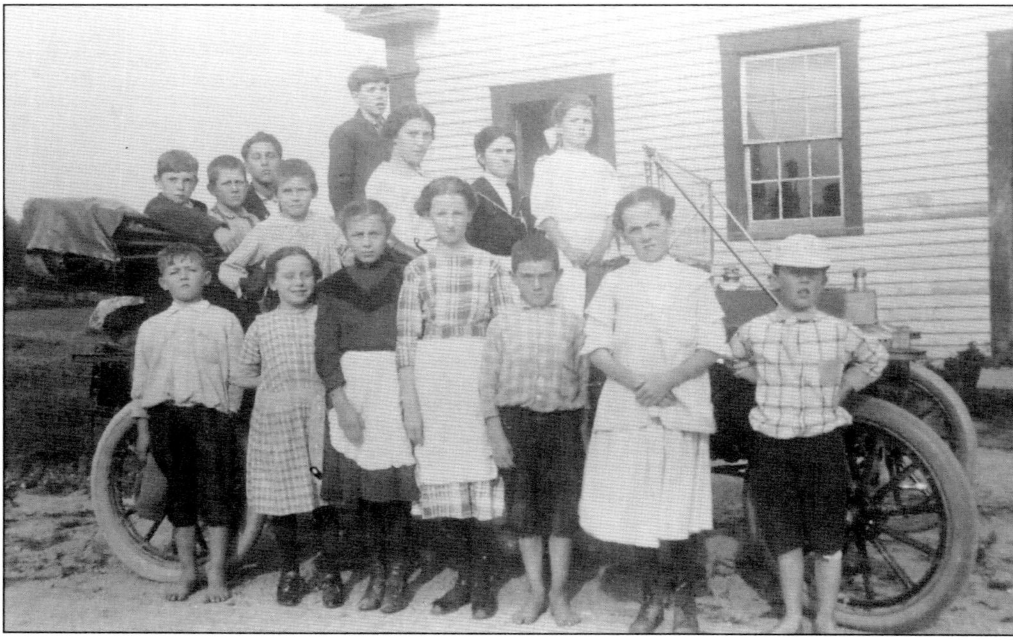

Surry Had Its Share of Old Cars. This *c.* 1915 photograph shows teacher Lizzie Gray and her class posing in her new automobile. From left to right are as follows: (front row) Manford Gaspar, Myrtle Shapleigh, Ruth Gaspar, Mildred Grindle, Edgar Ingalls, Marion Ingalls, and Harvard Sinclair; (back seat) Mannie Gaspar, Newton Clark, Gene Ingalls, Almon Smith, Carl Gaspar, Addie Carpenter, teacher Lizzie Gray, and Jessie Ingalls.

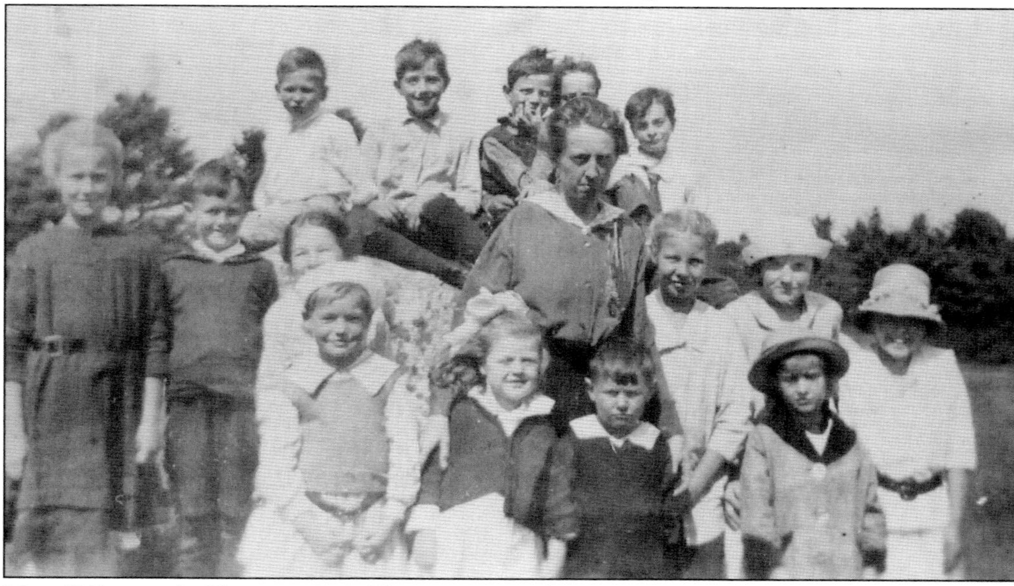

Myra Billington's Class, *c.* 1919. This appears to be an outing on the last day of school. The following students have been identified: (front row) Charlotte Gaspar, Mary Shapleigh, Chester Smith, and Winifred Gaspar; (middle row) Merle Jellison, Francis Smith, Clara Sinclair, teacher Myra Billington, Marguerite Jellison, Abbie Ingalls, and Dora Smith; (back row) Hazen Smith, Albert Gaspar, Charles Gaspar, Clarence Mann, and John Mann.

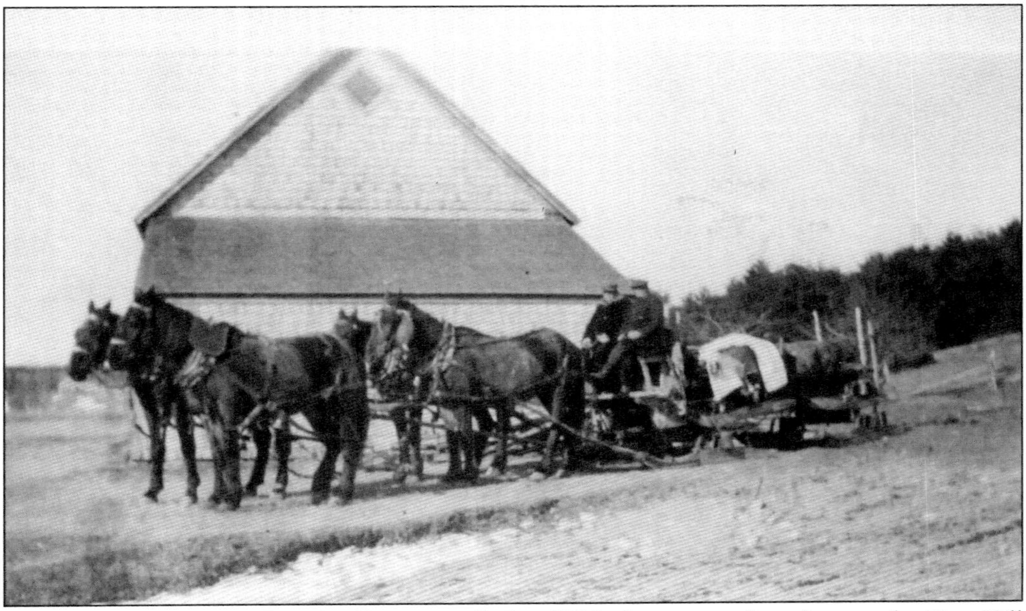

A Barn at Surry—Gone but Not Forgotten. Before 1929, this commodious barn at the Pine Hill Farm was always filled with hay and the farm animals. Gaspar's horse team is shown here pulling a double-runner sled used the haul wood out to the mill.

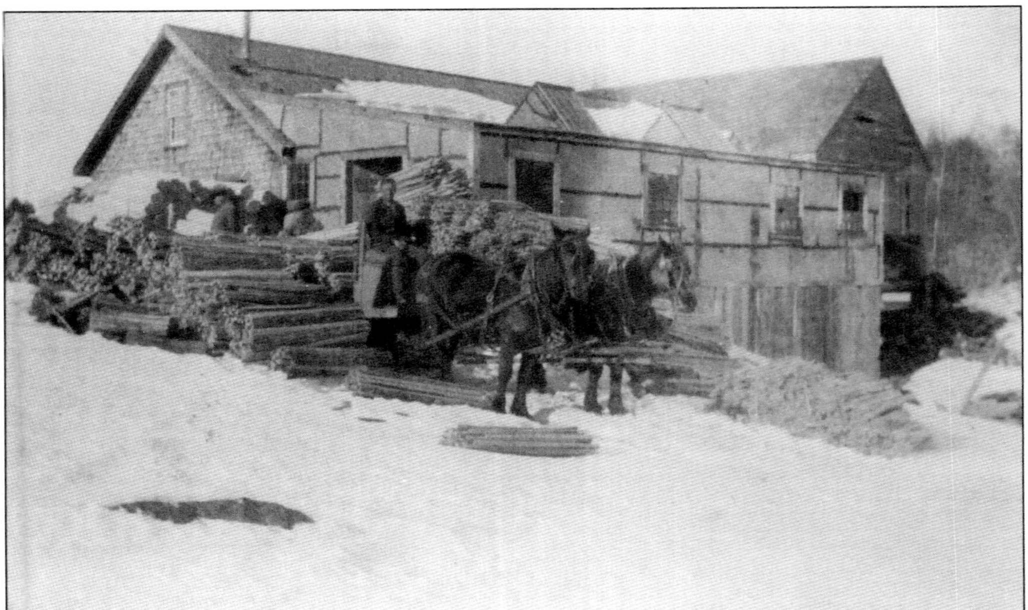

The Gaspar Mill, c. 1920. Manoel Gaspar's mill was located at the North Bend in Surry. The bundles of wood appear to be fencing used to keep snow from drifting across the road.

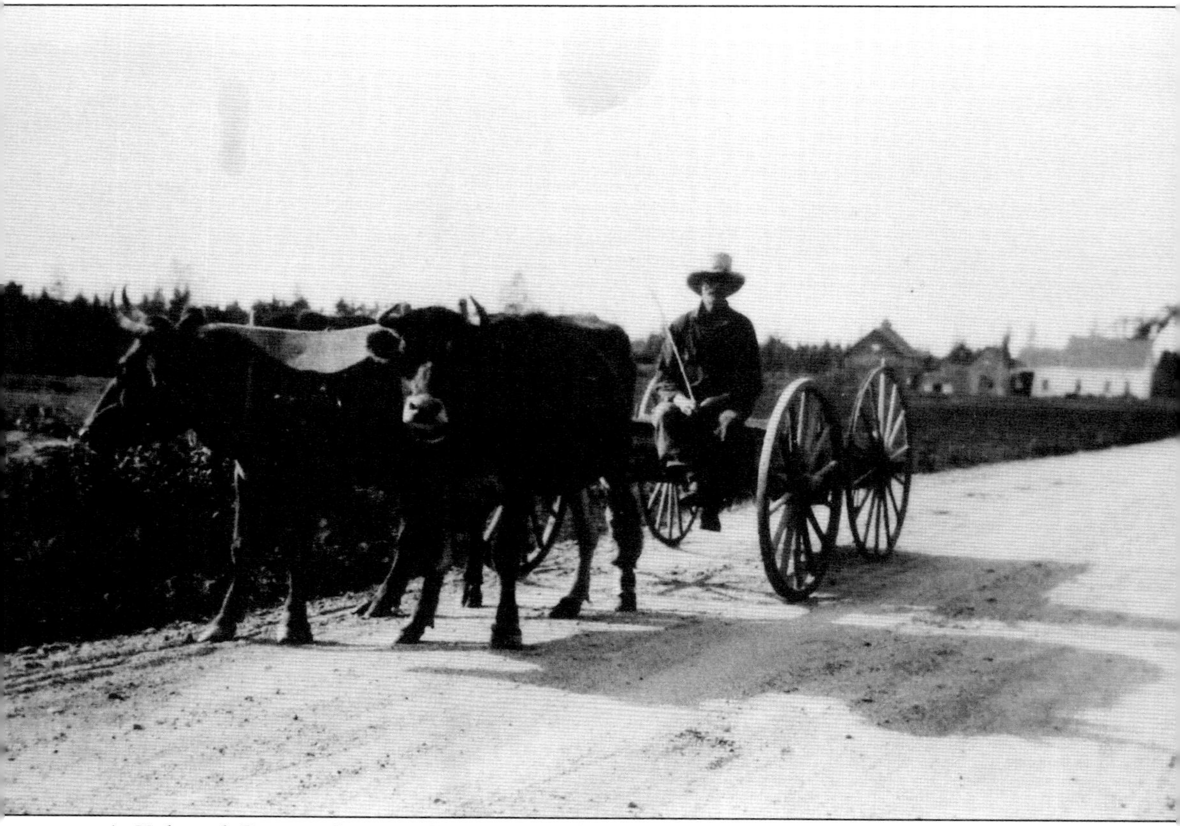

A Yoke of Oxen—Once a Common Sight. Lincoln Treworgy, shown here about 1870, was a skilled manager of a yoke of oxen. These animals were much easier to drive in and around the forests of Union River settlements then horses were, and were less expensive to feed as well. Lincoln was a descendant of the Trueworthy family (which came to be spelled Treworgy over the years), who came to Union River by 1790 and settled on the west side of the river at #6, or Surry.